Praise for Professional Networking For Dummies

"Remarkable! There are more tips, tricks, insights, and secrets in this one volume than you can find in a dozen books or tapes on the same subject. I loved the chapter on how to talk to people. It showed me ways I had never thought of before. The title is misleading, though. The only dummy is the one who doesn't get this book! Fantastic stuff!"

— Joe Vitale, marketing specialist; author of *Spiritual Marketing* and numerous other books and tapes

"*Professional Networking For Dummies* is not only informative and educational, but it provides entertaining insight into often overlooked aspects of communication and developing relationships. Donna Fisher has covered a myriad of topics that can help the novice and the old pro networker alike, illustrating and reminding us that we all have unique strengths and abilities to share. An easy read with extensive information, I could hardly wait to turn the page."

— Susan Luke, CSP and author of *Log Cabin Logic*

"Whether you're a beginner or a seasoned networker, you will gain extensive benefit from this book. The great tips for extroverts, introverts, and gender differences are extremely useful. I highly recommend this book."

— Melissa Giovagnoli, co-author of *Networlding: Building Relationships* and *Opportunities for Success*

"From the novice to the expert, this book has something of value for everyone. It shows that networking is an attitude, a spirit, and a way of life, not a set of techniques or tactics. Yes, networking produces business benefits, but the bigger message is that networking is really about living a full and fulfilling life — contributing to others, building communities, and participating in all spheres of life."

— Wayne Baker, author of *Achieving Success Through Social Capital;* Professor of Organizational Behavior, University of Michigan Business School; Director of Research, Humax Corporation

"If you're just starting out in a business career of any kind, and want to be successful, this book is a *must* — even if you think you already know everything there is to know about networking. This is one of those books you can pick up, start reading for ten or fifteen minutes, and come away with great tips."

— **Bob Littell, co-author of *Power NetWeaving: Good Things Happen When People MAKE Good Things Happen***

TM

References for the Rest of Us!™

BESTSELLING BOOK SERIES

Do you find that traditional reference books are overloaded with technical details and advice you'll never use? Do you postpone important life decisions because you just don't want to deal with them? Then our *For Dummies*® business and general reference book series is for you.

For Dummies business and general reference books are written for those frustrated and hard-working souls who know they aren't dumb, but find that the myriad of personal and business issues and the accompanying horror stories make them feel helpless. *For Dummies* books use a lighthearted approach, a down-to-earth style, and even cartoons and humorous icons to dispel fears and build confidence. Lighthearted but not lightweight, these books are perfect survival guides to solve your everyday personal and business problems.

"More than a publishing phenomenon, 'Dummies' is a sign of the times."

— The New York Times

"...you won't go wrong buying them."

— Walter Mossberg, Wall Street Journal, on For Dummies books

"A world of detailed and authoritative information is packed into them..."

— U.S. News and World Report

Already, millions of satisfied readers agree. They have made For Dummies the #1 introductory level computer book series and a best-selling business book series. They have written asking for more. So, if you're looking for the best and easiest way to learn about business and other general reference topics, look to For Dummies to give you a helping hand.

Hungry Minds™

6/01

Professional
Networking
FOR
DUMMIES®

Professional Networking FOR DUMMIES®

by Donna Fisher

Hungry Minds™

Best-Selling Books • Digital Downloads • e-Books • Answer Networks • e-Newsletters • Branded Web Sites • e-Learning

New York, NY ◆ Cleveland, OH ◆ Indianapolis, IN

Professional Networking For Dummies®

Published by:
Hungry Minds, Inc.
909 Third Avenue
New York, NY 10022
www.hungryminds.com
www.dummies.com

Library of Congress Control Number: 2001091996

ISBN: 0-7645-5346-1

Printed in the United States of America

10 9 8 7 6 5 4 3 2 1

1B/QX/QY/QR/IN

Distributed in the United States by Hungry Minds, Inc.

Distributed by CDG Books Canada Inc. for Canada; by Transworld Publishers Limited in the United Kingdom; by IDG Norge Books for Norway; by IDG Sweden Books for Sweden; by IDG Books Australia Publishing Corporation Pty. Ltd. for Australia and New Zealand; by TransQuest Publishers Pte Ltd. for Singapore, Malaysia, Thailand, Indonesia, and Hong Kong; by Gotop Information Inc. for Taiwan; by ICG Muse, Inc. for Japan; by Intersoft for South Africa; by Eyrolles for France; by International Thomson Publishing for Germany, Austria and Switzerland; by Distribuidora Cuspide for Argentina; by LR International for Brazil; by Galileo Libros for Chile; by Ediciones ZETA S.C.R. Ltda. for Peru; by WS Computer Publishing Corporation, Inc., for the Philippines; by Contemporanea de Ediciones for Venezuela; by Express Computer Distributors for the Caribbean and West Indies; by Micronesia Media Distributor, Inc. for Micronesia; by Chips Computadoras S.A. de C.V. for Mexico; by Editorial Norma de Panama S.A. for Panama; by American Bookshops for Finland.

For general information on Hungry Minds' products and services please contact our Customer Care department; within the U.S. at 800-762-2974, outside the U.S. at 317-572-3993 or fax 317-572-4002.

For sales inquiries and resellers information, including discounts, premium and bulk quantity sales and foreign language translations please contact our Customer Care department at 800-434-3422, fax 317-572-4002 or write to Hungry Minds, Inc., Attn: Customer Care department, 10475 Crosspoint Boulevard, Indianapolis, IN 46256.

For information on licensing foreign or domestic rights, please contact our Sub-Rights Customer Care department at 212-884-5000.

For information on using Hungry Minds' products and services in the classroom or for ordering examination copies, please contact our Educational Sales department at 800-434-2086 or fax 317-572-4005.

Please contact our Public Relations department at 212-884-5163 for press review copies or 212-884-5000 for author interviews and other publicity information or fax 212-884-5400.

For authorization to photocopy items for corporate, personal, or educational use, please contact Copyright Clearance Center, 222 Rosewood Drive, Danvers, MA 01923, or fax 978-750-4470.

Hungry Minds is a trademark of Hungry Minds, Inc.

About the Author

Donna Fisher found out early on that she was an introvert — and yet, she also knew that she had a strong desire to connect with people and didn't want to be so shy. She noticed, time after time, that shyness would get in the way of her doing things she wanted to do. Through hard work and intense concentration, she gradually began to step outside her comfort zone. Now, she's a world-renowned networking expert and teaches others the networking skills that have made her a success.

Donna started her own business because she wanted to speak to groups and teach people how to connect, communicate, and create success together. She wanted people to see how the true spirit of networking could change their life in a positive way. By putting her networking skills to use, she grew her business from zero to six figures and has continued to grow it by approximately 30 percent every year.

Donna has developed *People Power* programs that are conducted at corporate meetings, conferences, and conventions around the world. She has also written four books, including *Power Networking* and *People Power,* which have been translated into four languages, and *Power NetWeaving*.

As a member of the National Speakers Association, Donna received her designation as a Certified Speaking Professional (CSP) in 1998. At that time, she became one of 295 speakers in the world to receive the CSP designation. Her programs, *Drumming Up Business* and *Powerful Connections: The People Side of Business,* are often presented as the kick-off presentation for meetings, conferences, and conventions.

Her company, Donna Fisher Presents, focuses on connecting business with people and people with life. Donna helps companies bring out the best in their people and works with people to help them build strong alliances with each other.

Author's Acknowledgments

Special thanks to my literary agent, Carol Susan Roth, for seeing and seizing opportunities. Thanks to Holly McGuire, Suzanne Snyder, Ben Nussbaum, Pam Mourouzis, and everyone at Hungry Minds for their dedication, professionalism, commitment, wisdom, and talent. Thanks to Susan RoAne for being a friend and mentor who walks her talk.

I appreciate the support of my Mom, Betty Fisher, who worried as much about my deadlines as I did. My heartfelt thanks goes to Mike Henry for providing a daily dose of connection and encouragement. Thanks to my colleagues Carolyn Harvill, Lyn Salerno, and Steve Brown for keeping my business going and growing while I was busy writing. Thanks to everyone who so graciously shared of themselves by contributing their stories, experiences, and ideas to add richness and reality to this book. Also, thanks to all the people who have attended my programs and thus given me courage and inspiration to continue my path.

Thanks to everyone in Windsor for being my networking support group for over ten years, with special thanks to our monthly roundtable group. Thanks to everyone in Mastery for continually challenging me to step into new possibilities. Thanks to my brother Randy and family Linda, Valerie, and Leslea just for being there. Also thanks to everyone in Wisdom and Landmark who have contributed to my life in numerous ways. Thanks to my friends and buddies in the National Speakers Association, for your generous and valuable friendship and support. Thanks to Stan for giving me my theme song, "writing, writing, writing, keep those fingers typing." To Vicki for the strength your love gives me. Thanks to everyone who has so graciously provided endorsements for this book.

Publisher's Acknowledgments

We're proud of this book; please send us your comments through our Online Registration Form located at www.hungryminds.com

Some of the people who helped bring this book to market include the following:

Acquisitions, Editorial, and Media Development

Project Editor: Suzanne Snyder

Acquisitions Editor: Holly McGuire

Copy Editor: Ben Nussbaum

Acquisitions Coordinator: Tonia Morgan-Oden

Technical Editor: Richard Petitte

Senior Permissions Editor: Carmen Krikorian

Editorial Manager: Pam Mourouzis

Editorial Assistant: Carol Strickland

Cover Photos: John Lawlor/FPG

Production

Project Coordinator: Maridee Ennis

Layout and Graphics: Amy Adrian, Jackie Nicholas, Jacque Schneider, Brian Torwelle, Jeremey Unger

Special Art: Trish Strangmeyer

Proofreaders: John Greenough, Marianne Santy, Charles Spencer, TECHBOOKS Production Services

Indexer: TECHBOOKS Production Services

General and Administrative

Hungry Minds, Inc.: John Kilcullen, CEO; Bill Barry, President and COO; John Ball, Executive VP, Operations & Administration; John Harris, CFO

Hungry Minds Consumer Reference Group

Business: Kathleen Nebenhaus, Vice President and Publisher; Kevin Thornton, Acquisitions Manager

Cooking/Gardening: Jennifer Feldman, Associate Vice President and Publisher; Anne Ficklen, Executive Editor; Kristi Hart, Managing Editor

Education/Reference: Diane Graves Steele, Vice President and Publisher

Lifestyles: Kathleen Nebenhaus, Vice President and Publisher; Tracy Boggier, Managing Editor

Pets: Dominique De Vito, Associate Vice President and Publisher; Tracy Boggier, Managing Editor

Travel: Michael Spring, Vice President and Publisher; Brice Gosnell, Publishing Director; Suzanne Jannetta, Editorial Director

Hungry Minds Consumer Editorial Services: Kathleen Nebenhaus, Vice President and Publisher; Kristin A. Cocks, Editorial Director; Cindy Kitchel, Editorial Director

Hungry Minds Consumer Production: Debbie Stailey, Production Director

◆

The publisher would like to give special thanks to Patrick J. McGovern, without whom this book would not have been possible.

◆

Contents at a Glance

Cartoons at a Glance

By Rich Tennant

page 5

page 35

page 123

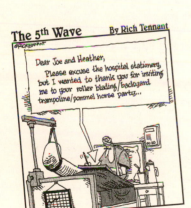

page 199

page 251

Cartoon Information:
Fax: 978-546-7747
E-Mail: richtennant@the5thwave.com
World Wide Web: www.the5thwave.com

Table of Contents

Part II: Building and Maintaining Your Network 35

Chapter 3: Expanding Your Circle of Influence through Networking Events 37

Chapter 4: You Are the Source of Your Network 55

Chapter 5: Let's Talk: Networking Happens through Conversation 67

Chapter 6: Cultivating Your Network by Making Requests 85

Chapter 7: Listen Up! 99

Chapter 8: Using Follow-Through to Maintain and Grow Your Network 109

Introduction

*T*hroughout your life, you will find yourself in situations where you are expected to be personable, friendly, interesting, and a great conversationalist. Instead, you feel uncomfortable, your palms are sweaty, your heart is fluttering, and your mind goes blank. What's a person to do?

Realize that you are not alone. Most people at some time and in certain situations feel shy, uncomfortable, awkward, and ineffective at connecting and communicating with others. No matter how shy or uncomfortable you feel, you can develop the confidence and ease that others portray.

Or perhaps you don't have any problem being with other people. You love to be around others and you light up when you walk into a room full of strangers. But you don't really feel like you have a *professional* network — a group of people who can help you work smarter and better to get ahead professionally.

Whatever your strengths and weaknesses are, you can learn to be a better networker. Learn how to be with people, talk with people, stay in touch with people, and build powerful relationships. Learn to network. Your network has a direct influence on the success and satisfaction that you experience in all areas of life.

You already network, so it's not like we're starting from scratch. Every time you ask for a recommendation for a good restaurant, movie, auto mechanic, or business consultant, you are networking. And every time you recommend someone, whether it's a realtor, printer, graphics designer, or doctor, you are networking. Networking is building connections with other people for the opportunity to give and receive value to each other.

It's really not so difficult. In fact, you may discover it can be fairly simple — and fun. Yes, you may need to step out of your comfort zone and practice your communication skills. And developing some new habits will be important so that your networking can be an easy, natural part of your life.

Learning to network effectively can be the single biggest factor that contributes to your professional success and personal satisfaction. Give yourself a chance. Networking is the chance of a lifetime — the chance to establish valuable contacts and a powerful support system.

About This Book

Between these covers, I attempt to cover everything you need to know about networking. I try to answer all your questions and give you the information you need to be successful. You'll notice some chapters focus on the attitude and philosophy of networking, while others focus on the skills — listening, asking, praising, being organized — that are important when networking. And some chapters focus on various situations and times in life when networking is important.

Ideally, this book will become your networking workbook. Use a highlighter to mark the sentences and examples that are most meaningful to you. Jot down your ideas in the margins and between the paragraphs. Every place where I give an example, take a minute to write down your own example. Take the ideas from this book and put them into your own words and your real-life situations.

Every time you find an idea that you want to implement in your life, highlight it and then go to the back of the book, to the Appendix, and list that action as part of your networking action plan. This book is designed to be a catalyst for action and results in your life.

How This Book Is Organized

Although you may choose to read the book from cover to cover, it is organized so that you can easily find the chapters and sections that relate to your specific interests and needs. So feel free to jump in wherever you choose.

Part I: Networking: What It Is, What It Isn't, and What It Can Do for You

In Part I, I give you a chance to review your thoughts, attitudes, and beliefs about networking. You are encouraged to get rid of the misperceptions and misunderstandings about networking that you may have so that you can develop a style of connecting with people that is effective and beneficial.

Part II: Building and Maintaining Your Network

This part gives you specific information on how to network. I give you information on how to introduce yourself, ask for support, initiate small talk, listen effectively, and follow through appropriately. You are given examples that you can customize for yourself and ideas on the habits that will best support your networking goals.

Part III: Using Your Network: Networking Opportunities

This part covers how to network throughout life — when starting your career, during job transition, in the corporate world, as an entrepreneur, as you move into retirement, and during times of personal and professional growth.

Part IV: Networking Challenges

If you think that you're too shy or too busy to network, then this part of the book is for you. You discover the challenges and strengths of introverts and extroverts and how both styles can use their strengths to enhance their networking. I also write about the unique challenges faced by men and women. I give you information on how to use technology appropriately as a tool for connecting with others. You even discover the etiquette associated with handling business cards and hosting a business event.

Part V: The Part of Tens

Finally, I give you these short, easy-to-read chapters with information on small talk, name recall, avoiding networking turnoffs, and becoming a masterful networker.

Icons Used in the Book

One of the features of *For Dummies* books is the use of icons that highlight useful information to make it easy to find. To help guide you through this book, here are the icons to watch for with information on what each icon represents.

 This icon calls to your attention the information that is important to always keep in mind.

 This information is a warning of things that can easily go wrong with your networking. Take these cautions seriously, and you will have a smooth, successful networking experience.

 These are real-life stories of people just like you who have experienced networking success.

 This icon highlights helpful hints and ideas on how to increase your networking effectiveness.

 The ideas in this book are only as good as the actions you put behind them. This icon represents where most of the value of this book gets created — in your actions. When you come to this icon, it's time to put into practice what you've been reading about.

Where to Go from Here

This book provides information that can enhance your success and satisfaction starting today and continuing throughout the rest of your life. Every piece of information put into action creates a result — that result may show up immediately or in the future. You have started the process by picking up this book and reading this far. You may want to continue from here and read straight through the book, making notes as you go. Or you may want to review the table of contents and pick the part or chapter that either seems the most interesting or the most scary — and jump in. Allow each chapter or section to lead you to what's next for you. Networking is a process of meeting people, making connections with people, and being a resource for people. It is a never-ending process because you will always be meeting and interacting with people and your interactions with people will always create a ripple effect of results. Thank you for choosing this book as part of your networking process.

Part I

Networking: What It Is, What It Isn't, and What It Can Do for You

The 5th Wave   By Rich Tennant

"I added a bunch of new people to my network today. They were standing behind me in the express check out line at the grocery store."

In this part . . .

This part identifies the basic philosophy of networking. I show you how to shift your attitude and awareness to generate more networking opportunities. You find out what your core network is and who is involved. There's also information about how networking, selling, and marketing are all related — and yet different.

Chapter 1

Networking Defined

Can you recall the last time someone told you about a good movie? Or maybe a friend suggested a great vacation spot, a wonderful book, or a fabulous new restaurant? What about the time someone told you about a great place to purchase a computer, a car, some furniture, or clothes? Every time someone gives you a recommendation, suggestion, or idea about something that's of interest or value to you, that's networking. And every time you do the same for someone else, that's networking. Networking is the passing along of information from one person to another for the purpose of being of value and service.

Networking involves creating opportunities through meeting people, making contacts, and building strong relationships. These relationships grow and deepen over time, leading to other contacts, relationships, and opportunities. As human beings, we have a natural need to be in relationships with others. Honoring that natural desire to connect with and develop camaraderie with others is up to each of us. That need for connection can be fulfilled through networking.

By fostering the power of cooperation, networking links people to one another for the mutual benefit of everyone involved. Those who are truly masterful at networking do it in a very quiet, yet powerful manner. These people know the power of grace and respect. They've developed their personal power and know how to connect with people to share their power. You have that personal power within you. Your potential network is unlimited.

What Networking Is

Networking is the passing along of information, ideas, and contacts from one person to another, and then possibly to more people. Every time someone shares an idea or contact with you, you are on the receiving end of networking. Every time you give someone support, encouragement, or a recommendation, you are on the giving end of networking.

Most of the time we don't think of networking as networking. If I call a friend because I've had a tough day and need the comfort of a caring person and a familiar voice or I offer to give a friend a ride to the airport when he leaves for his two-week dream cruise to Greece, I might think of these actions as just being a part of friendship or a friendly gesture. Or if I recommend my chiropractor to all my friends simply because I am so pleased with how much better she has helped me feel, I might categorize the action as common courtesy.

Networking is as simple as friendship. It's about people sharing and caring for one another. People become friends because they share certain things in common and connect with each other in ways that are pleasing to both people. Over time, friendships tend to grow and deepen. Friends provide support, information, and comfort and add fun to one another's lives. Friends also typically introduce their friends to their other friends, interests, hobbies, and businesses. This type of introduction is networking operating at its most natural level.

Make a list of all the times over the last week that you have done someone a favor, given someone encouragement, provided someone with a valuable or interesting piece of information, asked for help or advice, made a recommendation to someone, or given a referral. Pat yourself on the back for already being an active networker.

What a Network Is

A network is a group of people with links to one another. These links may be due to similar job situations, career activities, friends, neighbors, hobbies, schools, communities, religious activities, and so on. A network is a support system of people that you can reach out to for help, support, advice, or friendship. A network is an intricate web of people who are related in some way and thus connected to each other directly or through the links of other people in the network.

Your network is working when there is a constant flow of information, ideas, and contacts among you and the people around you.

You've heard of networks of computers that are connected via cables and communication lines that allow people to access and share information. A professional network is similar; it gives people a way to connect with one another for the purpose of accessing and exchanging information.

Actions Associated with Networking

Networking involves action. In fact, you must take action for the power of your network to become manifest. Without action, your network is like a field of grain that's been planted but is never harvested. There can be great value and worth in that field, but without the appropriate action, the good that the grain can do for others is never fulfilled.

Networking requires conscious action along with clear intention. As a way of life, networking incorporates attitude, awareness, and action. You can have a great attitude about wanting to be of service to others, but people only get served through action. You can be very aware of people and opportunities, and yet it is only when you take action to bring those people and opportunities together that results happen.

✔ **Giving and receiving information, contacts, and referrals.** Networking is a two-way street of giving and receiving. You are a wealth of information, contacts, and referrals and so are the people in your network. By accepting and offering support, you enhance the flow of networking, strengthen your relationships, and give people an opportunity to experience the satisfaction of giving and receiving support. This giving and receiving of information, contacts, and referrals can be done in person, over the phone, or via mail or e-mail. However, some type of action must take place to generate the interaction and exchange of information called networking.

You are the center and source of your network. You have available to you a multitude of resources to exchange, share, and pass along to others. Being a resource means that you are proactive about looking for ways to pass along what you know.

People may not always take you up on your offers and the information or contacts that you offer to others may not always turn out to be what they need. But the act of offering, whether or not you turn out to be helpful, generates goodwill.

Networking is a form of recycling — sharing what you know and have so that it can also be useful to others.

✔ **Introducing people.** From a networking perspective, introducing people to one another is like planting a seed. You take the initiative to link two people together and they then have the potential to generate growth by creating some value out of their having met. Because you are the common denominator for all the people in your network, you have the opportunity to create links between people, groups, and organizations.

Your network becomes even stronger when the people in your network know one another and do business with each other.

✔ **Making requests.** Ask your network for help. You can ask for information, names, ideas, validation, encouragement, recommendations, and so on. The process of making requests helps you find the resources that you want and need. And you help your network get into action by giving people a chance to respond to your requests. Chapter 6 gives further information on making requests and contains examples.

✔ **Sending notes.** Sending cards, letters, and e-mails are actions that help you to stay in touch with your network. Whether it's a note of thanks or congratulations, a request for support, or an offer of information, your taking the time and effort to send the note represents networking in action.

Thank people on a regular basis with your words and actions. Praising, acknowledging, expressing appreciation, and saying thanks are a vital part of building and nurturing powerful, long-term networking relationships. Appreciation is at the heart of networking.

✔ **Exchanging business cards.** Business cards are a tool for exchanging information and providing people with information on how to contact you. See Chapter 16 regarding how the exchange of business cards should happen as a natural part of the conversation that you are having with others.

✔ **Attending community, professional, and networking events.** Suit up and show up! Networking involves attending events at which you can meet and interact with people to generate opportunities. (See Chapter 3.)

✔ **Talking with people.** Take action to call people, walk up and introduce yourself to people, and engage in conversations with people. Networking happens through conversation. You have to open your mouth and your ears. I include tips on conversational skills and making small talk in Chapter 5.

The Four Components of Successful Networking

Networking is a way of relating to people. It encompasses being aware of people, having a positive attitude about people, having the ability to communicate with people, and getting in the habit of doing the things that build strong relationships.

You may discover that you're doing all the right things and that a shift in attitude will start your network snowballing. Or you may discover that, although you mean well and truly care about people, you need to be more proactive with your networking to start producing results.

Networkers are aware

Opportunities are all around you, and yet if you're not aware of them, they may as well not exist. Being aware means being in touch with the complex and ever-evolving world around you. As your awareness expands, you appreciate just how tremendously full of opportunity the world is — indeed, the world you live in expands.

For example, what if a student wants to go to college but doesn't have the funds? Even if a scholarship is available for someone in exactly the student's situation, if she or he isn't aware of the scholarship and doesn't apply for it, the scholarship doesn't do any good. The student could spend his or her whole life thinking, "If only I would have had access to the money for my education, I could have made something more of my life."

Awareness moves opportunities into possibilities. The student in my example had the opportunity, but the opportunity never became a real possibility because of a lack of awareness. Awareness is a critical part of effective networking.

Networking requires being aware of people and of opportunities. Notice the people around you, what they are talking about, and what they are doing. Rather than being self-focused, create a radar system that is able to easily detect what is going on around you so that you can respond to happenings as a networker. Doing so will help you be aware of what the people in your network want and need. In addition:

✔ Be aware of the network you already have and how vast and powerful it can be when utilized effectively. Because of all the strengths, skills, information, contacts, and expertise that you have to offer others, and that others have to offer you, your network can create a multitude of opportunities for yourself and others.

✔ Be aware that it's human nature that people want to give and contribute to you and to each other. They may be hesitant, scared, or too shy to offer their support or ideas, but know that the desire to be of value is natural.

✔ Be aware of the almost unlimited nature of your network. Every individual in your network has a network that you can access.

> ✔ Be aware of what you're thinking and not saying, what you need but are not requesting. Often, if you say what you're thinking, you can create an opportunity.
>
> ✔ Be aware of how networking can be an easy, natural part of your life. Remind yourself that networking is an accepted and expected way of relating to others and doing business.
>
> ✔ Be aware that almost everything you could possibly want or need is available and right around you . . . it's yours for the asking!

Networkers have a helpful attitude

Being an effective networker isn't just about what you do; it's also about your attitude toward what you're doing. It's about how you relate to others — yet, it's also about how you relate to yourself. Your attitude influences everything in your life — the goals you set, the risks you're willing to take, the way you approach people, your willingness to approach people, the way you respond to people, and much more. Your attitude sets the tone for your life. It's like the background music of a TV show.

Your attitude not only affects what you do; it also affects the way people respond to you. Your attitude can create a barrier and turn people off, or it can communicate with people that you want people to interact with you.

Your attitude is the way you think and relate to yourself and others, to what happens to you and around you.

Networkers have an attitude of contribution, service, possibility, and opportunity. They look for ways to be of service and contribute. They tend to think that there is a way, rather than "No way." They enjoy contributing to others and allow others to contribute to them.

What is your attitude when you walk into a room of people?

A. There's nobody interesting to talk to here.

B. This looks like a great group of business professionals.

C. I'd rather be home watching television.

Imagine if three people walked into a networking event, and they have the three attitudes above. Picture what each one would do and say, how they would look and behave based on their attitude. Think about the different experiences and results they would have as a result of their attitude.

Your attitude serves as a filter. Everything that you see and hear goes through your attitude filter. If you meet someone new and your attitude filter is "Here's someone who probably has nothing to offer me. This is useless," then you will probably not really listen to what the other person has to say and you'll miss out on learning and discovering anything that she could offer to you. She may even offer something of value, and because of your attitude you blow it off — another missed opportunity!

If you meet people and hear what they say through the attitude filter "I am open and receptive to discovering the value that this person has to offer and I want to know how we can contribute to one another," you listen in a way that creates connection and opportunity.

A simple shift in attitude is enough to change and enhance your life. Your attitude is not set in stone. You have the opportunity at every moment to become aware of attitudes that you have that aren't in sync with what you want to be experiencing in life and then change them.

Think of someone you know whom you respect as a networker. Identify what it is you appreciate about his networking attitude. Identify how you will strengthen that particular attitude within yourself.

Networkers hone their communication skills

Networking happens through conversation. It is through conversation that we connect with each other, learn about one another, and share information. After mastering the art of small talk, you will feel more comfortable meeting new people and developing rapport. By developing rapport with people, you will be able to turn small talk into opportunities to make requests and be a networking resource. See Chapters 5 and 17 regarding small talk and conversation skills.

Most people tend to partially communicate. When networking, it is important to give complete and accurate information when you are making requests or giving referrals. By developing an assertive communication style, you generate respect and dignity for yourself and others in your networking interactions. See Chapters 6 and 7 for in-depth information on two important communication skills: making requests and listening.

Assertive communication requires that you speak in a way that honors your own needs while at the same time you respect the rights and needs of others.

Networkers develop relationship-building habits

A network exists as a series of relationships and connections between people. People must relate with and respect one another in order for a valuable networking exchange to happen. Building relationships is your first priority when networking.

Considerate, respectful, caring behavior builds strong relationships. These behaviors, practiced on a consistent and regular basis, become the relationship-building habits that guarantee a long-lasting, fulfilling network. Some of the caring behaviors that make for powerful relationship-building habits include saying thanks, appreciating people, sending notes of encouragement and support, paying attention when people are talking, calling to say hi, and honoring people by doing what you say you will do. For more information and ideas on powerful networking habits, see Chapter 4.

What Networking Is Not

Networking is commonly misunderstood. As a result, networking is often misused. Although many actions, activities, and communications are related to networking, networking's heart is the desire to serve and contribute to others.

Networking does not involve

- ✔ **Manipulating people into doing what you want.** People in your network do things for you because they want to. Often, we think we have to manipulate to get what we want when all we have to do is ask in a clear, upfront, no-strings-attached manner.

- ✔ **Keeping score.** Tit for tat is an old form of false networking: You do this for me, I'll do that for you. Now, negotiating with people is fine, and finding ways to be of mutual value and benefit and to reciprocate is great. But a you-owe-me attitude is detrimental to the flow of networking.

- ✔ **Obligating others.** If I think that the only way people will help me out is if I make them feel obligated, then networking is arduous and limiting rather than fun and unlimited.

  There is no need to feel obligated or make others feel obligated when you focus on doing the best that you can for others and trust others to do the best that they can for you.

✔ **Putting people on the spot.** Networking is about serving people, not about putting people on the spot. In order to build strong relationships, you must learn to put people at ease, develop trust and rapport, and be an advocate for others.

✔ **Being demanding of others.** Sometimes, people get what they want by demanding it of others. Networking, however, involves giving people an opportunity to share with you — but never making demands. Even if you get what you want, if you had to demand it, then you've missed the opportunity to develop a deeper level of respect and appreciation in the relationship.

Networking is a lifestyle, not a thing that you can do from time to time.

Networking, Marketing, and Selling — How They're Related

If you own a business or are in the fields of marketing or sales, your duties and activities may include networking, marketing, and selling. These three activities are related. Each one is an essential ingredient of business success.

Marketing encompasses all the activities involved in presenting a business to the marketplace via brochures, advertisements, Web sites, mailings, and so on. The goal of marketing is to get business and product information in front of people so that consumers buy the products you're selling.

Networking is a specific marketing tool that is very effective in getting the word out to people. It's a very direct, personal, and credible marketing approach because it involves people talking to people. In fact, it may be the way that many people hear about your business. And it's cheap — I mean it's cost-effective!

Selling requires offering a product or service for purchase and asking people to spend money. The process of selling involves describing how your product will fit the needs of a potential buyer. Networking does not involve an exchange of money, but rather an exchange of information, ideas, or contacts.

Just as networking is helpful in marketing, networking is also helpful in selling. Networking builds relationships that may lead to sales. Although networking can be very beneficial in creating opportunities for selling, knowing when to network and when to sell is important. With networking, the focus is on building connections and being of value. With selling, the focus is on matching a product with a need and securing a commitment to buy. Great information on selling is available in *Selling For Dummies,* by Tom Hopkins (Hungry Minds, Inc.).

Marketing, selling, and networking each have a time and a place. They feed into one another and should support each other. Don't focus on one element at the expense of others, and don't try to market or sell in an environment that's better suited for networking.

Networking is a vital people skill for everyone, from sales reps to administrative assistants to entrepreneurs to corporate executives.

When salespeople are not trained in effective networking, they fail to take advantage of opportunities to meet people who could either become customers or refer them to potential customers.

Network marketing is a term you may have heard. Network marketing is a way of doing business. People grow their network marketing business by bringing other people into the business, typically as distributors. It's a business growth plan based on people bringing in other people, and networking is a vital skill for making those contacts and building successful distributor relationships. For more information on network marketing, see Chapter 11 in this book or check out Zig Ziglar's *Network Marketing For Dummies* (Hungry Minds, Inc.).

Networking's Benefits

We are in an age where appreciating and utilizing the power that comes from combining ideas and resources is crucial. You've probably engaged in brainstorming sessions during which the ideas start building on each other and the end result is magic. Networking sort of works along the same lines: The power of many is greater than the power of one.

The value of networking shows up in all areas of life. It fulfills a basic human desire to connect, belong, and be part of something bigger than yourself. It generates a sense of well-being and respect. Networking isn't just important in the business world. It's important to you personally because it helps to shape your future, your experience of yourself, and your mental, emotional, physical, and spiritual well-being.

Here are some other benefits that networking provides:

> ✔ **Greater and easier access to information, ideas, and contacts.** Through your network of contacts, you have access to far more people than you could reach on your own. Also, those people have information far beyond what you alone could possibly know — information regarding all areas of life. By staying in touch and keeping your network strong, you are able to reach people more quickly and easily.

✔ **Friendships and professional relationships.** Some of the people you connect with through networking will become great friends and powerful professional allies. Through networking, you develop partners and advocates and a support system that is as committed to your success as you are. Your allies enable you to pursue your dreams, give you constant encouragement and reminders that they care about you, remind you to get back on track when you get distracted from your goals, energize and inspire you by their successes and courage, and provide you with role models.

✔ **Fun approaches to getting things done.** Have you ever noticed how tasks that are normally drudgery can be fun when other people help? When we help each other, even with mundane tasks, we have the ability to create joy in being together and a sense of play. Moreover, as you become more familiar and comfortable with people through networking, you are able to be yourself and learn to enjoy yourself even more.

✔ **Opportunities to give and contribute to others.** People want to be of value and contribute to others. Any time that we give of ourselves in a way that helps someone else, the act of giving enhances our self-image. Although we live in a culture that tends to honor measurable accomplishment as the ultimate giver of satisfaction, the human heart and soul yearn for the sense of satisfaction that comes from helping others.

✔ **Increased efficiency and productivity.** Having access to people and information via your network allows you to be efficient and productive. With a strong network, people are more likely to return your phone calls, respond promptly to your requests, and sometimes even jump in with their support.

✔ **Results and accomplishments.** Your network should enhance and expand your results and accomplishments. By working together effectively with others, and utilizing the resources and support of others, you can accomplish more than you could accomplish by yourself. With consistent networking, quick and major accomplishments can become the norm.

✔ **Opportunities (job, career, business, personal).** The people in your network expand your scope and outreach, creating new avenues and links to new opportunities. Constantly encountering these opportunities keeps you optimistic that another opportunity could be just around the corner.

✔ **Peace of mind and a sense of security.** Life is full of unexpected twists and turns. Having a strong support system gives you the comfort of knowing that people will be there to help, no matter what comes your way.

✔ **Resources for everything you want and need in life.** Having a full network means that anytime you need or want anything you can turn to someone you know as a resource to help you fulfill that want or need. Whether you're dealing with a career, financial, or health challenge, someone from your network will have information that helps you deal with the situation or a recommendation regarding someone who can provide you with assistance.

✔ **Trust and faith in the good of people.** By accepting help and support from others, you bring out the good in people and are constantly reminded of the goodness that is available.

✔ **Less stress in all areas of your life.** When you're utilizing your support system, rather than trying to do everything on your own, life is much more relaxing and enjoyable. The typical aches, pains, and illnesses that are brought on by stress and that are rampant in our society become less of a problem. The support and camaraderie of your network contributes to your mental and physical well-being.

Networking addresses and satisfies many basic human needs and desires. The benefits of networking go beyond the tangible results. Actually, the feeling of connectedness is the greatest reward that networking brings. In all of the networking groups that I've belonged to, people typically join for the business opportunity. Yet, those same people later indicate that they value the relationships and camaraderie that they get from their membership above everything else.

The heart of networking is people caring about people. Networking is truly powerful when genuine human caring animates it.

Business benefits of networking

Business success requires satisfied customers, people working together effectively, quality products and services, profitability, and strong leadership. The one asset you have that supports all these aspects of business success is your network. Your network is your source for customers, problem solving, encouragement, and industry information.

Networking is a marketing tool for growing your business. Through your network, you can create a word-of-mouth marketing stream that reaches people you would never be able to reach on your own or by other means. Here are some of the ways networking can be a powerful resource for business growth:

✔ Happy and satisfied customers tell others about products and services they like. This gives businesses access to new customers through current customers.

Customers are part of your network. If you own a bookstore and your customers recommend your store to their friends, they have been a valuable networking resource for you and their friends.

✔ Participation in community activities and industry-related activities creates community goodwill and exposure to individuals who can be potential customers and resources for the business.

✔ Businesspeople discover opportunities to partner and collaborate with each other, which can lead to sharing facilities, resources, and even sending customers to one another.

Being well-connected means you get to leverage your outreach and your results. People whom you know allow you to extend into areas, organizations, and venues that you may not normally have access to. They provide you with a strong foundation for growing your business or advancing your career.

Gaining business wisdom from your network

In the business world, people often learn as they go. They make mistakes and then recover as best they can. Business people with a strong network, however, are able to learn from their network and avoid many of the mistakes they may have otherwise made. With a network, the learning curve becomes both steeper — meaning that people learn quicker — and longer — meaning that people learn more overall.

You don't need to make the same mistakes that your friends and acquaintances have made. If you share your experiences with other people, and they share their experiences with you, everyone is more successful as a result. Some of the ways your network provides you with business wisdom include

✔ Experts can provide feedback or validation regarding ideas or help with new ideas. They're only a phone call away.

✔ You can create an advisory board of businesspeople that is regularly available to you and that's committed to the growth and success of your business.

✔ People are available to brainstorm with, so you get outside of your normal way of thinking and create new and innovative ways to grow your business.

✔ People in your network can connect you with potential employees.

Community connections through networking

What has happened to our communities? Do you know and talk with your neighbors? Maybe, maybe not. Even though our hectic lives may appear to make us more isolated, we still have a basic human desire to connect in a safe, supportive environment that provides respect and honor and allows us to live with dignity and harmony. We create that environment through our network. We create our environment by the people who we draw into our lives and choose to spend time with.

We can't help but be influenced by the people and the environment where we live. Even though we may tend to think of ourselves as independent individuals, we are part of a very intricate and interdependent community of individuals influencing each other in major ways. Rather than attempting to protect your independence, work on understanding and enhancing your connections.

Here's how networking contributes to building stronger communities:

- ✔ People feel connected and become more approachable and available to each other.
- ✔ A sense of community pride develops and people begin to work together on projects that improve the community.
- ✔ A sense of safety and camaraderie develops, which enhances everyone's sense of well-being.

Serendipity and divine connections in networking

Consistent networking creates opportunities that seem to magically appear at just the right time, in miraculous ways, and with unexpected people. A person's name pops into my thoughts. I call them and something wonderful happens as a result of the phone call. Or I attend a meeting and happen to be introduced to the perfect person for the project that I'm working on. Such events lead to a sense of serendipity, a feeling that everything is in order and that some things are meant to be. No matter what your faith or beliefs, be aware that if you network faithfully you may find yourself serendipitously at the right place, at the right time, meeting the right people.

When you develop a networking lifestyle, you may find serendipitous events happening on a regular basis. Trust the process of networking to give you connections to everything you want and deserve. Look around. Stay alert. Your network is at your fingertips and is eager to give you the gift of having your dreams fulfilled.

Timing and trust pay off

After living in Austin for six years, Leslie and Kathy decided to sell everything, buy an RV, and head to San Diego for what looked like a great opportunity to work with friends who had started a training company. They found an RV park on the beach, set up their new lifestyle, and had a great time for about nine months — all the while charging most of their living expenses to their credit card. When things didn't go as they hoped, they decided to head back to Texas. They arrived back in Austin with no jobs and continued to live in their RV. Kathy went to work for an outplacement firm and Leslie got a job with Relax the Back, a company that offers products for people who have back problems.

About that same time, some friends of theirs started a company called CyberCorp, developing software for stock market trading. These friends said that they wanted Leslie to come work for CyberCorp, but they weren't quite ready to hire more people.

One day, Leslie got called into a meeting at Relax the Back and was told that he was being laid off because the company was being bought and moving to California. At the same time that Leslie was getting word that he was out of work, his friend Philip from CyberCorp was leaving him a phone message saying, "It's time . . . we're ready for you to come onboard."

Leslie thus got his severance package with Relax the Back and immediately went to work for CyberCorp — the seventh person hired by the company. For three years, Leslie worked for CyberCorp and accumulated stock in the company. Then the owner decided to offer some of his own stock for sale to create additional cash for the company. Leslie thought it sounded like a good opportunity, so he approached Kathy about buying the stock. Even though they didn't have any money and the stock wasn't really worth anything at the time, they decided to take out a loan to buy the stock. Eventually, CyberCorp was bought for millions of dollars. Leslie and Kathy went from living in an RV to being millionaires. When they look back at the situation, they figure that for every month Leslie worked there, he made a million dollars. And yet during that time, he had no idea that his friends were developing a technology that would be so valuable and that would provide him with such financial freedom.

Chapter 2

Your Core Network

Your network is your support system. It consists of family, friends, and people you grew up with, went to school with, worked with, and so on. Actually, your network consists of everyone you have ever met or known. Now, of course, some of those people don't remain active in your network. Nevertheless, they are part of your network because you have made contact with them and could probably reconnect with them.

Your *core* network consists of those people closest to you whom you have regular contact with. They are the ones who influence you and support you on a regular and ongoing basis. People in your core network have a strong bond with you. They are available to you and are sincerely interested in how you are doing. They tend to return your phone calls promptly. They trust their relationship with you to be mutually supportive.

Some of the people in your core network have a single specific role that they play in your life: accountant, financial planner, banker, hairstylist, minister, and so on. At the same time, there are people in your core network who are close friends or family and tend to be supportive in numerous ways rather than one specific way.

Family Support

Your family is your original core support system. Even as you get older, your family can continue to be a powerful support system throughout your life and in all areas of your life. Often, you take on certain roles and characteristics when you're with family members and you get used to your family members being a certain way. As a result, you may begin to limit how you relate to them. (A later section of this chapter addresses this problem — and its solution.)

Even though they're "just family," your family members are like all the other people in your network. They know a lot of people, have mastered various skills, performed various tasks and jobs, and developed expertise in certain arenas. Quite possibly, you have relatives who can be valuable resources for you (and you for them).

This is not about hustling family members for business! Remember: Networking is about building relationships in which people are valued and honored and in which there is mutual support. Don't rule out your family members as great networking allies. They have contacts, skills, and expertise just like all the other people in your network.

Determining how your family can network

Many families already network effectively with one another. You can probably think of various times when a family member has referred you to someone or something. Maybe it was when you were looking for a new dentist, wanted to find a reliable auto mechanic, were looking for a new job, or wanted suggestions for a vacation you were planning. Chances are that you already network effectively with some of your family members. The challenge is to see how you can expand your networking approach to create even more opportunities for being of service to one another. Here's an exercise that may help:

Create a family inventory by making a list of your family members in a way that helps to identify how they can be resources. Your family inventory might include

- Family members who have worked or currently work in the same industry as you or in a similar industry

- Family members who have worked or currently work in a similar business structure as you (corporate, entrepreneur, contract work, and so on)

- Family members who have had or currently have an identical or similar job position as the one you have (manager, sales rep, administrative assistant, purchasing agent, and so on)

- Family members who have developed a skill or attained a level of success or accomplishment that you admire

- Family members who have a vast network and broad circle of influence

- Family members who participate in various community, charitable, and professional organizations

Knowing what each other do for a living

For a family network to function effectively in the areas of career and work, family members need to know what other family members do. In many families, this is a problem. Do your parents, children, or cousins understand what you do? When their friends ask what you do, can they speak clearly about the work that you do? Or do they just mumble, "Oh, she does something over at XYZ Company"?

If your family members don't have a basic understanding of what each other do, then how can you possibly network with one another? If the people around you do not understand what you do, then networking opportunities are being missed. Your family doesn't need to understand everything about what you do and how you do what you do. However, conveying to your family at least a simple understanding of what you do is crucial.

Making your conversations with family count

People sometimes get so comfortable around their family and friends that they are lax in their communication. You may think that you already have a connection and an established relationship with the members of your core network and that you don't have to keep working at it. You may think you already know everything there is to know about them. Yet the truth is you don't know what's happened to them that day or since you last saw one another. Something major could have happened in their lives since last you talked with them.

In the case of elders in the family, you could learn about what they did or what they were like before you came along.

Consider talking to family in new ways rather than falling into familiar conversational patterns. For instance, a common question in families is "How are you?" The common response is "fine." But you can stop the cycle of unhelpful small talk by taking that person's habitual response and having it lead to your next question: "Great. What's been the finest thing about your day?"

Explore and be curious. Don't just take their comments or responses at face value. Be playful and creative by responding in a fun, unusual, or energetic manner. By taking what others say to a new level, you generate deeper, more intriguing, and more personal interactions.

Here are some other specific questions you can ask:

- ✔ "So what about that XYZ project I read about that your company is conducting, are you involved with that?"
- ✔ "So you've been with this company for X years now; you must really like the work, eh?"
- ✔ "Last time we talked you were planning a trip to Cancun. How was it?"
- ✔ "I thought about you when I heard about XYZ happening in your area of town. Were you affected by that?"

Show an interest by asking specific questions and mentioning things that you already know about that person or have previously talked about.

Likewise, when family members ask you how you're doing or how business is going, don't just come back with a pat answer like "Great." Take the opportunity to tell them a little bit about your business and the projects that you are working on. Don't go into a long, detailed, boring, and technical monologue or presentation. But answer their questions with more than one word and give them some interesting information. If they listen, seem interested, and ask further questions, then this could evolve into an interesting and valuable conversation

Rather than sharing data, facts, and information, share a piece of you. Include the person you're talking with in new areas and aspects of your life. When you talk with Aunt Susie, do you always talk about the weather? What if you told Aunt Susie about your newest work project, most recent vacation, or new hobby? You might think, "Well, she wouldn't be interested in talking or hearing about that." But you don't really know that. Chances are she will be interested, simply because she's interested in you. Let people be part of your life so that you can deepen your relationships and be resources for each other.

List ten things that you feel strongly about. Think about whether or not your close friends and family know that these are things that are important to you. Think about how giving them this insight about you might deepen your relationship.

Being present in body, mind, and spirit!

Give your presence to family and friends. Don't just go through the motions or be physically there and yet mentally somewhere else. If an opportune moment came along in the conversation — for sharing, connecting, offering support, or asking a critical question — you might miss it entirely!

Notice who you're talking to or sitting across from. Remind yourself of the importance of this moment in time (this is popularly called "being in the moment"). Remind yourself of where you are physically. "Oh wow, I'm at my first NSA national convention!" or "This is our first family gathering in our new home" or "Here I am at my reunion with my best friend from 20 years ago." Don't let special moments slip by. Let your energy and awareness be present — in other words, be both physically and mentally there for the people in your network.

Every family is a network of links of people connecting with one another through the generations. The richness of our family connections can be cultivated with some attention and by focusing on listening, learning more about one another, looking for commonalities and opportunities to support each other, and expressing appreciation.

Being a resource for your family

Networking *for* your family members is just as important as networking *with* your family members. Your resources can be a valuable aid to the members of your family. Your resources can even, at times, be a lifesaver for someone you love. Be interested in what is going on with others so that you can be there for them in whatever they need.

Friends in Time of Need

Networking happens most easily, naturally, and automatically with your friends. A friendship carries with it trust, rapport, and caring, which are basic elements of a successful networking relationship. You naturally want to be with friends because you like them, enjoy them, and experience some kind of pleasure being with them. You typically wish friends well, and desire success, health, and well-being for them. You are probably pleased to be of help.

Friendship is a healing force. It has been repeatedly documented that people with strong friendships tend to recover more quickly from illness, and even have lower rates of contracting certain illnesses. A lack of friends leads to isolation, alienation, and depression, and can adversely affect your health, success, and well-being. The experience of being loved and cared for by others contributes to our esteem, our health, and our overall experience of life being worthwhile.

Have you noticed how people come together when there is a crisis? When there is a tragedy, people tend to rally around to be of help. That is part of human nature.

Networking your way to health

Chaka's networking story happened because she found that she was dealing with breast cancer. Even though her doctor wanted to remove the breast, Chaka wasn't convinced that this was absolutely necessary or the path she wanted to take. Being a great networker, she decided to do some research regarding her options.

She got on the phone and reached out to her friends who responded with information, contacts in the medical community, prayers, and support. She also got on the Web to research the medical recommendations, treatments, and clinics that were available. She immersed herself in the many books and articles sent to her by people in her network. By doing this, she gathered a wealth of information and at the same time discovered that the treatment she desired was going to be very costly and only partially covered by her insurance.

As word of Chaka's situation got out to her friends, they began to rally around her. A dear friend of hers who was a musician had lost his mother to breast cancer the year before. He initiated a fundraiser for Chaka and many of her friends responded by pulling together a beautiful concert. People not only helped out with organizing and promoting the event, they also donated items for a silent auction. Over $5,000 was raised for her treatment.

Another friend in Austin, Texas responded by asking for Chaka's mailing list and sent out a letter to everyone, letting them know of the situation and the need for support. She requested money, prayers, and anything else people could offer. Chaka says, "Every day when the mailman came, there would be envelopes of donations ranging from $20 to $1,000." She received the financial support and the medical care that she needed. Her treatment was successful and she is very grateful for her health and the network of friends who rallied around her.

Your friends would rally around you if only you would give them a chance. Let people know what you need and want so that they can be there for you. Ask for help and support. (See Chapter 6 on making requests and allowing others to help.) It is not uncommon for someone to have experienced a crisis and everyone (including best friends and family) goes, "Well, I had no idea." Don't leave your friends with no idea of what's going on with you and in your life. Share your successes, your celebrations, and your wins, but also be willing to share your challenges, difficulties, and struggles. You cannot utilize the help that is available and all around you unless people know to reach out and offer their help.

Create Support Systems for Each Area of Your Life

Your network is your life-support system. A balanced and fully functional network is the best way to a balanced life. Some people network easily when it comes to career, jobs, and business opportunities, but when they have a health or personal challenge they withdraw rather then reach out to their network. Create a core network that includes people you can call on and count on for all areas and aspects of your life. Don't wait until you have a need to build your network. Don't wait until you hit rock bottom to call for help. Don't wait until there's an emergency to put a backup plan in place.

Creating a full network

Think about all the areas of your life and identify whether you have a core network in place to provide support for you in all those areas. If not, start finding people who have skills and expertise in that area and bring them into your life and start building a relationship with them.

Having a full network means that you have people you can call on and count on in all areas of your life. To see how full and balanced your network is, create a list of the important areas of your life and your corresponding network. Here's how to do it:

1. **In the first column, list the various facets of your life: career, hobbies, health, finances, spirituality, personal development, family, community involvement, volunteering, relationships, or whatever.**

   Pick the categories that relate to your life (your list will be different from mine or anyone else's list). And don't worry about which category is first or last on the list. The order doesn't matter

2. **In the second column, list the people you already know who are influential to your success, happiness, and full self-expression in that area of our life.**

3. **In the third column, list people who you could bring into your core network for that area of your life by building and deepening your relationship with them.**

Table 3-1 is an example.

Table 3-1:	Charting a Full Network	
Area of Life	*People Already in My Network*	*People to Bring into My Network*
Career	Joe	Mathilda
Hobbies	Martha	Gary
Health	Mark	Natalie
Finances	Nina	George
Spirituality	Vicki	Marilyn
Relationships	Pat	Jose
Personal development	Carmen	Harry

Call the people in column two and let them know that you appreciate them being in your life and let them know how important they are to you. Call the people in the third column to invite them to join you for coffee, ask them for advice, or initiate some way to further your connection with them.

This list is designed to have you consciously focus on building your network You can have a vast network just like you can have great talent, but if you don't use it what good does it do? Without use, ultimately your talent and your network will be wasted.

Because "Anne" lived in New Jersey and worked in Pennsylvania, she felt like she never had any real connection with anyone. Because she didn't work in the town in which she lived, she had a hard time making connections there. She didn't want to have to move to another city or change jobs in order to feel more connected, so she began to consider other ways that she could develop some friends in the area where she lived.

She heard about an organization called Business and Professional Women (BPW) and became interested. After asking a member about the organization and visiting one of its meetings, she decided to join a local BPW chapter. She later became an officer of the organization and got to know a lot of the members. She enjoyed the group and found that it helped her to feel not quite so isolated, though she still hadn't really found ways to offer or ask for support from the members.

Then her father got sick and she needed to go to the courthouse to handle some paperwork. Her problem was that the courthouse was a 40-minute drive from work and there was no way she could get there during normal work hours. When one of the members of her BPW chapter heard about Anne's situation, she contacted another member who works at the courthouse. The woman who works at the courthouse handled everything for Anne and even helped her fill out the various applications. Several other members of the chapter happened to work at the hospital and helped out with Anne's father's appointments. Anne said she was totally surprised and grateful. She had no idea how valuable that group could be to her until she had a need.

If someone had asked Anne before her father got sick what the importance of networking was, she would have said business success. But what she discovered was that her network helped to relieve the strain and pressure of dealing with a situation she had never had to deal with before, the illness (and eventual passing) of her father. Her chapter friends made it easier for her to get through a very difficult situation. She said the whole experience helped her see how important people are and that people really are willing to help, but they won't know how to help if they don't know you and don't know what is going on in your life.

Mentors and buddies

You can have mentors and buddies for all areas and aspects of your life. Mentors are the people whom you respect, admire, and call on for advice and support. They may be role models for you in some way. They embody some qualities or have characteristics that you desire to develop within yourself. (See Chapter 10 for information on mentoring in the corporate arena.)

You can have mentors for your relationships, your hobbies, basically any area of your life. They are typically people who have attained a level of success or expertise that you admire and desire. They are also people you have a relationship with that allows you to learn and grow through accessing their experience and assistance.

Buddies are the people whom you enjoy hanging out with and with whom you share some common interest or hobby. Dancing is one of my hobbies, so I have dance buddies. Some of them I see only when I go dancing, although I have developed friendships with some of my dancing buddies that go beyond our common interest in dancing. Develop buddy relationships with people who have the same interests and avocations that you have. If you want to take yoga, take cooking classes, play golf, or participate in other activities, you can find people with similar interests to join you. Get involved in those activities and make a point to meet the other people who enjoy the same activities and thus develop some friendships.

Utilize the buddy system!

Having buddies can make your participation in activities much more enjoyable, and it expands your network in new ways. One of my dance buddies is a homebuilder. As we began to get to know each other, we would talk a little bit about our businesses. Once when I needed a plumber to check on a leak in my kitchen, I called him and he was able to refer me to someone whom I could call to get prompt, reliable service. There have been various other times that I have called to ask his advice about a home repair problem. As a single-woman homeowner, knowing that I can call on him with my questions and problems is a great relief to me.

Make a list of your hobbies and interests. You can do this by modifying Table 3-1. Here's how to do it.

1. **Create another 3-column table.**

2. **List your hobbies and interests in the first column.**

3. **Start a second column and by each item list the people you know who share this same hobby or interest.**

4. **Start a third column and list the people you know who have attained a level of success with this hobby or interest that you admire.**

Turning acquaintances into buddies

Everyone starts out as a stranger. Until you meet someone, you call him or her a stranger. After you meet the person, you may call him or her an acquaintance. Then, it is up to you to take the steps to turn the person into a friend, buddy, mentor, client, or whatever.

How do friendships happen? You meet a person and discover that you like him, enjoy him, feel good around him, and have fun with him. You engage in small talk with him (see Chapter 5 for ways to initiate conversations and draw information from people) and find that you have some common interests or hobbies. You choose to spend time with him and the process of getting to know each other continues. As you get to know each other better, you begin to trust the person and reveal more about yourself and the friendship deepens. You call on each other for support and to do fun things together. It's a process that can happen relatively quickly and easily with some people. With others, the friendship develops gradually, slowly, over a long period of time.

Using the Grapevine Responsibly

The grapevine (your network) is often how you hear about deaths, illnesses, marriages, babies, celebrations, pending contracts, job transitions, and other important events. The grapevine is useful to networkers because networking involves gathering information, not just gathering contacts, and then acting on that information in a manner that is useful to yourself and others.

There are times, however, when it is best to check the validity of the information you hear through the grapevine. You may need to further clarify the facts in order to make clear choices on how to respond and offer yourself to someone as a resource. Know how to distinguish a rumor from a fact from an opinion by asking questions such as "How did you hear about that?" or "How can I find out more about . . .?" or "Do you think that's hearsay or that it really happened?"

Grapevine information can be distorted. Listen and check it out. Do not participate (*listening* to it is one form of participating) in malicious grapevine information or negative gossip. Remember that gossip tells more about the person speaking it than it does about the person being spoken of.

Part II
Building and Maintaining Your Network

The 5th Wave   By Rich Tennant

PROFESSIONAL NETWORKERS PICNIC

"Don't forget your conversation generators."

In this part . . .

Networking is about people connecting, communicating, and creating success for each other. This part covers the skills and actions that are required to communicate effectively and build networking relationships. Check out the information on what to say when making small talk, asking for help, following through on a request, and introducing yourself to others. I also include tips on how to fine-tune your listening skills and even how to ask others to listen to you.

Chapter 3

Expanding Your Circle of Influence through Networking Events

• •

In This Chapter

▶ Knowing how to mingle gracefully and comfortably

▶ Broadening your network by attending networking events and trade shows

▶ Establishing new relationships through memberships in networking clubs

▶ Forming networking focus groups

• •

*B*y expanding your network, you bring into your life more people who can be influential to your success. You also expand the number of people who you may have a chance to influence in a positive way.

You can expand your network and circle of influence by participating in networking clubs, trade shows, and networking focus groups. Use this chapter to help you discover how to utilize networking events to expand your network. You can find information on how to prepare for an event, mingle like a pro, and follow up effectively.

Your network includes people who can contribute to your success and fulfillment. They may use their influence to help you avoid pitfalls that they have encountered or to steer you towards a great opportunity.

Knowing Where You Can Meet People

Obviously, you can meet people almost anywhere and everywhere. In this chapter, I review information about how to make good use of trade shows, networking clubs, and various types of networking events. Some common networking events might be sponsored by organizations such as:

✔ Alumni associations

✔ Industry associations/trade associations

- Chambers of commerce
- Neighborhood associations
- Civic organizations
- Business associations

Mingling Like a Pro

When you're at a trade show, networking club, or any other networking event, much of your time is spent mingling. This means you will be meeting people and talking and then moving on to meet others and then moving on to meet someone else.

Mingling involves taking the opportunity to meet and talk with people throughout the room or the event. The word *mingle* implies that you will not stay in conversation with one person or one group of people the whole time. It implies that it is your duty to make the rounds — and to make the rounds so that you are sincerely connecting with people, not just making obligatory or superficial contacts.

Think of mingling in terms of how it relates to dating. It may be that a best first date is a one-hour lunch. You have time to begin to get to know one another. It is a safe way to find out if you have anything in common and an attraction for one another. The second date gives you additional time together, probably in a different environment and for more than just one hour. You discover if you want to invest more time together. It is a gradual process of learning, exploring, and developing a relationship.

Mingling at networking events often provides the initial opportunity for making the connection that represents the beginning of a networking relationship. You have a chance to meet in a safe, supportive environment. You needn't spend more than 15 to 20 minutes in conversation with one another before moving on to talk with others. And during that time, you and the person with whom you are conversing can ask each other questions and gather information. Through mingling, you both can learn about each other's business and discover if there are reasons to be in touch with each other in the future. If so, then one of you contacts the other to have further conversation or schedule a meeting, lunch, or appointment.

Mingling is not the place to sell to someone. It is the place for meeting people. Once you have met, the ball is in your court for further interaction. You can take the next step with a phone call, e-mail, note, or letter.

A little preparation goes a long way

Here's a common networking-event scenario:

> Jack walks into the hotel ballroom and heads straight for the refreshments. On his way he passes by people he knows without evening noticing or stopping to say hi. He gets his drink and plate of food and sits down at a table where he sees some people he knows. They talk, chat, laugh, possibly have a good time. He may, by chance, be introduced to someone at the table whom he didn't already know and they might even exchange business cards — because they are at a networking event and that's the thing to do.

> The next day, Jack gets to the office, glances at the business cards he collected the day before, and doesn't even remember most of those people. Most of the cards get tossed in the wastebasket.

This is networking? No. This is partying, socializing, waiting on something to happen, and hoping magic will take over your life. This is thinking that maybe if you show up at enough of these events, one will pay off — just like a numbers game. Maybe at some point you'll meet someone who can be of value and benefit to you. However, with this attitude you are missing countless opportunities! You can create value and meet interesting people at every event you attend. Doing so is up to you!

A little preparation makes a major difference with everything in life, including your effectiveness while networking. Prepare yourself and think ahead. Even if the preparation is as simple as thinking about the event while you're driving there, by getting mentally prepared you will be more present and available to be with people once you arrive at the event. Mental preparation clears your mind — making you more likely to see opportunities that you might not have noticed otherwise. Preparation also helps you feel more comfortable and relaxed.

Here are some things to think about before attending a networking event:

> ✔ **Who do you want to meet and with whom do you want to talk?**
> Identify the types of people you want to meet. Maybe you want to meet people who can be centers of influence for you or sources of support for you. If you are a realtor (or banker, or musician . . .) what types of professionals are good for you to know? If you own a moving company, you may want to meet realtors. If you have specific people in mind, think about what you know about them. Clearly identify why you want to meet them, what you have to offer them, and what they have to offer you.

- **Who is the sponsor and what do you know about the sponsoring organization?** Recall any information that you can about the organization, who the leaders are in the organization, the purpose of the organization, and the purpose of the event. With all of this information in the forefront of your thinking, you will be more effective at conversing with people in a way that is meaningful and respectful.

- **Who will possibly be there whom you already know?** Who do you want to make sure to say hello to? Who do you want to see because you want to ask them something or offer them something? A networking event can save you time and phone calls when you think ahead about things that you can handle while there. Can the person you already know introduce you to the person who you want to meet?

- **Do you have your networking supplies handy?** Make sure you have lots of business cards in a place where they are easy to reach (see Chapter 16). Likewise, make sure you have a pen handy so that you can jot down notes or reminders for yourself regarding the people you are meeting.

- **What are some fun and interesting conversation openers and small talk topics?** Attempt to identify topics that are appropriate to the event, the sponsoring organization, or the reason for the event. Think about noteworthy things that are happening in the host organization, the industry represented by this group, the community, or the noteworthy achievements of some of the people in attendance. Is there a theme or focus for this particular meeting and does it provide a good topic for conversation and inquiry? If you intend to talk to a particular person whom you haven't met, think of some conversation initiators that you can use.

- **What would you like to accomplish by being at this event?** If you could have it any way you wanted, what would the results of the event look like? Who would you meet? What would you say? What would they say? How would you feel? What would happen as a result of meeting these people?

- **What is your intention?** A strong intention will give you focus, strength, and direction. Your intention may be to meet three new people and give them your full attention while talking with them. Or your intention could be to find two people for whom you can be a resource in some way. Or your intention could be to enjoy the event and set aside business for a couple of hours. What would serve you the most? It's your party . . . your networking party. You can use it in whatever way best serves you.

Mingling basics

Good networkers mingle with such grace and ease that you never notice they are networking. Of course, they have almost always spent many years learning and practicing the skill that they have mastered and have typically integrated the skill into every cell of their being until networking is a natural part of who they are. And they are always fine-tuning their skill and ability, continuing to develop their communication and relationship-building skills.

Here are some mingling suggestions:

✔ **Greet the people around you.** I am amazed at how many people will walk right by someone they don't know without even saying hi — or hello, good morning, good afternoon, or even good evening! Acknowledge the presence of the people around you. When you walk up to someone you know and they are talking or standing next to someone you don't know, be sure to speak to everyone who is present.

✔ **Smile.** A great smile can be a great asset. A smiling, friendly face makes you more approachable and increases the chance that people will feel comfortable talking with you. This must be a genuine smile, not a fake smile. Some people say you can smile with your eyes. Ideally, a smile comes from your heart and emanates throughout your whole being.

✔ **Shake hands.** Your handshake is often your first chance to convey your personality. It creates a physical sense of connection. Review the information in Chapter 5 regarding handshakes.

✔ **Generate conversation.** Be willing to generate conversation by responding to others with some interest. Practice the art of small talk. See Chapter 5 for small talk tips.

✔ **Introduce the people you know and meet to other people.** Be the initiator of connections. When you meet Jay, who enjoys dancing, introduce him to other people you know who enjoy dancing. When you are talking with Bob and discover he is from the Northwest, introduce him to your coworker Robert, who is also from the Northwest.

✔ **Call people by name.** As soon as someone is introduced to you, call him or her by name and sprinkle the name throughout your conversation in an easy, natural manner.

Breaking in on conversations

When you see some people you want to talk with and they are already engaged in conversation with others, you can break in using several techniques:

✔ If the group (group is two or more) appears to be in an intense interaction, it may be a wise choice to let them be and check back later. Go talk to someone else.

✔ If people seem to be engaged in lighthearted conversation and they are not rigid or intense in their stance or appearance, you may wish to approach the group and see if there is an opening for you to join them. Maybe someone from the group makes eye contact and nods to you as a greeting, or sees you and slightly shifts his or her stance in such a way that creates some space for you to merge into the group. Consider this an invitation and step in. Someone may even stop his or her conversation, say hi, shake your hand, and introduce you to the others.

✔ If you approach a group and there seems to be no opening and no response, that's okay. Don't take it personally. Keep walking. Look around. It's okay to casually take your time as you find the next person to talk with.

Bowing out gracefully

Mingling means you talk with someone, end that conversation, talk to someone else, and end that conversation. Don't be afraid to end a conversation. It is an expected part of the process when you are mingling. In fact, the close of the conversation is very important. Giving closure allows you to reinforce the connection you just made and move on freely to be available for the next interaction. You can graciously end a conversation by saying "Good to meet you" or "Nice to visit with you. Good luck."

Don't slip away from a conversation hoping your exit won't be noticed. You want people to notice you today and remember you tomorrow (in a positive way). By giving closure to a conversation with a "goodbye" or "see you later," you reinforce the connection you just made.

Following up

Mingling is the first step in making the most of a networking event. The next step — your follow-through — is critical and is up to you. The quicker you respond to people after meeting them, the better. A short note that arrives within two days sent to the people you talked with at an event saying you're glad to have met them is very impressive. You can follow up with a note, an e-mail, a phone call, or a meeting. See Chapter 8 for more information on follow-through.

Networking Events

Although any encounter can be a networking opportunity, in this chapter I write about networking events as specific events that are organized with networking as one of the key benefits and opportunities. Whether the event is called a mixer, reception, or whatever, the event is designed as a way for people to meet and mingle.

Whatever it is that you do, there are networking events that can be of value to you. There are organizations for executives, administrative assistants, and business owners. There are associations for most any industry that you can imagine. These organizations and associations are an already established network of people with a mission that relates to that particular industry or profession.

Associations may be geared to a specific type of businessperson but not be industry specific. Examples include the American Business Women's Association, which has a membership of women from all industries and everything from business owners to administrative assistants to corporate executives. The American Association of Home-Based Businesses is another example of an association that draws people from a broad base of industries. If you join one of these associations, you will have something in common with the other members, but the other members will also be a mix of potential prospects, vendors, and friends.

Industry associations provide a great opportunity for networking with your peers. Talking and networking with your peers can lead to sharing best practices, outsourcing and contracting business that is not a fit for you, and developing strategic partnerships.

You may also consider joining the association that represents your target market as an associate, vendor, or supplier member. For example, if you are a hotel manager, you can join a travel association in order to be around travel agents who can book their clients at your hotel. If you are a musician, you might join an organization for catering executives because they have clients who want to book music for parties or events.

Networking at trade shows

Every day, around the world, exhibitors greet, meet, and talk with all the people walking through the aisles of a trade show. Trade shows are networking showcases. Unlimited opportunities exist for both the exhibitors and the attendees to make contacts that lead to business.

Being the exhibitor

Companies may spend megabucks on their trade show exhibit. However, having a well-located booth with an enticing display doesn't necessarily make for a successful show. What makes the difference is the attitudes of the people working the booth and their ability to attract people, connect with people, and gather information. If you are working the booth, you need to go out of your way to be warm, approachable, friendly, conversational, playful, energetic, and engaging to the trade show attendees.

It's better not to have more than two or three people managing the booth (depending on the size of your booth) or your group may appear intimidating and scare people away. Also, realize that a trade show is a time to make connections, not to sell.

You want to attract prospects to your booth and develop that first stepping-stone of relatedness. Learn as much as you can about your visitors in a very short amount of time. Give them enough information to pique their interest and identify what type of follow-up is appropriate based on their interests and needs.

You can have games, gimmicks, and giveaways that will attract people to your booth. However, realize that the people stopping by might be more interested in your games, gimmicks, and giveaways than in your products and services. Think about how you can attract qualified prospects to your booth and how you will know them when they come. You might consider sending a postcard, notice, fliers, or invitation to the buyers you are targeting. When they bring the notice to the booth, they can receive something that will help them learn more about your products and services.

Just because someone drops by your booth does not necessarily make him or her a qualified prospect. If you follow up on every person who drops by as if they were a hot lead, you may spend a lot of time getting frustrated. Find some way to distinguish a prospect from someone who is just stopping by.

Trade show attendees

Look through the trade show materials and make note of the vendors that you know you want to visit for sure. Think about what you want to learn and what you need to ask when you visit their booths. Ask as many questions as necessary get the information you need. If they cannot answer your questions sufficiently, get their card and write on the back the name(s) of whom they recommend you contact to get the information. Even if they ask you for a card and say they will have someone contact you, be sure you get their contact information as well so that you can be in control of making sure the follow-up happens. Many trade show exhibitors have great plans about following up with all the people who come by their booth; however, they get busy once they get back to their offices and the follow-up often falls short.

Also, be aware of the people right around you while in the booths and walking through the aisles of the trade show. Striking up a conversation with someone who is standing right next to you while reviewing information at an exhibitor's booth can be very easy.

How small a world it is!

Julie Lyon was attending a convention in Las Vegas. She casually struck up a conversation with the guy sitting next to her by noticing his nametag and saying, "Oh, I see you're from Los Angeles. I have a consultant I work with in Los Angeles." He responded by saying, "I live there but I'm not a Los Angeles native. I'm originally from Wyoming." Julie's surprised response was "I went to junior high school in Wyoming!" It turned out they went to the same junior high school and he was one year ahead of her. And here they were in Las Vegas some 20 years later, sitting next to each other and striking up a conversation in a networking seminar.

This prompted them to have lunch together before going on to their afternoon session, which gave them a chance to reminisce and learn about each other's lives and businesses. It turned out that he was able to give Julie some valuable information regarding some of the California companies that she works with.

When Julie told her husband about running into the guy who went to the same junior high, he said, "You can't go anywhere without seeing someone you know." Julie seems to have that knack. She says she likes that. It's nice to have that feeling of familiarity when you run into people that you know everywhere you go . . . a great example of the truth of the phrase "It's a small world, isn't it!"

Follow-up at trade shows

Follow-up is critical for both the exhibitor and the attendees. Often, exhibitors seem focused on how many cards or names they can collect, rather than on making contacts with quality prospects where their follow-up is really worth the time, effort, and money. Have a follow-up plan in place before the trade show ever happens. Otherwise, the follow-up can easily get delayed and take so long that it loses some of its impact.

Here are some trade show follow-up ideas for exhibitors:

- ✔ Send a thank-you note to people who stopped by your booth. This could be a letter with a brochure included, a notecard with a business card included, or an e-mail with a link to your Web site and information on how the recipient can subscribe to your e-zine or download your free articles.

Do not automatically include people in any regular e-mail announcements or e-zines that you may send out unless they subscribe to your e-zine or ask to receive your e-mail announcements.

- ✔ Include the people you are able to identify as qualified prospects in a monthly mail campaign for at least three months, sending informative articles, product announcements, gift certificates, and other literature that could be of interest to them.

✔ Make sure that anyone who came by your booth and expressed a strong interest and gave out buying signals ("This is what I've been looking for" or "I'd like to talk with one of your reps") gets a phone call within the next week.

Here are some follow-up tips for attendees of the trade show:

✔ Sort through the business cards, brochures, and other literature that you collected to identify the people or companies that you want to get back in touch with. You may want to call some immediately to talk or set up an appointment. With others, a notecard or e-mail would be an appropriate next step.

✔ After you identify the people you want to keep in your network, add their information (name, address, phone numbers, e-mail, trade show where you met, and anything else you want to remember about them) into your computer database program. Make a note to yourself regarding any follow-up action that you take.

Getting Involved with a Networking Club

If you want to stay inspired, focused, and on track with your career or business, surround yourself with inspiring, powerful, caring people who are on a path to success. One of the ways to do this is to join a networking club.

Whatever your business goals are, you deal with similar challenges, fears, obstacles, and dreams as other businesspeople. You don't need to reinvent the wheel. You can learn from other people, encourage other people, and be part of a group that supports each other's success.

There is great power in people coming together based on a common goal of growth and success. Imagine connecting with even a handful of people to share knowledge, expertise, and support.

A lot of business takes place among the members of a networking club. Lots of long-term friendships develop too. And all this happens because the members make a commitment to one another. Which comes first, the business or the friendships? Neither. What *actually* comes first is the vision and the commitment . . . then the opportunities. As you grow, your network grows, and as your network grows, you grow and your business grows.

Networking clubs provide a safe haven

Mary Ann Bryan joined the Dover Club at the invitation and encouragement of her friend, Marilyn Hermance. Marilyn owns a plumbing supply business, and Mary Ann owns her own interior design firm. It wasn't that Mary Ann needed business. She is one of the top interior designers in Houston and has had a successful business for over 30 years. However, when she visited the breakfast club, she felt a sense of camaraderie and safety that she had never experienced among a group of men and women business owners.

Mary Ann believes that the success of this club is due to the level of acceptance and support that the members offer each other, creating an experience of family and community. The group gives entrepreneurs and small business owners a safe place where they can talk about the challenges they face.

Understanding the nature of a networking club

A *networking club* is an organization that has the purpose of bringing together businesspeople to meet on a regular basis in order to do business with each other, refer business to each other, and support each other. It is a group of professionals who commit to working together to attain mutual growth and success. There are bylaws, dues, regularly scheduled meetings, and attendance requirements. Participating in a networking club helps you realize that your fears, challenges, and problems are not unique. As a business owner, it gives you a way to be connected with other business owners. Everyone in the club is responsible for growing their own business so everyone can relate to the challenges and goals that each other deal with day to day. As business owners, they all have the authority to choose to do business with each other and will have many opportunities to refer business to each other. The caterer may refer clients to the florist, the florist uses the photographer for her brochure, the photographer uses the delivery service, and so on.

Every successful person has a support system of people who have provided him or her with emotional, physical, intellectual, and spiritual support.

Here's the nitty-gritty on how most successful networking clubs work:

- ✔ The members are owners, officers, and key decision makers of companies.
- ✔ Each member represents a different industry or business category.

  Whereas a professional association is typically made up of people from the same industry or profession, a networking club is typically made up of business owners from different industries.

✔ Members invite and sponsor new members into the club.

✔ After visiting one to three club meetings, a prospective member turns in an application (with a check for membership dues), which the board reviews and votes on. In some clubs, the board votes on membership, while in other clubs the board approves the applications and presents the applicants to the membership for a vote.

✔ Weekly or bimonthly meetings are held at a facility or club with a private meeting room.

✔ The meeting agenda includes time for introduction of guests, announcements from the board, introductions, acknowledgements, and announcements from members.

✔ Individuals from the community are invited to speak regarding business and community topics that are of interest to the members.

✔ The focus of the group is to get together on a regular basis in order to become familiar with each other's businesses and build relationships with each other. The end result is that members do business with each other, refer business to each other, and support each other in whatever way they can.

✔ Membership is for a minimum period of one year, with renewal on a yearly basis. The first year is an important time for getting to know the other members, because the results and benefits of being a member build over the long term.

✔ Social activities are scheduled to provide members (and spouses or significant others) a chance to gather for fun while getting to know one another in a social environment.

✔ Board members are elected by the membership annually, in a manner designated by the club's bylaws.

✔ Roundtables are generated by members to create a five- to seven-person advisory board of club members who meet monthly to give focused support to each person regarding his or her business's growth and success.

Networking clubs go back a long way

Networking groups are nothing new. Benjamin Franklin's autobiography mentions his involvement in a "club of mutual improvement" with his "most ingenious acquaintances." His fellow networkers included a mathematician, shoemaker, composer, copier of deeds, surveyor, mechanic, merchant's clerk, bookbinder, and farmer. For 40 years this group met on Friday evenings. According to Franklin, although they were interested in "exerting themselves in recommending business," they turned out to be the "best school of philosophy, morality, and politics that then existed in the Province."

When you are a member of a networking club, you are encouraged and expected to network with all the members. Being a member of a club can be like adding a board of directors, advisory board, and 20 to 40 salespeople to your organization.

Finding the perfect networking club for you

The best way to find a great networking club is through your network of contacts. Ask around about clubs in your area. Find out which ones are highly regarded and which ones have been around long enough to have proved themselves. Determine which ones attract powerful members and keep their members for the long time. Discover which clubs your clients, associates, and friends belong to and find out enough about the clubs to know which ones would be a possible fit for you.

Here are some other suggestions:

- Visit each club that interests you until you find one that you know you are interested in belonging to for the long term.

- Look for a group that you enjoy being with and whose purpose supports what you are looking for in a group.

- Be aware of the group's energy and dynamics and the type of meeting it conducts. Is the atmosphere friendly, professional, focused, and productive? Or are they gossiping about each other?

- Be aware of how people interact with each other and whether there are indications that they are actually doing business and referring business to each other.

- Ask about dues, attendance requirements, and the goals of the club.

- Look for clubs with active, successful business professionals.

- Think about how you felt being there. Did you feel welcomed? Were you inspired and energized? How were you treated, and how did the members treat each other? Was there warmth in the interactions, or was it very formal and strictly business? Did you get value from being there? Are the members the kind of people you can imagine yourself wanting to be in a group with for 10 to 20 years?

- Think about the level of participation that you are willing to give and how that relates to the level of participation that the group requires (and the level of participation required to produce the results that you want).

Consider scheduling breakfast or lunch meetings with members of the club to get to know them, learn more about the club, and give them a chance to get to know you as a prospective member.

Getting your needs met through networking clubs

Clare Jackson belonged to a networking breakfast club during the early stages of owning her own business and says that her involvement helped her not only to grow her business but also to effectively deal with the problems and challenges that came from growing a business. When she needed to expand her office to a new site, when she lost her sense of direction after a difficult project, and when she decided to develop a new image and market herself in a new way, her network came through with the support to help her fill those needs and move her business to the next level.

She happened to mention to her dentist (who was one of the members of her breakfast club) that she was ready to hire additional staff. She says that if they had not been in the breakfast club together, chances are slim that she would have made the comment about hiring staff to him. Yet he happened to know of someone looking for a job, and through his recommendation Clare easily and effortlessly got her staff person.

Making the most of your membership

After you apply for membership in a networking club and get accepted, you need to jump in and get involved. You must participate, participate, and participate. The quicker you jump in and get involved, the more likely you are to start getting benefits and have those benefits continue for the long term.

Here's how to ensure the productivity of your membership:

- ✔ **Make a long-term commitment to the group.** The opportunity and value represented by the club doesn't manifest itself in immediate results.

- ✔ **Make it a priority to attend all the meetings and activities of your networking group.** Mark them in your calendar and consider them as important as sales calls with your most valued prospects.

- ✔ **Focus on getting to know the other members and building relationships with them.** Don't wait for people to call you or approach you. Reach out to generate conversation that helps you get to know people better so that you discover ways to send business to them. Here are some suggestions:

  - • Sit next to different people at each meeting.

  - • Schedule one-on-one breakfast, lunch, or coffee meetings with each member to have focused time to get to know each member and create a strong connection.

  - • Do all the same courteous things you would do in any networking situation — send thank-you notes, clip articles of interest, and so on. And do these things even more than you normally would.

> ✔ **Invite other business owners from your network to attend the club as prospective members.** Bring guests and prospective members on a regular basis.
>
> ✔ **Reach out to the members by calling to ask for help and support.** Also, notice and acknowledge the value of the intangible support you receive, which includes the encouragement, sense of belonging, and friendships provided by the members.
>
> ✔ **Offer leads, referrals, support, encouragement, and business opportunities to the members.** Always be on the lookout for opportunities to be a resource for the other members. When you hear someone in your network say, "I need to update my brochure before next month's trade show" refer him to the graphic designer who is in your networking club.

Don't expect people to knock your door down with business the moment you join a club. Reaping the full benefits of a networking group takes patience, diligence, and commitment.

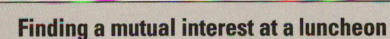

Finding a mutual interest at a luncheon

Jane Pollak reluctantly followed her friend Ellen to her first women's networking luncheon back in 1990. Jane felt like she did not have good "meet-and-greet" skills. Not only did she not particularly like having to encounter new people, but she wasn't the least bit sure that she would gain anything from the experience. After all, she had been an entrepreneur for ten years and had been doing perfectly well, thank you. So Jane admitted that she walked into the event skeptical and reserved.

The hospitality chair presented her with a nametag that listed her name, Jane Pollak, followed by her business name, An Egg by Jane. Immediately, other women approached her to ask about An Egg by Jane. Jane discovered that she liked the attention and enjoyed the opportunity to tell people about her work and her business. Her unusual product, hand-painted eggs, was fascinating to these women. Jane was challenged to describe what her business was all about succinctly and entertainingly. She began to realize that there could be something to this networking thing.

Jane discovered the thing she likes best about the networking groups is that the groups are usually focused on some area of mutual interest. When she's with women business owners, they tend to talk about how their businesses are faring; when she's with her friends who are professional speakers, the focus is on developing as speakers. Jane realizes now that she has a spiritual network, a college alumni network, and a network that focuses on writing. The conversation in each of the groups adds to her knowledge base and increases her value to her colleagues in the other networking groups.

Jane says, "Were I to start a new business today, finding out what connections I could make through networking would be one of my first steps. Networking has become a cornerstone of my business success, offering me leads, sales, information exchange, and friendship. I look back on that first lunch experience and wonder at my own naiveté. I wonder how I could have not known about the power of networking."

Creating Networking Focus Groups

A *networking focus group* is a group of business owners who sell to the same target market. They agree to meet on a regular basis to share contacts, clients, and business and marketing ideas with each other.

A networking focus group typically has anywhere from 7 to 15 members, whereas a networking club typically has anywhere from 20 to 60 people. The focus group has regularly scheduled meetings, probably monthly, although it could be six times a year or even four times a year. It's up to the group or the person organizing the group to make decisions about size and the frequency of meetings and set guidelines for the group. At each meeting, one member gives a presentation about his or her business, which helps the members better know how to refer business to each other.

Forming a networking focus group

To develop a networking focus group that works for you, you need to answer a few questions:

- What are your business's target markets? Which of your target markets do you want to have as the focus of your group? Pick one!
- What other professionals and businesses provide products and services to that same target market?

Suppose you're a photographer who markets to couples who are engaged. Who else markets to these couples? Jewelers, florists, caterers, travel agents, limo services, musicians, reception facilities, tuxedo rental services, wedding gown stores, and bridal registries. The owners of these businesses are who you would target as potential members in a networking focus group. A networking focus group usually consists of one person representing each of the relevant businesses. The members recommend the other service providers to their clients. The members of the group grow their businesses through the recommendations.

Let's say your target market consists of people who want to buy a new home. Your list of providers could include the following:

- Realtors
- Movers
- Title companies

- Mortgage companies
- Home-cleaning services
- Appraisers
- Pest control companies
- Landscapers
- Painters and contractors
- Interior designers
- Furniture stores

Chapter 4

You Are the Source of Your Network

Everything about you — your attitude, behaviors, actions, and conversations — influences the people around you. What you do and don't do, say or don't say can make the difference in someone getting a job, making a career decision, or pursuing a dream. You are the center of your network and your actions and interactions ripple out from you and throughout your network.

You are the motivating force that fuels your network to be active and effective. Because it's your network, it's your responsibility to be a positive source of influence and make it work. A network that's working is one where people are actively engaged in conversations and opportunities and are of mutual value and benefit.

When I say that you're the center of your network, it's not about being the center of attention or putting yourself on a pedestal. Being the center of your network means that you are the central link to everyone else.

Developing Yourself

When you are growing personally and professionally, your network is most likely growing in strength and effectiveness also. Develop your faith, your strength, and your self-esteem. Love yourself. Be accepting of yourself and others. Expand your capacity for giving and receiving love, appreciation, and support. Expand your ability to enjoy life and people. Enhance and deepen your willingness to be generous and grateful.

Be real. Be genuine. In every interaction, stretch your capacity to respect yourself and others. Honor yourself and others. Acknowledge that everyone, including you, has worth. Know that everyone has the right to have needs, feelings, and opinions. As you expand your own confidence, you will be more accepting and trusting and more available to others.

You have the power to have a phenomenal network and live a fulfilling life. You have the power to use your network for the greater good of the people in your life.

Having a vast network provides you with more options because you have more people to call on. You have access to more ideas, information, and opportunities. The more options you have, the more power you have regarding how you respond to circumstances and situations.

Being influential

You influence people by the way you speak, what you say, and how you respond to people. You can influence people in a positive, negative, or neutral manner. To influence in a neutral manner is to be of no influence. To be a consistently positive and powerful influence requires awareness and commitment on your part. Influence is developed when you consistently prove yourself to be someone who can make connections, produce results, and be a powerful resource.

Answer the following to identify your I.Q. (influence quotient):

- ✔ Do you get approached regularly to contribute and be of support to the people in your network?

- ✔ Do the people in your core network know that you want to be as influential in their lives as they are in yours?

- ✔ Are there people in your network who have your phone number in their cell phone, palm device, or daily planner for frequent and easy use?

- ✔ Are you frequently and respectfully asked to participate in worthy causes or charitable events?

- ✔ Are you considered an expert in your profession or industry?

- ✔ If your local newspaper, radio station, or TV stations were doing an article or segment on something related to your business or life, would they know that you are someone who they should interview?

✔ Do people know you well enough to be able to say, "What I've heard Gary say about that is. . . ."

✔ Do you have a Web presence that is easy for people to find, link to, and access valuable information from?

✔ Do people notice you? Do you attract positive attention?

✔ Do people pay attention to what you have to say?

✔ Do people take your advice and put it into action?

✔ Do people feel empowered, motivated, and inspired around you?

Your network gives you access to sources of influence, thus granting you personal and professional power.

Your habits become you

You are a creature of habit. You go on automatic every day when it comes to certain thoughts and behaviors. When you get in your car, you probably don't even have to think about reaching for the seatbelt. You just buckle up automatically because it's a habit you've developed.

Habits define who you are and dictate what you do through your day. Habits also define how you network. Do you consistently wait a couple days to return phone calls or think to yourself that no one is really interested in your career? These are habits that you need to change. Do you send thank-you notes on a regular basis and check to make sure that you have plenty of business cards before showing up at a networking event? These are habits that help your networking go more smoothly.

Realize that you are a conglomeration of productive and unproductive habits. Some of your habits contribute to your sense of confidence, happiness, and well-being, while other habits contribute to a lack of confidence, unhappiness, and frustration. Don't become a victim of your habits. You are the one who is actually in charge of choosing, changing, shifting, tweaking, or implementing the habits that will best serve you.

Your power in life lies in your ability to choose your habits. Your habits determine what you do and how you do it.

Networking habits to cultivate

You can develop certain habits that make networking easy, efficient, and natural. With the right habits, you won't have to *think* about networking — you'll just do it. Networking can become the automatic way that you interact and relate to people. However, the only way something becomes automatic and natural is through repetition and consistency — through practice.

The basis of networking is the little things that you do on a consistent basis that contribute to your awareness of people and your connections with people.

This book is full of suggestions for great networking habits. Habits worth developing include calling people by their names, keeping a back-up stash of business cards for times when you run low, and reintroducing yourself to people you haven't seen in a while. Be aware as you read the book of the habits that you could implement in your life. Here are three to consider:

✔ **Say thank you.** Say *thanks* throughout your day. In every conversation, think of something positive, supportive, and appreciative to say. Make sure that you are giving and receiving positive feedback in your life on a daily basis. Put your words of appreciation in writing. Tell people specifically how they influence your life in a positive way.

✔ **Encourage and congratulate.** You have the opportunity to be an empowering influence on the people around you. You never know when a few simple words of encouragement may make a difference in someone's life, so seize the opportunity whenever you can. Tell people how they have contributed to your life. Celebrate and acknowledge the successes and the accomplishments of others.

✔ **Introduce yourself to people who you don't know.** What if you made a point to introduce yourself to people you don't already know at every event that you attended? Even if it were just one person per event, you would expand your network and improve your likelihood of having influential connections (see Chapter 5 for more on introductions).

Networking habits to lose

Be vigilant against falling into unproductive habits. Remember that a repeated action becomes an automatic habit and influences your entire life. Check yourself on a regular basis to clean out old, unproductive, or stale habits so that you are constantly enforcing your good habits.

Some unproductive habits to be aware of include

✔ **Putting off phone calls.** Obviously, the new habit would be to call people when you think of them or as soon as the need arises.

✔ **Postponing responses to invitations.** You get an invitation or announcement to an event or activity that would be good for you to attend and you set the information aside somewhere never to be seen again. Instead, RSVP and make a notation in your calendar.

✔ **Letting business cards stack up on your desk, in your briefcase, or in your pockets.** On a daily basis, input information into your contact management system from business cards that you have collected. Do this when your recall of the person and the conversation is fresh.

> ✔ **Leaving your business cards in your briefcase, which is in the car or at the office.** Every day, put a supply of business cards in one of your pockets so that you always have cards handy — just in case!
>
> ✔ **Going to an event and hooking up with people who you already know and staying with them the whole time.** It's easy to get comfortable and lazy. A new habit to implement would be to make sure you meet at least two new people at any event that you attend.

Start a list of networking habits to develop. Pick ones that would help you create a more natural and effective networking style. Keep adding to the list as you read through this book and at the end you will have a great networking action plan. See the Appendix for a template for a networking action plan.

If you want to change your life in any way, take a look at your habits. Tweaking, shifting, or replacing a habit can enhance your life in a major way.

Being Clear and on Track with Your Vision

Your network can help you expand your outreach and consciousness. Your network can be the resource that lets you see beyond your current thinking. What new thing would be exciting for you to learn? What recognition would be most meaningful for you? If you could create any future you desired for yourself, what would it look like? If you could create fame for yourself, what would it look like?

What would you like to accomplish in your life that seems beyond your reach? If nothing were impossible, what would you be doing with your life? If you had a support system to back you up in anything you attempted, what would you do? Be visionary and look beyond the horizon to see the big picture.

How building relationships can build success

Inspired by her daughter, who has Down syndrome, Sherri O'Keefe had been on a three-year journey to learn how to effectively raise money for people with disabilities and how to partner with the government regarding policies that affect the disabled. Every year she would attend a Down syndrome conference, put a lot of effort into meeting people and gathering information, and then leave the conference feeling discouraged and drained.

After attending one of my Power Networking workshops, she shifted her attitude about networking and began to look forward to the next conference as an opportunity to implement her new networking skills. At the conference, Sherrie was more comfortable approaching people, introducing herself, and asking questions. She met two women from Nevada who invited her to go sightseeing one day. Normally,

she would not have accepted an invitation to go sightseeing with people she hardly even knew; however, she thought about the importance of building relationships and decided to join them. During their time together, they told her about an advocacy class that would help her fulfill her desire to work with the government on policy issues. This was exactly what she had been looking for over the past three years.

Sherri had always wanted to be a spokesperson for people with Down syndrome but she hadn't been able to figure out what she needed to do. By shifting her attitude about herself and others, moving out of her comfort zone, and joining with others to pursue her passions, she made two new friends and discovered how to fulfill her dreams and make a difference for children all across the country.

Set goals for yourself

Goals are the steppingstones and means of achieving your vision. And your network is a great resource for helping you accomplish your goals. Goals give you direction and focus. You won't always accomplish all of your goals, but chances are that you will accomplish much more in life with goals to give you direction and motivation than you would if you didn't set goals.

Your network can be your greatest asset and resource for help in accomplishing your goals.

Establish goal-setting criteria

Make your goals measurable and give them a timeframe so that you will know when you have accomplished them and can celebrate your success. If you tend to have goals like "I want to make more money," your goal is so nebulous that there is always more to do. You'll never reach your goal. But how about "I want a yearly salary of $75,000 by December 31, 2002? In order to qualify for a higher salary, I plan to improve my sales by 15percent each month." You have a measurable goal and you can begin to identify the actions you need to take to fulfill that goal. Keep track of your progress as a way to stay focused and inspired.

Here are some more examples:

- ✔ "My goal is to bring in eight new clients each month starting in April and going through the end of the year."
- ✔ "My goal is to have lunch with coworkers at least three times a week so that I improve my network within my corporation."
- ✔ "My goal this year is to place 20 percent of my income each month into savings."

Make your goals measurable, specific, and definable.

Clarify your goals

Make sure you commit to goals that you truly believe in and that make the best use of your time, energy, and talents.

Make sure your goals are *your* goals rather than ones that someone else has assigned to you. Your goals should mean something to you personally. They should be important to you. They shouldn't be something you think you should do or feel that you have to do to be good enough, successful, or whatever.

Inspire yourself with the goals that you set. Don't set goals that are a burden to you. The idea is to have goals that energize you and bring forth the passion inside you. When you have goals that bring forth your passion, everything else in your life will begin to fall into place much more easily. When you focus on things in life that you don't have passion about, things that don't really make much difference, or things that are complaints, you drain your energy. Positive results don't happen and there is very little fulfillment.

For example, let's say your goal is to exercise a certain amount each week in order to lose weight because you think you *should.* If you don't have any passion or vision, exercising will feel like drudgery and chances are it won't happen. What you can do instead is think of something that you love to do, that you have a passion for, and that would be a good way for you to get exercise, lose weight, do something that you love, and accomplish your goal. (For me, it's rollerblading and dancing. I still have that membership to the gym, but it's very seldom that you'll find me there.)

My first sales job (many years ago) was with McDonnell Douglas Automation Company. After going through a six-month training program, I was about to start calling on prospects and clients. My manager called me into his office and started asking me about my goals in life. He asked questions like "What's the dream car that you would like to own?" and "What kind of home do you want to buy for yourself?"

What I realized later was that he was getting me to think about my dreams and desires so that I would have a strong motivation to make a lot of sales, be successful, and have the money to buy that dream car and dream home. Well, it worked.

This was in the 1970s, and my dream car at the time was a Datsun 280Z. I thought it was the coolest sports car around. I knew exactly what color I wanted — sky blue. I had dreamed about that car, but until then hadn't given much serious thought to having one of my own. The morning after that meeting with my manager, as I was driving to the office, I noticed Datsun 280Zs all over the freeway. Now, I knew that all those people hadn't gone out and bought those 280Zs the night before. Those cars had been all over the freeway all along. But that morning, that's where my mind was focused so I noticed them. And eventually I bought that sky blue Datsun 280Z for myself.

That's the power of clarity and focus. You will see, perceive, and experience whatever your mind is focused on. You have the power to focus your mind so that you have access to everything you need to accomplish your goals and fulfill your dreams.

Your network develops as a natural outgrowth of your life, your goals, and your accomplishments.

Assess your goals

You can further clarify your goals and determine if they match you, your mission, and your purpose in life by asking yourself the following questions regarding each goal:

- What is the reason this goal is important or exciting to me?
- How is the accomplishment of this goal in alignment with my values, vision, and purpose in life?
- How will the accomplishment of this goal be of value and benefit to me and others?
- What will be required of me in terms of my current strengths and skills?
- What will I need from others to accomplish this goal?
- Who would most likely encourage and support me in achieving this goal?
- What must I keep in the forefront of my thinking to keep me on track to accomplish this goal?
- What are the future opportunities that the accomplishment of this goal will provide for me?

Taking the first step

Wishing and hoping do not make dreams come true. Vision, focus, intention, and *action* are the guarantees for turning your dreams into your reality. You can have lots of great ideas and influential contacts, but without taking action you'll have lots of potential and little results. (See Chapter 1 for more information on taking action via your network.)

Stephen Mayers, who owns a company that sells office furniture, visited my professional networking group one day. One of the people who he happened to meet during the program was Joan Portman, an interior designer and feng shui consultant. Stephen immediately realized that there could be a potentially great networking relationship between them if they referred clients to one another. He called Joan to express his interest in developing a mutually supportive referral relationship and set up a meeting with her. Stephen obviously came to that professional networking group with a clear vision of what is possible with networking and a desire to discover new networking relationships. His awareness led to new opportunities. Lots of people would have attended that meeting and walked away with no opportunities because they were waiting rather thinking — waiting for something to happen or waiting for someone to approach them.

Involve your network

You can wander through life or you can fulfill your passions, desires, and God-given talents. You must set the direction. You should then be able to rely on your network — your support system — to make sure you stay on track and on the path to fulfilling what you have declared as your life goals and aspirations.

If you don't let your networking contacts support you in accomplishing your goals, you are just networking for the sake of networking. Networking for the sake of networking is okay. But think how much better it would be to use this powerful resource called your network to further your goals in life while at the same time furthering the goals of the people you know! But — and this is key — it is only when you speak about your goals and take the first step in achieving them that people know how to be of support to you.

At times, obstacles will appear to get in the way of you accomplishing your goals. Some circumstances are out of your control (road construction makes it difficult for people to get to your store or the weather gets in the way of that big event you've been planning). You can't do much about those circumstances, but you do have a choice about how you respond to those circumstances. Reaching out to your network for creative solutions to unexpected problems can make your life easier.

Using your network to achieve your vision

After 14 years in her family's car rental and self-storage business, Debbie Allen left to build her own business. She really had no idea what she would do next; she just knew it was time to do something new and different. She was concerned that not having a college education or varied business experience could be a huge obstacle, but she took the plunge anyway.

Her business opportunity showed up in the form of a ladies apparel store. Debbie had never worked in retail and this store had not turned a profit in the six years of its existence. Debbie had no idea how to turn this store around; however, she felt like this opportunity was the right one for her.

When Debbie told others of her plans, she received comments like "You have no experience," "I don't know how you think you're going to have this work," and "Are you crazy?" She realized that some of these comments made sense. Along with the comments came a fear of the unknown and failure. Debbie took all that frustration and fear and turned it into motivation — motivation to make the business work no matter what. She was determined to fulfill her dream of owning her own business, no matter what anyone else said.

Debbie realized that she needed to learn the business and learn it fast. And an opportunity to

do that came her way. She was invited to join a group of networking retailers called the Fashion Alliance. The members met once a month and shared their expertise, strategies, and success tips with each other. None of the members were in direct competition with one another, so they felt free to share their knowledge and expertise.

Debbie soaked up their knowledge and information like a sponge. The members of the Fashion Alliance became her mentors, teachers, coaches, and friends. And although she was concerned about what she could give back to them, she discovered that her enthusiasm was contagious and was something that they all appreciated about her. Some of the members had lost their own enthusiasm over many years of being in business, and her energy added a new level of excitement and interest for them.

Within three short years, Debbie grew her business's sales from $87,000 to nearly 2 million dollars annually. She acknowledges that she never could have accomplished this on her own — "My Fashion Alliance group took my retail career to a much higher level of success."

Debbie has taken what she learned through her experience and now speaks internationally on how to outmarket, outsell, and outprofit the competition.

Training Your Network

Having a masterful network involves not only training yourself in the art of networking, it also involves training the people in your network. Imagine what would happen if everyone in your network were continually being a resource, expressing appreciation, and expanding his or her outreach. Now imagine what would happen if everyone you know were building his or her network for the greater good of everyone!

You train the people in your network by the way you communicate with them and the way you network with them. Training does not always happen overnight. So don't think that just because you are suddenly acknowledging people and sending them articles and offering them information that they will respond in kind right away. It will likely take consistency on your part to get the networking ethos firmly established with your network.

Train your network to call on you and refer to you when anyone has a need for your product or service. Keep yourself in front of your clients, customers, prospects, and networking contacts. Provide gentle reminders to them of your existence in their networks. Everyone has a vast and powerful network. Yet, if you don't stay in touch, the communication lines get weak and rusty from neglect.

Determining Your Vision of Your Network

Because you are the source and creator of your network, you get to determine your own vision of your ideal network. You can make your network into a valuable support system for all areas of your life. You can include in your network a diverse mix of people from various backgrounds, cultures, age groups, and professions, or you can focus on creating a network of go-getters, movers, and shakers. You can focus on bringing in people who are kindred spirits who share your philosophies and way of life.

Here are some possibilities for your network's vision:

- ✔ My network includes friends whom I can talk to about anything and everything.
- ✔ My network includes mentors who are as committed to my success as I am.
- ✔ My network helps to keep me active and involved in fun social events.
- ✔ My network includes peers in my profession who are readily available to me.
- ✔ My network includes peers who call on me as a resource and know that I am available to them.
- ✔ My network consists of family connections that are strong, loving, and supportive.
- ✔ My network supports me in having balance in life and fulfillment in all areas of life.
- ✔ My network supports me in having everything that I want and deserve in life.

Networking is a powerful lifestyle. Network effectively to accomplish your goals. Let networking serve you in having the life you've always wanted, the life you've dreamed of, the life you deserve, and the life you would create if you could create any life you wanted.

You're not just building a network for yourself. When you build a powerful network, everyone in your network is served by the power and value of the network that they have available to them through you.

Chapter 5

Let's Talk: Networking Happens through Conversation

In This Chapter

▶ Understanding that conversations create and nurture your network

▶ Learning how to make small talk effectively

▶ Getting off on the right foot: Introducing yourself

Networking happens through conversation — and someone has to initiate the conversation. That someone is you! Get into conversations with people. Initiate conversations with the people around you. Call people. Talk and listen. Be aware of the people all around you and find easy, natural ways to strike up a conversation. Networking is that simple — talking and listening.

Every time you have a conversation with someone, there is the possibility of networking. It is through conversation that we get to know each other and build a relationship. It is through conversation that we share and exchange ideas and information.

This chapter covers everything from how your handshake influences the first impression people get of you and how to make small talk in a seemingly effortless way, to how to draw a person out and build rapport, to how to introduce yourself in a way that makes you stand out. The basic ideas regarding talking and interacting apply whether you're in a formal or informal setting.

Networking through Small Talk

Grace seems to have a natural ability to talk to anyone, anywhere, about anything. Whether she's at the shopping mall, the cinema, the grocery store, the dentist's office, or a business meeting, Grace regularly chats with people. She knows how to make small talk. Her interactions are examples of how small talk can happen almost anywhere, with anyone. You can strike up a casual, short conversation with someone standing in line with you at the grocery store who you never see again. Or you can initiate a conversation with someone sitting next to you at a business luncheon and as a result make an appointment to meet with the person the following week.

Small talk is often considered to be insignificant, a waste of time, or frivolous. Yet in some cultures, small talk is essential before you begin to talk business. And in almost any culture, small talk is a valuable and respectful way to develop trust and rapport, which are prerequisites for moving into the business of networking.

Small talk helps you create frameworks for relationships with people. It is about taking little steps in conversation in a safe and non-threatening way so that you can build rapport with others, put them at ease, and create a comfortable space that allows you to venture into their world and vice versa.

Small talk is an important conversation skill in formal and informal situations. Mastering the art of small talk enhances your ability to connect with people and begin the process of building relationships.

Initiating conversations

One of the sports that I enjoy is tennis. So I'm going to use a tennis analogy regarding small talk. If you and I were to go out to the tennis courts and you were serving the tennis ball to me, you may have to make several serves before I return the ball back across the net to you. Imagine small talk the same way. You may need to throw several topics out to me before I pick a topic to volley back to you. So don't give up on small talk if people don't respond immediately. At least give the game a chance by giving people the opportunity to warm up to you and the game — give them a few chances to jump in and play.

Observe the other person — what he or she is doing, saying, wearing, reading, and so forth. Then "serve" a question or open-ended comment:

> "That's a great travel bag. Where did you get it?"

> "Great question you asked at the project meeting this morning."

> "I can tell you've been dancing a long time. How did you get started?"

> "How's the book?"

> "I noticed you know a lot of people around here . . ."

Be proactive. Initiate conversation rather than waiting on others. Think about what the other person would possibly like to talk about. For more information on ways to initiate conversation, see Chapter 17.

Open-ended questions encourage people to speak freely and at length if they wish. Ask what, how, why, or in what way.

Start with easy questions or comments to put people at ease. Create comfort. Then you can shift the conversation, if you wish, by asking more specific questions, as discussed later in this chapter. Here are some questions that you can ask in different settings to start a conversation:

- ✔ Office: "That's a great picture of you and your family. Looks like a fun ski trip!"

- ✔ Business conference: "This is my first time to this conference. Are there certain sessions that you recommend for first timers?"

- ✔ Wedding party: "Hi, my name is Ann. I work with Jane. How do you happen to know Jane and Bill?"

Make a list of five questions you can ask people that can lead to fun and interesting small talk. See Chapter 17 for more information on how to draw people out.

Building rapport by discovering common interests

Rapport is present when two people speak easily with each other, with a natural rhythm and flow of conversation. It is the experience of being kindred spirits. Having rapport doesn't mean that you agree on everything; it means you can discuss most anything with respect.

Rapport is created through conversing and relating. You know how with some people you meet and you just seem to click? Ever wonder what that's about? When you click with people, you have found rapport. Being able to connect, relate, and communicate easily creates a feeling of comfort and safety.

Here are some questions that you can ask people that they would enjoy answering and that would assist you in developing rapport:

- ✔ Where are you from?

- ✔ What business are you in?

- ✔ How did you get into the . . . business?

- ✔ What do you love most about your business work?

- ✔ What do you do for fun?

For more topics of common interest to explore, see Chapter 17.

Using the three-deep small-talk plan

Fritz Koehler has mastered the art of small talk and turning small talk into opportunities. He attributes his ease and success with networking to the habits he developed in college. As a freshman in the Corps of Cadets at Texas A&M University, he was required to follow a mandatory protocol regarding how to greet and get to know other students on campus. As a freshman in the Corps, he was required:

✔ To know every upperclassman in his dormitory *three deep* — their name, their hometown, and their major.

✔ To speak to the upperclassmen in his dormitory every time he saw them.

✔ To greet every upperclassman he knew anytime he saw one of them. And if they were with people he didn't know, then Fritz had to introduce himself three deep to the new person.

✔ To greet people by name without any prompting.

Fritz acquired some valuable habits from his Corps-mandated interactions. After graduating, Fritz translated the three-deep plan into:

✔ Name

✔ Hometown

✔ Occupation

Focusing on those three pieces of information, he consistently creates connections with people. Opportunities seem to magically appear. Here are some of his responses:

Name:

✔ "That's an interesting name, how do you spell it?"

✔ "I've never heard that name before, what is the origin?"

✔ "Are you by any chance related to (a person with the same last name)?"

Hometown:

✔ "I used to spend a lot of time in . . . which is near (the other person's hometown)."

✔ "I hear that (hometown) has a great . . ."

✔ "I'm not familiar with (hometown). How did you get from (hometown) to here?"

Occupation:

✔ "Oh, I know somebody who works for (name of company)."

✔ "I just had a meeting with . . . who's in the marketing department over there."

✔ "I saw an article in a recent copy of the business journal about (company's) expansion into other states."

A typical small talk conversation for Fritz might go like this:

Fritz: "Joe, where are you from?"

Joe: "Beaumont."

Fritz: "Beaumont, I drive over there for business about once a month. In fact, I've been attempting to reach someone at XYZ Company. Do you by any chance happen to know Jim Keller?"

Joe: "You're kidding. Jim and I went to high school together. We were on the baseball team together for four years and then years later coached little league together for our kids."

Later, Fritz contacts Jim Keller:

"Jim, I was at a meeting recently and met one of your high school buddies."

Small talk can be simple, fun, and very powerful. Don't make it difficult. Fritz's plan focuses on three pieces of information. The questions are easy to ask and easy for people to respond to. And yet, each of the three pieces of information is likely to create some way of relating and connecting. Fritz says that it amazes even him how he is able to create a connection of some kind with almost everyone that he talks to. And oftentimes those connections lead to unexpected results and opportunities!

Create your own three-deep small talk plan. You could choose to always find out name, college, industry; or name, company name, favorite sport; or name, job, favorite vacation. The options are unlimited. Think about three things that you would like to know about people so that you can create productive small talk that leads to connections.

We are all connected in some way, and our commonalities are more abundant than our differences. You can choose to look for and focus on how people are different from each other or on how they're similar to each other. In every conversation, you can fairly quickly find something that you have in common with the other person. The fact that you're talking with one another shows that you have something in common — something brought you together to have a conversation in the first place.

Responding to and getting a response from others

Small talk can be easy. Sometimes all you need to do is listen and respond with simple questions or statements like:

- ✔ "Really?"
- ✔ "Tell me more about . . ."
- ✔ "Oh?"
- ✔ "Interesting!"

A conversational tool recommended by Jeff Slutsky in one of his Street Fighter Marketing programs is the *echo technique*. This tool helps to keep the conversation focused on the other person. You use the echo technique by repeating the last few words of what the other person said, with either an exclamation mark or question mark at the end. Here's an example:

Jill: "We are in the process of producing a new audio program."

Mark: "A new audio program?"

Jill: "Yeah, it's going to have six cassettes."

Mark: "Six cassettes!"

Jill: "Yeah, we want to make sure there's enough information to produce major results."

Mark: "Major results?"

Small talk attempt that goes nowhere

Whether the conversation goes anywhere or not can depend on the response you get to your questions and comments. Likewise, if you are on the receiving end of the questions, your responsibility is to respond in a way that makes for interesting conversation and the opportunity to get to know the other person.

Person A: "Where are you from?"

Person B: "Fridley."

A: "Where's that?"

B: "Outside of Minneapolis."

A: "How long have you lived there?"

B: "All my life."

A: "Oh."

In this example, Person B answered all the questions, but certainly didn't contribute much or show an interest in conversing. Maybe the respondent didn't mean to be rude or unfriendly, but these short, limited responses are a turnoff to the person who is attempting to initiate a conversation.

Small talk attempt with willing participant

Here's an example of responses that take you to a deeper level of conversation:

Person A: "Where are you from?"

Person B: "Fridley, about 20 miles southeast of Minneapolis. It's a great place for the XYZ corporate headquarters in that we're close to the big city and yet don't have to deal with the traffic to get to and from the office."

A: "How long have you lived there?"

B: "All my life. I hired on with the corporation right out of school and have worked my way up into management. It's one of those American dream stories that you always think happens to other people!"

See how this conversation has already developed some rapport and interest and could continue in a lot of different directions?

By revealing something about yourself to others, you encourage others to share with you and thus relate to you.

If you don't respond to people's attempts to converse with you, you may appear aloof, arrogant, rude, or non-approachable. When someone asks you what's new, think of something interesting to say. Beware of falling into the automatic trap of answering with something like "oh nothing," "not much," "just working," "working hard as ever." Think about recent or current successes that you've had, projects that you are working on, trips you've taken, and so on.

Small Talk Do's and Don'ts

Making small talk is all about making people comfortable. If you utilize these suggestions and make them habits, you'll be successful at engaging in conversation with people and creating relationships with them that can lead to opportunities.

Do's

- ✔ Do ask open-ended questions.
- ✔ Do attempt to include everyone (if in a group) in the conversation.
- ✔ Do comment on mainstream, non-controversial topics that are easy for other people to converse about.
- ✔ Do stick with topics that are appropriate to the situation.
- ✔ Do have some familiar topics in mind that help you feel at ease.
- ✔ Do keep up-to-date on current events.
- ✔ Do comment or ask about hobbies or interests that you know the other person has.
- ✔ Do speak in a respectful and professional manner.
- ✔ Do help make the conversation interesting.
- ✔ Do respond to comments and questions of others.

Don'ts

- ✔ Don't comment on or ask about something that is personal or could be embarrassing (money, relationships, and so forth).
- ✔ Don't wait on others to initiate the conversation.
- ✔ Don't monopolize the conversation.
- ✔ Don't use jargon, curse words, or inappropriate language.

Avoiding clichés

Frequently asked questions can become cliché, which means the phrase has become common-place and relatively meaningless. Clichés usually generate another cliché or automatic response. When both people are being automatic, the conversation will be cold, impersonal, and go nowhere. Here is a list of common clichés and typical responses they generate:

- How are you? (Fine.)
- How was your day? (Okay.)
- What have you been up to? (Same old, same old.)
- What's up? (Not much, how 'bout you?)
- How are things? (Same as usual.)

- Don't gossip. Don't talk about people.
- Don't get on a soapbox, teach, preach, or attempt to impress.
- Don't continue a conversation if the other person is obviously bored or not responding.

Being a great conversationalist requires a combination of listening skills and conversing skills. You don't have to know a lot to carry on a great conversation. What will make you a great conversationalist is your ability to listen, respond, and make a connection.

Everything about You Communicates!

If you think communication just has to do with the words that you use — wrong! You communicate with your words, with your body language, your appearance, your tone of voice, your gestures, and even with what you *don't* say. Everything communicates. Even the clothes you wear and the adornments you may put on them. The power that you have is you get to choose the words, body language, tone of voice, and so on that best communicate what it is you want to convey to others.

For more information on how you communicate non-verbally, see Marty Brounstein's *Communicating Effectively For Dummies* (Hungry Minds, Inc.).

Communicating approachability

If you want to communicate to others that you are friendly, approachable, and available for conversation, do the following:

> ✔ Smile. Allow your face to relax into a genuine smile — not a forced or canned smile. Even over the phone, a smile helps to generate a sense of friendliness.
>
> ✔ Maintain eye contact while conversing.
>
> ✔ Maintain an open posture: arms relaxed and by your side rather than crossed.
>
> ✔ Make friendly gestures.
>
> ✔ Be relaxed in your pace and energy.
>
> ✔ Speak in a friendly tone and manner.
>
> ✔ Focus your attention on people.

Location, location . . .

Where you stand or sit at an event can make a difference in how likely you are to have people to talk to. Make yourself approachable by being where people are most likely to gather. Be visible. Don't hide behind tables, columns, decorations, or groups of people. If you hang back against the wall or off in a corner, people will be hesitant to approach you.

Consider where you will be visible and near the flow of people. People tend to gather and be open to conversation while they are standing near the entrance, in the registration area, at the refreshment table, and so on.

Let's shake on it

Not every conversation starts out with a handshake. Often, you will be in an informal environment like a grocery store line, a sporting event, a school play, and so on when you begin to talk with the person beside you. The conversation may get to the point where you introduce yourself to one another and shake hands or it may not. In business situations, the handshake is, however, typically the initial contact you make with the other person as you introduce yourself to each other. It is the physical connection that you make when formally meeting and greeting someone.

Your handshake is often the first opportunity you have to connect with the other person and make a positive first impression. So make sure that your handshake conveys the image you want it to.

Don't offer a limp, wimpy handshake. Doing so makes you appear weak and ineffective. Likewise, your handshake should not be bone crushing or overbearing, which gives the impression of being too eager or controlling. First impressions are very important. Make sure the physical contact you make with someone via your handshake conveys a message of confidence, warmth, and professionalism.

Guidelines for shaking hands

Everything about you communicates, your handshake included. Because your handshake is often your first connection with a person, it's an important element in creating a positive first impression. It may seem like a simple thing, and yet a weak handshake can create hesitancy or doubt in the other person's mind. Here are some guidelines regarding handshakes that will help get you off to a good start:

- Offer your hand equally to men and women.
- Make eye contact at the same time that you are shaking hands.
- Smile and have a pleasant facial expression and tone of voice.
- Give the handshake full contact — web to web (the web part of the hand in between the thumb and first finger touches), palm to palm.
- Make it a solid, friendly handshake with two to three light pumps.

Here are some unacceptable handshakes and the impressions that they make:

- **Cold fish:** A limp and lifeless handshake makes you appear unavailable, weak, not happy to be there, and without substance.
- **Pump:** You appear aggressive, overbearing, and demanding if you pump your arm up and down too vigorously.
- **Arm grasp:** If you grab the person's arm — not just the hand — you appear aggressive, overbearing, too personal, too friendly, and invasive
- **Tips of fingers:** If you just barely make contact when you shake, you appear cold, detached, not friendly, unavailable, and weak.

The two-handed handshake, where you grab the person's hand with both of your hands, can be too friendly or overbearing when you're meeting someone new. However, it can convey genuine warmth with someone you already know and sincerely care about.

Turning Small Talk into Big Business

You have the power to direct every conversation to topics that are interesting and can lead to opportunities. The key is to focus, listen, and be aware. Often, people wait on others to make the conversation interesting. Be proactive and be willing to direct the conversation. This is not about taking over or monopolizing the conversation. It is about participating and contributing to the interaction with an intention of creating and discovering value.

Imagine that you're on a treasure hunt and you're listening and looking for the clues to the location of a very valuable treasure. You would pay very close attention to everything that is being said. You would pick up on things you wouldn't normally notice. Networking is like a treasure hunt. Jewels are out there everywhere.

The fun part of networking is the process of exploring, figuring out, and discovering where the treasures are. You meet new people, talk to friends and family, and, yeah, sometimes those conversations don't seem to lead to any particular jewels. But maybe they have a clue for you on where to find the treasure. And then all of a sudden, from somewhere totally unexpected, you hit upon something great!

The idea with small talk is to have the conversation progress. It's taking little steps in conversation to develop trust and rapport. Each step allows you to get a little closer to the other person.

Here are some questions you can ask that lead the conversation in a business direction. Notice how the questions progress from casual to more revealing.

- ✔ "What type of business are you in?"

- ✔ "How did you get into that (industry/career/company/business)?"

- ✔ "What do you most like about your job?" or "What appealed to you about being a (job title)?"

- ✔ "What advice would you give to someone considering getting into this business?"

- ✔ "What (trends/goals/future) do you see for your (industry/career/company)?"

- ✔ "What would you like to be doing with your business that you are not currently doing?"

Small talk can lead to big results!

It's part of Rich's personality to mingle and talk with people in the church courtyard after the Sunday-morning service. And it's not uncommon for him to seek out and approach some of the people who appear to be a bit shy or quiet or off by themselves. In doing so, Rich struck up a conversation with a man who had recently started attending church in a desire to turn his life around.

Every Sunday, Rich would say hi and visit with this man for a little bit. Each time he would get to know him a little better. The man shared with Rich that he had six months of sobriety and that it was especially important to him at this time in his life to have support for his recovery and his commitment to create a good life for himself.

Rich offered his support. He invited the man to call him every week just to let Rich know how he was doing. The friendship grew and they would occasionally meet for breakfast. Rich knew the man didn't have a car and rode the bus to work. He also noticed the he was always courteous and professional. The man was always appreciative and even sent Rich a note thanking him for his friendship and support.

Then one day, out of the blue, the man told Rich he had received a six-figure inheritance from relatives and needed assistance with his investments. Rich was a stockbroker . . . you guessed it, the man wanted to know if Rich would be his stockbroker.

Rich never thought that befriending this man would lead to business. His offer of friendship and support was never about anything other than being there for someone else. It never would have mattered to Rich if the man could give something back, because Rich benefited just from extending friendship and support.

Their friendship and professional relationship has remained intact. This man is now teaching art to children at the church and is blossoming in many ways: personally, spiritually, and professionally. Like everyone else, he has those tough days. Rich is pleased to know that he's considered the kind of friend and confidant that the man can call on those days to talk.

Networking more effectively isn't necessarily about talking to more people. It's about paying closer attention to the conversations that you have as a natural part of your day. You don't have to create a canned script; you simply pay attention, are aware, are ready, and flow with the conversation. Allow networking to happen easily and naturally. Most networking opportunities are missed because people let something in a conversation pass by without commenting on it.

My Name Is . . .

Most of your conversations don't start with you giving your name. However, somewhere in the process of talking with someone new you will likely introduce yourself. It is typically at this point that you take the conversation to the next level.

After you introduce yourself, the conversation tends to get more focused than the initial chitchat. You typically start to talk about topics that give you a chance to find out more about each other. It's common for one person to ask the familiar question, "So what do you do?" People tend to respond to these questions automatically with their title.

Instead of responding with a title, respond by telling people what it is that you *do*. Give people an interesting description of your business or your job. Have it be a natural part of the conversation. And let the conversation continue to be a dialogue. Don't go on and on and create a monologue. Speak, listen, respond, be aware, and create opportunities!

Here are some examples of how to answer the what-do-you-do question:

> ✔ **Bad response:** "I'm a photographer."
>
> **Good response:** "I photograph families, everyone from babies to great-grandparents. I love capturing the spirit of the family in a portrait."
>
> ✔ **Bad response:** "I'm an organizational consultant."
>
> **Good response:** "I'm in the business of helping people get organized so that they can find what they want when they need it."

Notice that the good response actually answers the question. What do you do . . . I photograph families. The good response provides specific information in a conversational tone and thus generates a continuing flow of conversation.

Many of your friendly conversations with strangers — the conversations that happen at grocery stores, sporting events, and so on — never get to the introduction step. That's okay. There's a place for casual, friendly conversation with the people who cross your path during your day.

Decide what you want to accomplish in your self-introduction

No matter what business you're in, you will very likely have many opportunities throughout your career to introduce yourself to individuals and groups of people. In the past when you've introduced yourself, you probably say whatever comes to mind at the moment. It's called "winging it!" But I recommend thinking ahead, planning, preparing, and practicing what you will say so that you're ready when the opportunity comes along again.

Think about what you want to accomplish with your introduction. What impression do you want to make? Do you want to make yourself memorable? Approachable? Do you want to generate more conversation with the person you're talking to?

To be approachable, use a strong, friendly tone of voice and use common everyday words and phrases. To make yourself memorable, you can use light humor or a catchy phrase. If you're talking one-on-one with someone and want to generate more conversation, tell the person something interesting about your business in a concise statement and then give him or her a chance to respond.

In their introductions, people often downplay the value of who they are and what they do. Notice how sometimes when you ask people what they do or what kind of business they're in, they respond with "Oh, I *just* do such and such." Please don't ever, ever use words in your introduction that devalue who you are. You are important and what you do is of value.

Imagine if the people within your company spoke with pride and confidence about their work every time anyone asked them what they did or what kind of business they were in. Imagine the effect in terms of creating positive visibility, goodwill, and powerful public relations for your company. The way you and the other people in your company introduce yourselves is almost the most powerful public relations tool available. The only thing better is when every customer that you have is saying great things about you.

When introducing yourself to a group

Think about the last time you were at a meeting and you were asked to stand and introduce yourself to a group of people. Do you remember what you said? And how you felt? And what kind of response you got from the group? Most people introduce themselves formally by giving their name, title, and the name of their company. Now there's nothing necessarily wrong with that. However, it's like giving people data — dry information — and it comes across that way. It doesn't build rapport.

Give yourself permission to speak with pride and confidence regarding yourself and your work. This is not about braggadocio or being aggressive. This is about letting people know who you are so that you can get to know each other well enough to network with, and thus serve, one another. When I work with people on their formal group introductions in my workshops, I ask them to tell me what they do. And then I just keep asking questions: "And what do you actually do?" "And what does that mean?" "What do you love about that?" "And what is most satisfying about what you do?" "And what's the most important value and benefit that you provide to others through your work?"

After a few of these questions, the participants stop talking as if they are giving a report and they light up. They actually begin to say what's real for them — their personal pride statement — rather than all the empty words that they think are the right things to say.

At that point, they begin to find the perfect words for their introductions. I then have them write their introductions down so they can become aware and conscious of what they said and can use it again when they introduce themselves. Here are some examples:

> "Hi. I'm Trish Strangmeyer of Trish Strangmeyer Photography. I love getting children, parents, grandparents, and even great-grandparents together to capture the essence of a family in a portrait."

> "Good morning. I love helping people organize their lives to find what they need when they need it. I'm Jan Limpach of Organizing Plus."

> "Hi, I'm Genie Fuller, America's Referral Coach. I help you get your phone to ring (pause) prospects calling *you* for a change."

Notice that the above examples follow one of these formats:

- ✔ Greeting, name, company name, personal pride statement
- ✔ Greeting, personal pride statement, name, company name

Make sure you aren't using a generic introduction. If anybody in the industry could be saying those same words, it's a bad introduction. Make your introduction be about *you*. Find the words that touch your heart, inspire you, remind you of the value of what you do, and make you grateful for your job. I call this *finding the words that light you up*.

Creating your self-introduction is as important as creating your company name, choosing a brand, developing an advertising campaign, and launching a public relations project. You are your own best PR person. And you know best what others need to know about you and what you offer.

The way you introduce yourself will turn people off, leave people cold, or draw people in. It's up to you! Your words, mannerism, and tone of voice create connection or distance. You can take the same words and use several different tones of voice and they will come across totally differently and thus create different results. Learn to be a master of communication by having your words, mannerisms, and tone of voice be congruent and true to the image and message you choose to convey.

Ways to spice up your self-introductions

Here are some tips and techniques you can use to make your self-introductions more memorable and interesting:

✔ Make a list of words and phrases that make you excited about what you do. Then identify various ways you can use those words in a phrase that describes your business.

✔ Get a friend, family member, or coworker to listen to your introduction and give you feedback regarding the impression that you create.

✔ Write out the version you choose to use and post it in a place where you will see it.

✔ Practice saying your new introduction by rehearsing it in your head and saying it out loud when you are by yourself (or practice saying it to yourself in the mirror).

The next time you have a chance, deliver your new introduction with pride and confidence!

Introducing others

Be sure to introduce the people you are with to one another. Including some information in the introduction that helps folks begin to talk with each other is always helpful.

"Jack, I would like you to meet Eddie Carver. Eddie's an optometrist. He just moved to Chicago and is looking for a networking breakfast club."

To Eddie: "Eddie, this is Jack Spratt. He's the founder of our networking breakfast club and the president of his own travel agency."

For more information regarding the etiquette of introducing people, please see Chapter 16.

I've forgotten your name

If you can't recall someone's name, be upfront about it. Occasionally forgetting a name is normal, especially when you encounter a person in a different environment from the one in which you originally met him or her.

Don't pretend that you know someone's name when you've forgotten it. You will be so busy trying to think of the name that you'll miss what the person is saying.

Here are some ways to extract yourself from this situation with dignity and grace:

- ✔ "Hi, I remember you from . . . tell me your name again."

- ✔ "Hi, I know that I know you. It's just that right now I'm drawing a blank."

- ✔ "Hi, I keep thinking I know you from somewhere . . ."

- ✔ "Hi, I'm John Caldwell. I think we met at the XYZ networking breakfast last month. Tell me your name again, please."

By practicing the name retention techniques suggested in Chapter 19, you won't be forgetting names nearly as often!

Chapter 6

Cultivating Your Network by Making Requests

Ask for what you want! Doing so is actually very simple. Yet, it's amazing how many people are hesitant to ask. What's the worst that could happen? You've probably heard the phrase "Nothing ventured, nothing gained." Chances are very high that you won't get what you want if you don't ask. And sometimes you won't get what you want when you ask. But for sure your chances of getting what you want increase dramatically when you master the art of asking.

Identifying Your Wants and Needs

If you were given a magic lamp and had the opportunity to be granted three wishes, do you know what you would ask for? Maybe you don't. Life can be so busy that you lose sight of your goals, dreams, and desires.

A frequent problem people have when making requests is that they don't take the time to think through their request and clearly identify what they want and need. Clarity about what you want and need always makes your requests more powerful and effective. See Chapter 4 to review information about setting goals.

Make a list of 25 goals that you have. Compile them from all areas of your life (your career, health, finances, hobbies, and so on).

For each of those goals, list three different networking requests you can make to help you accomplish those goals easily and efficiently. Then list some of the people who it would make sense to call with your request.

You have now identified what you can request from the people you talk with every day. Here are some examples of how you can frame your requests once you have your goal in mind.

Goal: Get job with an environmental engineering company in Knoxville, Tennessee

Requests:

Who do you know in the environmental engineering industry?

Who do you know who lives in Knoxville, Tennessee?

I am an environmental engineer and want to move to Knoxville, Tennessee. Who do you recommend I contact?

Resources:

Jack, Ray, Ginger — members of the environmental association

Terry, Jim — friends in the engineering industry

Tom & Mary — neighbors who moved here from Knoxville

Goal: Sell 12 drum sets per month through the end of the year

Requests:

Who do you know who plays the drums?

Who do you recommend I talk with about musical instruments for the students at the local high schools?

Who within the church (theater, community playhouse, school, drama department) is in charge of purchasing instruments for the musical productions?

Resources:

Jim, Harry, Jane — current customers who are respected by the musicians in the area

John, Frank, Bill — band directors at three of the local high schools

Jack, Howard, Vicki — drum and percussion teachers

Get clear about your goals; identify the requests to make and the people who can best fulfill your requests. By thinking ahead, you will create a mental awareness that reminds you to make those requests more often of the people in your network.

Everything you could possibly want or need is available and right around you. The more you stay aware of what you want, the greater the likelihood that you will discover those resources.

Requesting What You Want

Networking is about giving and receiving, exchanging information, offering and responding, and being resources for one another. One person must ask so that someone else can respond. If you're not asking for what you want and need you're actually blocking the flow of networking. By asking, you initiate action, interaction, and exchange and open a door for opportunity. Asking is about your words, your attitude, and making it easy for people to respond.

Why making requests is important

If someone handed you a computer that had 1) the contact information of every person you would ever want or need to contact, and 2) information on everything you would ever need to know to have a full, rich, and successful life, would you learn how to use that computer to access all the marvelous data? Or would you just let that computer sit there with all that data inaccessible to you?

This analogy may sound silly. Yet, the people around you can provide you with access to all the contacts and information you ever dreamed possible. The people around you can give you everything you ever wanted and needed in life. And yet, some people say, "I'm too shy" or "I don't want to bother them."

Making requests is important because doing so:

✔ **Helps you to get what you want and need.** By asking, you put the word out there so that people know what you want and need. Don't assume that people know. Inform people of what you are looking for and increase the chances of connecting with the right person so that you get what you want.

✔ **Gives other people permission to also ask for what they want and need.** You influence the behavior of the people around you. You have the chance to lead the way, set the stage, and be an example for others. When you ask for help, then others are more likely to think, "Oh, if she can do that, so can I."

✔ **Helps to build relationships with others.** If I call and ask you for help or support, I am including you in my life. Even if I don't get what I am asking for, I have strengthened my relationship with you by calling you. Positive interaction enhances relatedness. Finding ways to support and contribute to one another enhances relatedness. And asking gives you an excuse to call people and be in touch.

When you call someone from your network, even if you don't get what you're asking for, you have strengthened your relationship with him or her by reaching out and asking. By strengthening your relationship with the person, you have increased the chances of networking effectively in the future. When you realize there is value in asking even if you don't get what you're asking for, you feel less pressure to get results.

Asking also strengthens your relationships because it acknowledges the importance and value of the other person.

✔ **Starts the flow of networking.** Asking sets things in motion. You ask for something, the person responds, you offer something, the person thinks of something to ask for, and so on.

✔ **Gives people an opportunity to contribute and get involved in your life.** It is human nature to want to be valued and to have an opportunity to give and contribute to others. You are inviting people to be part of your life and your network.

✔ **Gives you a chance to offer your support to others.** Any time you ask for support is a perfect time to also offer your support. Even when you don't have something in particular to offer, you can say, "Thanks, how can I be of support to you?" or "What can I do for you?"

✔ **Gives you a chance to expand your network.** When you make a request of someone, that person may refer you to someone else. At the same time that you're getting what you want and need, you're also meeting new people and expanding your network.

What you want and need may be right around you. Yet, if you don't ask, you won't access it. Asking is like a magnet. It draws to you what is right around you that is a fit for your needs and desires.

Making requests strengthens relationships and benefits everyone

Marty works at a company where I conducted a series of networking training sessions. She was caring for her husband, who was recovering from a stroke. Being an organized and efficient person, she had developed a system and a plan for taking care of him and was adjusting to this new situation in her life. Then she had one of those days where nothing worked as planned and her whole schedule went out of kilter and she had to work late. Because he wouldn't be able to eat until she got home, she became concerned about what to do. As a last resort, Marty called one of her neighbors and asked for help. She asked if her neighbor would be willing to go to Marty's house and make sure that her husband had a chance to eat (she always had food prepared ahead of time). The neighbor responded with a sigh of relief. "I would be glad to . . . I thought you'd never ask." She had wanted to help but just didn't know how to offer her assistance.

Marty instantly realized the power and importance of asking and allowing people to help and contribute. It not only eased some of the stress for Marty, it allowed her neighbor to feel good about helping. Marty was able to develop a strong friendship with her neighbor. She shifted from feeling like "I've got to do this all myself" to experiencing a sense of community and support.

Thoughts that get in the way of making requests

It constantly amazes me how hesitant people are to ask for things and how difficult it can sometimes be for people to think of something to ask for. All of us, as human beings on this planet, can think of things that can help us in some way. Yet, we're so conditioned to just doing things on our own that we don't even think to ask.

Asking for help makes some people feel vulnerable. Just remember that being vulnerable means being real and vulnerability builds relatedness. Being vulnerable means I am willing to let you know me. It means I am willing to allow you to help me and contribute to me.

TIP

Start asking for more things more often. If doing so seems difficult, then start with what you would consider to be little things, small requests.

Often, all that gets in the way of asking are thoughts about why you shouldn't ask. These habitual thoughts can be replaced with a more productive way of relating to the power of asking. The following list combines reasons people frequently use to avoid making requests with new ways of thinking that enable them to make the requests.

I don't know them well enough to make a request.

I know them well enough to call, which will allow me to get to know them better.

I don't want to risk rejection.

I trust that people will do the best that they can do to help me and I do not need to take it as rejection if they cannot help me.

I ought to be able to do this without anyone's help.

I don't need to prove that I can do this by myself when it can be a lot more fun if I receive the help of others.

It wouldn't be fair to them since I can't be of help to them.

I won't prejudge or decide for others whether they want to help or not. I will always look for opportunities to support others even when I don't know what that support might be.

They're out of my league.

They are part of my network and have probably had others help them throughout their career in the same way that I'm asking them for help. I will approach people as equals in terms of human value and allow them to choose how they can be of service.

Asking is a sign of weakness.

I ask from a place of strength and acknowledge myself for my clarity, courage, and willingness to include others in my life and my successes.

Why would they want to help me?

I remind myself that it is human nature for people to want to be of help and service to others. I will be courteous, professional, and appreciative of any help they give.

They probably won't even take my call.

They may or may not take my call, however, at least I will know that I have not let myself be intimidated by my own thoughts and fears. I trust that by taking action I am setting my network into motion.

It would just be a waste of time.

I am willing to take a chance and trust the process of networking to be worthwhile, whether the results come immediately or in the future.

People are often hesitant to ask for help or information because they're afraid of rejection or concerned that they may be bothering people. In reality, most people feel flattered and acknowledged and are glad to help. You have to be the one to open the door and give them permission.

Sometimes it's all in how you ask

Your mind and the minds of the people you meet contain billions of pieces of data. This information is there for the grasping. All you have to do is learn how to access the data. With a computer, you have to learn the right command to enter. If you type it in wrong or spell it wrong, too bad, you will not get the response that you desire. The same is true with people. If you make your request long, cumbersome, nonspecific, or confusing, chances are you won't access the data. You can learn how to trigger and open people's "mental hard drives" through the way you communicate and connect.

Abracadabra! Using the magic words

Using certain words will enhance your networking and help you transition into making your requests. These words can help to make it easy and natural to request something from another person. Ideally, you want your requests to fit in with the natural flow of the conversation.

- ✔ **Oh, by the way:** At the end of a conversation in person or over the phone, say, "Oh, by the way" and transition into your request. "David, by the way, I had a question to ask you."

- ✔ **I just had a thought:** When you're in a conversation and someone says something that triggers an idea, you can say, "I just had a thought . . ." or "Something just came to mind that I've been meaning to ask you."

- ✔ **Would you help:** Using *would* instead of *could* indicates that you are asking about a person's willingness, not a person's ability. You are giving them a chance to choose to do something that would be of value to you. "George, would you help me with . . .?"

- ✔ **I need help:** This one is pretty obvious. It lets the person you're speaking with know that you are in a situation where you need some assistance of some kind. In general, people want to be of help and will respond to the words "need help." "I'm attempting to reach . . . and I need your help! Would you be willing to contact her for me?"

- ✔ **Who do you (know, recommend, or suggest)?** Rather than asking, "Do you know anybody who . . ." ask, "Who do you know?" The second way of phrasing the request implies that out of all the people they know, they probably know someone who can help you. "I'm looking for work with a law firm in Santa Fe or El Paso. Who do you suggest I talk with who is familiar with the law firms in those cities?"

✔ **What would you recommend?** This is a respectful term that lets other people know that you acknowledge their expertise. "I'm looking for help developing a marketing plan for our newest product. What would you recommend?"

People love to help and contribute. That is part of human nature. When you ask people for help, you give them an opportunity to be valued and to make a contribution.

Requests versus announcements

People often make an announcement thinking they are making a request and wonder why they get no response. An announcement is a statement providing information. The information could be of value to others. Or the information could let others know how they can be of support to you. With an announcement, there is no call for a response. A request, however, states what you want or need and issues a call to action that generates a response from people. Here are some examples:

Announcement:

> I am interested in meeting people who schedule meetings and conferences for their employees.

Request:

> I'm interested in meeting people who schedule meetings and conferences for their employees. Who do you suggest I talk with at your company?

Announcement:

> I have three tickets to the Tennessee-LSU football game, for anyone who is interested.

Request:

> I have three tickets to sell for the Tennessee-LSU football game. Who do you know who loves football who I could contact to let them know that these tickets are available for them or their friends?

Announcements are fine. They are a way to give people information. However, if you want a response and prefer to walk away from a conversation with information rather than just being the conveyor of information, making a request is better. Think about whether an announcement or a request better serves your purpose.

Your dream may be closer than you think!

A designation of Certified Speaking Professional is available to members of the National Speakers Association. When I initially got into the speaking industry, I remember thinking that earning the designation would be great. It was a dream that I didn't know how to accomplish, so I simply set about to develop myself as a speaker, become an expert at my topic, and grow my business.

Then one year at the National Speakers Association convention, one of my fellow speakers received her designation as a Certified Speaking Professional. After I went over to congratulate her, we began talking about what it had taken for her to reach that accomplishment. I left that conversation thinking, "I don't think I've fulfilled the criteria; however, I need to be willing to check it out to at least find out how far off I am and identify what it would take."

I went back to my office and started gathering the necessary data. As I gathered the information, I begin to think, "You know, I may be closer than I thought." And then at some point I realized I had fulfilled the criteria. I had accomplished much more than I had even realized.

I had to be willing to face the possibility of missing the mark to discover that I was on the mark.

I then proceeded to document my speaking engagements for a five-year period in order to submit the necessary paperwork to the CSP Council. This involved calling all of my clients who I'd had over that period and verifying with them that the data (names, addresses, phone numbers, program titles, fees, and so on) I was turning in to the National Speakers Association was correct and current. This was a major but necessary task.

On many of those calls I got voice mail. When that was the case, I would leave a message saying, "I'm applying for my certification as a professional speaker and I need your help." Those phone messages were returned more quickly than I expected and people were extremely helpful. As a result, I got my application in on time and received my certification at the next convention. Part of the thrill of receiving the certification was to send a special thank-you to all of those people, not only for their business over those five years but also for the prompt response to my calls and for their help in fulfilling my goal.

Criteria for a powerful request

The way you make your request can greatly influence what kind of response you get and whether you actually get what you are asking for. A powerful request is one that generates a result and creates value. Here are the criteria for making powerful requests of your network:

✔ **Be clear about what you want and need.** Your clarity makes it easier for others to respond. When you speak directly about what you want, rather than beating around the bush, you are most likely to get support that will be useful. And don't hint, hope, or suggest — ASK!

✔ **Let people know why they're someone who can help you.** Tell people what about them it is that makes you think they can be of help to you. You must respect, admire, or appreciate something about the person if you're making a request of them. As part of making your request, let people know what you admire about them.

✔ **Be specific.** When you make a request that is broad rather than specific, it is typically difficult for people to respond. The more specific you are with your requests, the more likely you are to trigger a response in the other person's mental computer.

✔ **Be succinct.** Too much information creates overload and is overwhelming. When you make a request and give people more information than they need, their mind may at some point check out. Give people just enough information so that they know how to respond. If they need more information, they'll ask. If they do ask, you are in a conversation with them rather than in a situation in which you do all the talking.

✔ **Be strong.** Don't ask from a place of weakness. Asking is a sign of strength, so make sure that you don't apologize for asking or ask in a way that is complaining, whiney, or wimpy. Ask from the place of strength. Know what you want and need to have to accomplish your goals and dreams and derive power from knowing that you are going to get there.

✔ **Ask expecting to get what you want.** Make sure that you don't come across with an attitude of "Well, (shrug) I'll ask but I bet you anything they won't respond and aren't going to be of help." Your attitude comes across. Honor other people by having a positive attitude about their ability to help and your ability to get what you want and need in life. Be open to the possibility that even if you don't get exactly what you want, you may discover alternatives or be pointed to other resources that can help.

✔ **Give people a chance to respond.** Ask and then be quiet to give them a chance to think and respond. Some people ask and then just keep on talking, until at some point the conversation goes in another direction and the question gets forgotten.

✔ **Ask in a way that people see the opportunity for you and the value of responding.** Tell people the difference that it will make for you if they help you. Share with them your dream, vision, or goal. Make people feel good about helping you.

✔ **Be real.** If what you're asking for is exciting, then ask with enthusiasm. If you are having difficulty with something, then ask in a way that lets people know the importance of what you are asking. If you've suffered a hardship in life and feel emotionally tender, ask for help from people who can be gentle and caring.

If you're not getting what you've asked for

If you consistently don't get what you ask for, you may be asking the wrong way or displaying the wrong attitude when you ask. Think about the way you normally make requests to discover how to improve your requests. Review this list of questions:

- Do you hint, hope, and beat around the bush with your requests? "It sure would be nice if you could call . . ."

- Are you being vague? "If there were some kind of way to maybe . . ."

- Are you stating what you want rather than asking? "I've got to find a new accountant by next Wednesday."

- Are you giving the person an excuse not to respond? "I know you're busy" or "I understand you may not have the time to help me."

- Do you give the person more background information than is needed, and the person gets overwhelmed? "I'm looking for . . . this is what happened last time . . . this is what I plan to do this time . . . would you help?"

- Are you complaining and whining rather than asking? "I'm having a problem with . . . it just seems like no matter what . . . if only someone would . . ."

- Are you apologizing for asking? "I hate to bother you, but . . ."

- Do you demand rather than ask? "You owe me . . ."

- Do you continue talking once you've made the request, rather than pausing for a response?

- Do you mumble or speak so softly that it's hard to hear you

- **Ask again and ask in a variety of ways.** Just because you asked once and didn't get what you were asking for doesn't mean that you have to stop asking. Ask other people. Ask the same person again at another time. Think of asking as a moment-to-moment process. In the next moment, someone may think of a response that he or she hadn't thought of previously. When you're speaking with a person, you may have to phrase your request a couple of different ways to trigger his or her thinking.

Asking for Referrals

If you're in sales or in business for yourself, you will likely be asking for referrals. In fact, you ought to be asking for referrals. Your network can be your greatest source of contacts, prospects, and new customers.

Let asking for a referral be a natural part of the conversation. Think ahead and practice asking so that your conversation about referrals flows easily and naturally. Here are the steps you should follow:

1. **Identify what you want to ask them for.** Be specific in your requests. Point people's minds in the right direction. Here are some possibilities:

   - You want names and phone numbers of people you can contact.

   - You want them to tell their friends about you or tell a specific someone about you.

   - You want help or advice on reaching or contacting someone.

   - You want an introduction to someone.

2. **Ask what they are willing to do.** Help them to be clear and straight about what they are willing to do. If you sense that they are not comfortable referring, either help to clear up their concern or give them a chance to graciously decline.

3. **Offer them your support.** You might be able to give them a referral. If not, at least offer to be of support. Ask, "What can I do for you?" or "How can I be of help?"

4. **Thank them.** Recap what they have offered to do and thank them. Acknowledge them. "Thanks for your help" or "I appreciate you taking the time . . ."

Here is an example of a request for referrals:

Person A: I've been thinking about how to expand my business into the banking industry and I know that you are well respected in that industry. I wanted to see if you would be willing to help me with some recommendations on who to contact.

Person B: Sure. Do you want to talk with loan officers, branch managers, marketing directors?

A: I think the best place for me to start would be marketing directors and then branch managers.

B: Jack Carlson is marketing director over at ABC Bank. Here's his number. Another good contact would be . . .

A: This is great! Thanks. What I plan to do is give these people a call next week. I'd like to let them know I got their name from you. Is that okay?

B: Yeah, that's fine. Tell them I say hi. And let me know how it goes.

A: I will. Thanks again. I really appreciate your help. So what can I do for you?

B: Well, since you asked . . .

Letting your referral sources know who your ideal client is may help. Then find out who *their* ideal client is! For more information on getting referrals, please see Chapter 11.

Ask-Offer-Thank

Imagine if in every conversation you asked for something, offered something, and thanked the other person for his or her support and contribution to your life! The *ask-offer-thank* method keeps the flow of networking present in every conversation. If we all practiced this method with each other all the time, incredible relationships would develop and a ripple of opportunities would surface out of every conversation.

Have ask-offer-thank be part of every conversation you have today. Doing so will take some courage and creativity on your part as you'll end up asking a lot. But remember that asking creates trust and opens the door to results. The power is in having all three components present in every conversation so that you are served, the other person is honored, and gratitude is expressed.

To put ask-offer-thank into practice, make a list of some of the things you can be asking for and some of the things you can offer. Doing so makes having things in mind easier as you talk with people. Then, in each conversation, pay attention to what the other person is saying and what request and offer is a fit for that conversation.

When you're not sure what to ask for, you can say, "I'm focused on accomplishing XYZ this week; any suggestions you might have for me?" When you're not sure what to offer, you can say, "I'd like to be of help in some way; what can I do for you?"

And the thanks part should be easy. Thank people for their time, their friendship, their business, and their support. Take a moment to identify what it is that you appreciate about them and the conversation that you had with them.

Write *ASK-OFFER-THANK* on a sticky note and place it somewhere so that it is your reminder throughout the day. And then be ready for your relationships to accelerate and your opportunities to multiply!

Chapter 7

Listen Up!

· ·

In This Chapter

▶ Training yourself to listen effectively

▶ Listening for chances to be of assistance

▶ Understanding what makes a good listener

· ·

Honing your listening skills is critical for enhancing your networking effectiveness. It is through listening that you build trust and rapport with people. It is also through listening that you gather information. Building trust and rapport and gathering information are essential parts of effective networking.

To really listen effectively requires giving someone your full attention. When you give someone your full attention, you are more likely to create a trusting relationship and learn information about that person. Listen as if you're on a treasure hunt and you're listening for clues — clues on how you can be of support to the other person and how that person can be of support to you.

When you fine-tune your listening skills, you begin to learn more about people and thus discover opportunities to be of mutual value and benefit to each other.

When people feel a connection with you and feel like you are really interested, they open up and give you more information.

Most of the times that you think you're listening, you're probably also thinking about other things, doing other things, and even possibly planning what you're going to say when it's your turn. Partial listening is a common occurrence. It leads to lots of problems and missed opportunities. With focused, attentive listening you build stronger networking relationships, have fewer misunderstandings, and create more sharing of resources.

True listening occurs when you are mentally fully engaged in what the other person is saying. You are not fixing, advising, or judging. The other person has your full attention and you are like a sponge for his or her thoughts and feelings.

The quickest way to develop trust and rapport with someone is through effective listening. Listening well also saves you time and stress, draws out valuable information, and lets you find value in others.

Listening well is a challenge, but it's a powerful skill once you acquire it. For more information on how to be a powerful listener, check out *Communicating Effectively For Dummies* (Hungry Minds, Inc.).

Becoming an Effective Listener

You are not inherently a good or a bad listener. Listening is a skill and you can improve it by developing the right habits. Think of people you know who are good listeners. Think about what they do that makes them good listeners. The odds are pretty good that if you follow the tips I give you in this section, you'll start emulating those people whose listening skills you admire.

Create a positive listening environment

Your environment can make it difficult to listen. If you are in conversation with someone and there's a lot of chaos, noise, and other distractions, listening well requires even greater discipline and focus than it normally does.

✔ **Avoid distractions.** You are bombarded by distractions almost constantly — cell phones, pagers, the stack of papers on the desk, the list of phone messages to return. When you make networking calls, set aside the distractions so that you can focus on the people you are talking to.

Create an environment that helps you give the other person your full attention. When listening and connecting with someone is very important, choose to have the conversation somewhere that has as few distractions as possible. Find a place where the normal distractions of phones ringing, people walking by, and so on are not part of the environment.

✔ **Clear space between you and the other person.** Get out from behind the desk, the paper, or the book. Don't have physical blocks between you and the other person. Create a clear space so that you can connect with each other.

Using the right body language

Your body language is a crucial part of how people perceive you. Here are some tips for how to use body language to put the other person at ease and put yourself in the right frame of mind to listen:

✔ **Turn your body toward the person.** Facing and turning towards the people you are listening to conveys respect and interest and is actually a gesture that "opens the door" and invites them in. You want to welcome their communication.

✔ **Have an open posture.** Let people know that you are open to hearing what they have to say by holding your body in an open and receptive position — don't cross your arms or legs.

✔ **Make eye contact.** Look other people in the eyes. Be aware of any tendency you may have to look everywhere but at the people you are listening to. Look gently and directly into their eyes, without staring. Even when you break eye contact, keep your eyes focused on their face.

Don't lock onto the other person's eyes to the point where it is overbearing and uncomfortable.

✔ **Have a pleasant, yet fairly neutral, facial expression.** Make your expression convey openness and a non-judgmental attitude. Express a pleasure in being there to listen. Obviously, a scowl, frown, or tight lips convey that you are not open to what the other person is saying and have already decided what you think is going to happen in the conversation.

✔ **Nod.** A nod is a gesture of encouragement. It does not necessarily mean that you agree with what the other person is saying. A nod can be an expression of *okay, I'm here, I'm listening, I hear that, I'm with you.*

✔ **Have a calm presence.** Don't fidget, jitter, rustle papers, twirl a pen, tap your fingers, and so on. As a participant in one of my programs said, "Being a good listener involves having quiet body language." Quiet the body so that you can be present.

See Chapter 5 regarding the influence that your body language has on small talk.

Having a listening mentality

You may know people who operate as if listening is simply a matter of not talking. Just because they're not talking doesn't mean they're listening. Often, although they *look* like they're listening, *act* like they're listening, and even *say* that they're listening, they're really focusing on what they're going to say when their turn comes! Listening requires that you give up being self-oriented in order to give your attention and focus to the other person.

✔ **Be attentive.** Give people delighted attention — whether you agree with what they say or not.

I learned a lot about listening, networking, and giving people delighted attention when I was the executive director of the Center for Attitudinal Healing. We provided support for children with life-threatening illnesses. Our volunteers went through a twelve-week training program, during which they learned how to give people *delighted attention* — listening without judgment. Delighted listening is when you give people your full attention with no agenda other than to be pleased to be able to be there for them. This allows people to feel as if they are heard, to release negative feelings, and to regain a sense of power in dealing with life's challenges. Listening is a gift that you give to the people in your network.

✔ **Be curious.** When you were a child, you were intrigued and interested in everything. You didn't make judgments — you didn't know what anything was for — instead you had an open and eager mind.

Try to reconnect with that childlike sense of curiosity so that you just naturally show an interest in people and listen with rapt attention and respect.

✔ **Be patient.** Don't rush people and don't let a concern about time get in the way of connecting with people. If you let your schedule become your ruler, you may one day find yourself feeling empty, alone, and unfulfilled.

At times, you may have to give people timeframes. If you only have ten minutes to talk with someone before you have to go to a meeting, tell him or her so. You can say something like, "I have an appointment in 10 minutes, and I really want to hear more; can I call you at 3:30 this afternoon?"

Setting timeframes is different than rushing people. When people are hurried, they tend to communicate partial information, feel unimportant, and are less likely to attempt to generate a conversation with you in the future.

✔ **Be present.** Rein in the tendency to daydream and let the mind wander. Learn to focus and be totally present in the moment with people.

✔ **Listen for what's not being said.** Behind every frustration is a commitment to excel at whatever is causing the frustration. Inside every complaint is a desire that can be fulfilled. People often ask for something that is only *related* to what they really want, but they are reluctant to come right out and state their desire. As a masterful listener, you can uncover what's at the heart of the communication.

✔ **Listen to gather information.** You never know when people will say something that brings an "ah-ha" into your awareness. Maybe you'll simply get to learn more about them — which gives you a greater chance of discovering reasons to be in touch with them later!

✔ **Listen to respond.** The number one communication pitfall is *reacting* rather than *responding*. Reacting is an automatic behavior when you speak or act without thinking. Responding involves giving thought to your words and actions and speaking with purpose and intention. Fully listen to what's being said and then give yourself time to think before you speak.

Give it away now

Certain things block your ability to listen well. Give up the following in order to enhance your listening skills:

- Give up judgment.

- Give up thinking you know.

- Give up your attachment to your opinions and your need to be right.

- Give up focusing on what you're going to say next.

- Give up thinking that listening is simply a matter of not talking.

- Give up thinking you can't be a good listener.

Multitasking may be great for computers, but it's not great for people who are attempting to network with and listen to one another. Don't think that you can only partially listen to someone and still get the full gist of what he or she is saying. Most of the time people don't fully listen to each other. Which means they take incomplete, inaccurate, made-up information and live their life as if it's complete, accurate, and factual. Not a good way to live and definitely not an effective way to build a network.

Interacting as a listener

Listening doesn't mean being passive. Listening requires active engagement. Some of the things you can do during a conversation to improve your ability to listen include

- **Encouraging the other person.** Communicating and opening up can be difficult. Letting people know that you are interested and providing a safe space for their communication is important. Don't be defensive, rush the other person, or be critical.

- **Not interrupting.** To interrupt is to break the flow of the conversation. Interrupting stops the continuity and hinders the completion of the communication. You may think that your interruption is helpful or valuable, but you can make a mental note of something that you want to say and wait your turn. Try not to speak until the other person finishes talking and gives you the go ahead.

- **Expressing an interest in what the other person has to say.** Actually tell people that you are interested: "I want to hear about your business" or "I am interested in learning more about what kind of clients you are looking for." You can express interest with your body language and behaviors, but actually putting your interest in words adds a whole new level of attention and respect.

✔ **Asking questions.** Ask only questions that relate to what people are saying. Make sure your questions express interest, not judgment. Ask in a way that invites the person to go deeper with the conversation. As a good listener, you actually must draw information out of the other person.

✔ **Being quiet.** Although you must respond and be engaged in conversation as part of listening, you must also provide intervals of quiet. Give yourself and the other person a chance to process the information that is being communicated. Quiet gives the other person a chance to get underneath the surface level of what he or she is saying and communicate at a deeper level.

After the conversation

Being a good networker involves remembering what people have told you. Effective listening increases the likelihood that you will remember the conversation later. Have you ever noticed how flattered you are when someone remembers a point from a conversation you had with him or her? Recalling your conversations with people helps you build connections. And when you've listened carefully, you will, just naturally, remember conversations.

After listening to someone, think about ways that you can respond to what you learned in the conversation. See what kind of opportunities you can create: How can I use this information? What have I learned here today? How can I be a resource for this person?

Using mental images to understand and remember

Effective listening involves being fully engaged with the conversation rather than having information go in one ear and out the other. Creating mental images of what is being said is a way to help you be fully engaged in the conversation and remember the conversation later. When you are networking with someone and they tell you what they need, you can actually create a mental picture of that need being fulfilled by the person you refer. For example, if Bill tells you he is looking for a landscape person to fix his sprinkler system, you can visualize a sprinkler system

going off. That prompts you to think of your friend Ed, who owns a landscape company. So you get a picture of Ed driving up to Bill's house in his van that says "Ed's Lawn and Landscape Service" and working in Bill's yard. Mental pictures and images help you stay focused and engaged in the conversation. The mental picture will more likely trigger a mental response of other information that you have stored in your mind and will also help you remember what is being said so that you will call Ed to recommend that he contact Bill.

Getting Clear on the Purpose of the Conversation

Sometimes you, as a listener, need to know what the speaker expects of you. In the following examples, the speaker lets the listener know exactly what the speaker wants from him or her:

- ✔ "Do you have about ten minutes to *listen* and then give me your *opinion* of this marketing idea that I have?"

- ✔ "I am attempting to sort through an issue I'm dealing with. Are you available to *listen* to me? I find it very helpful to be able to *think out loud*."

- ✔ "Would you be willing to be a *sounding board* for me while I *review* my plans for my project?"

If the speaker doesn't clearly state what he or she wants from you as the listener, you can ask. "Tell me how I can best serve you here. Do you want me to be a sounding board or respond with advice?" If you're not sure what the person wants and don't ask, then you'll respond based on your assumption and may not give the person what he or she really needs or wants.

It's much better to ask the speaker what he or she wants from you rather than to guess or make assumptions.

This could go on forever . . .

A major concern people have is that giving their full attention to someone will encourage that person to go on and on. But being an effective listener doesn't mean that you have to be a doormat and allow people to ramble inappropriately. You can be fully engaged in listening and still give the conversation a timeframe. You can also be fully engaged and direct the conversation to a place of value and benefit for you and the other person.

Some people get lost in their own thoughts and seem to get in a verbal loop that they can't get out of. In those situations, you may say something like "You know, I've heard you mention . . . several times. What is it about that?" At other times, depending on the conversation, you may want to say, "This is very interesting, and I'd love to hear more. Right now I've got to . . . Would you like to schedule another time to get together?" (Of course, you only want to say this if you want to get back together to continue the conversation.)

Listening to Find Ways to Be of Help

Every time you hear people mention something that they want or need, the door is open for networking. Think about how you can be of help to people in accomplishing what it is that they want. When people have a problem, try to help them find a solution. Listen for phrases such as:

- ✔ I want to meet someone who . . .
- ✔ I'd like to know how to . . .
- ✔ I'm trying to . . .
- ✔ I'm having difficulty with . . .
- ✔ I'm looking for . . .
- ✔ For years I have wanted to . . .

These are trigger phrases that should tell you to sharpen your listening focus because these phrases indicate that relationship-building and networking opportunities are at hand. When you hear phrases like these in your conversations, pay attention. Ask questions to gather more information. Show an interest and explore how you can be a resource for that person. Be willing to offer a piece of information, an idea, a contact, or even just words of encouragement.

Probe for more information by asking questions like:

- ✔ Are you saying that if you could have . . . you would be able to . . .?
- ✔ Would . . . be of help to you?
- ✔ What if . . .?

It is through listening that you gather information and learn more about others — which helps you identify ways to be a resource for them as well as ways you can ask them to be of help to you. Listening, from a networking perspective, is not about doing things for others or fixing things or taking on others' problems. It is about being a source of encouragement, support, and ideas that empower others to be the best they can be and fulfill all their greatest desires in life.

When talking with or working with clients, listen for any non-business needs they have. If you are able to be a resource for them beyond your business role, you strengthen and expand your relationship.

SUCCESS STORY
#1

Counting to three makes for better listening

Out of my desire to always be improving my communication skills, I began to notice my tendency to finish people's sentences for them. Before I could stop myself, I would jump in and basically tell them what they were thinking. Because I was raised to be nice, courteous, and tactful, I was real nice about how I did it and even thought that I was helping them!

I realized this was an unproductive listening habit and decided to make a change and develop a new habit. So I decided to pay more attention, slow down my thinking, and stop myself whenever I was about to jump in with my "helpful" words. My plan was to give people my full attention and give them a chance to continue finishing their thoughts. So I started counting silently to three after they stopped talking and before I started.

Lo and behold, by the time I finished counting to three they usually had started talking again! At first I thought, "Oh no, they've started talking again. It was supposed to be my turn!" Yet what I noticed — nine times out of ten — was that what they said after that brief pause was very important for me to hear. My quietness had allowed them to go to the next level of information. By giving the speakers time and letting them articulate their own thoughts, my conversations with others became increasingly more valuable — both to them and to me.

Listening is one way for you to be there for others. It allows you to be a silent partner, at times, giving people a chance to think out loud and thus gain more clarity about what they want and need. Effective listening enhances your chance of being a networking resource for others.

Chapter 8

Using Follow-Through to Maintain and Grow Your Network

In This Chapter

▶ Knowing what to do next

▶ Taking action promptly

▶ Staying in touch with your network

▶ Keeping your commitments

You can have great people skills and communication skills, but without follow-through you won't have great results.

Networking happens through conversation. Opportunities are revealed and relationships are deepened as people interact with one another. Through conversation, you discover what people want and need and how you can be of help. The interaction reveals the action you need to take. The action creates opportunities and results. Plenty of people talk about networking, but don't actually network. For instance, they say they'll get together for lunch, they say they'll stay in touch, or they say they'll get involved in their industry's association. If they don't actually follow through, nothing happens. Networking works its magic only when you take the necessary action.

If you want your ideas to come to fruition, you must combine idea, intention, and action. Your ideas and intention are what help you determine the actions that are most effective in producing the results you desire.

It's All in the Follow-Through

Follow-through is the action you take after making a contact or discovering someone's need. For instance, in one of my workshops one of the participants mentioned that she loves reading and asked if anyone could recommend places to buy used books. At a recent church event, I had met Libbie Vaughan, the owner of Read It Again, Glenn, a bookstore that sells used books. A few days after the workshop, I sent an e-mail to the workshop participant giving her Libbie's name, number, and e-mail address. This is following through. The critical part of this networking scenario is remembering and taking the time to provide the information or action that brings value.

Follow-through is the next step to take that furthers a relationship or creates a valuable result for you or someone else. After you have information, it's up to you to use that information to create value. If you gather a lot of information through your networking but never pass that information along or get back with people, then you are only doing the front-end work of networking. The follow-through is what generates results.

Meeting people is easy. It happens as a natural part of life. Everywhere you go, you meet people. Some you actually make a connection with and some you simply meet in passing. Some may become great friends, clients, or associates. And then there are some that you connect with, and because there's no follow-through, nothing else happens. There may even be times when someone offers to meet with you, introduce you to someone, or give you a lead, and nothing ever happens because you or the other person falls short on the follow-through.

Prompt follow-through can make the difference in whether an opportunity comes to fruition or not. In networking, seizing the opportunity while the energy is hot and the moment is ripe is valuable. *Carpe diem!*

Timing may not be everything, but it certainly can be a critical component when opening doors and following up on opportunities. If someone recommends that you call Joe Smith about a job opportunity and you don't follow through because you forgot, misplaced the phone number, put off the call because you didn't feel confident, or got distracted by other things, the position Joe Smith is hiring for will possibly be filled by the time you make that call.

Doing the best you can do

Not all of your networking efforts will lead to results and satisfaction. And there's no way of knowing ahead of time which ones will lead to the pot of gold. Therefore, you must be willing to check them all out to find out which one leads to the riches.

Just like you can't expect every prospect to become a client, you can't expect every lead to generate your biggest deal ever. And you can't expect every person you follow through with to be a valuable resource for you. However, you can always be open to the possibility that every person could be a resource. With effective follow-through, at least you know that you have done your part to create an opportunity.

What good follow-through says about you

Good follow-through is one of the qualities that can easily set you apart from other networkers. By following up promptly on the things that you say you will do, you create a reputation for yourself as a world-class networker. When you put forth the effort to achieve good follow-through, others see you as:

- **Professional and dependable.** You show people by your actions that they can depend on you. You show up on time and you do what you say you're going to do. When people know that they can count on you, you are more attractive to them as a networking partner.

- **Responsive.** Some people, even though they seem to be present, never really respond to what is happening around them. Being responsive represents a level of awareness and aliveness. Observe what is going on around you and respond to the situations. When you are reading a magazine and find an article that reminds you of someone, clip it right then and put a note on it, address the envelope, and send it — that is prompt follow-through. Follow-through involves being responsive and taking action based on what you observe. If you're not fully present to what's going on around you, you won't even notice what action to take.

- **Organized.** If you are not organized, the chances of something falling through the cracks are multiplied. Have a place where you know you can find that name and phone number. Know where to put that reminder to call someone.

Keep notecards, stamps, stationary, business cards, and other supplies organized and handy to make it easy for you to follow up with people

- **Courteous.** Prompt and effective follow-through is good manners and good business etiquette. It is courteous to get back with people when you say you will and to thank people promptly after they have done something for you. For more on courtesy and etiquette, see Chapter 16.

Techniques for Effective Follow-Through

Follow-through happens when you take action to stay in touch with people, send notes, make phone calls, and keep your commitment to do what you say you're going to do. Effective follow-through helps you stay connected with people and keeps the process of networking alive.

Take immediate follow-through action

Taking immediate action can establish momentum. Take the energy that is present from an initial conversation and act on it right away. Sometimes when you delay taking action, the energy begins to fade away and motivating yourself to get into action can become more and more difficult. Let the current energy from your interaction be your motivator. Let it carry you through to the next step in the networking scenario. As I mentioned earlier in this chapter, being prompt and effective with your follow-through makes others view you as professional, dependable, and responsive.

I'm a very active member of a networking breakfast club in Houston. Our group has been together for ten years, and its members have become a big part of my life and my business. As a group, we are aware of the need to continue to grow in order to keep the group vibrant and alive.

We decided to have a special networking event to kick off the year 2001. Every member was encouraged to invite at least two people. Our focus was to have lots of guests, to create an energizing and valuable meeting, and to get the word out to people about our group so as to attract some great new members. Everyone brought guests and I conducted my Networking to the Music exercise from my Drumming Up Business program. Through the use of music and motivation, we had over 40 people circling the room and following the music to meet new people and make valuable connections with one another.

The next day I received a note in the mail from one of the people I had invited. It was a note of thanks and appreciation for the opportunity to be there and an indication that he was interested in a return visit and possible membership. He had to have written and mailed that note right after the meeting in order for me to have gotten it the next day. I was impressed and will probably always remember that about him. That action created an image of him as a responsive person who means business and is on top of things, someone who takes action and makes things happen — an impression formed by one little note. Although we had approximately 20 guests at the breakfast that morning, as far as I know he was the only one who took immediate action and sent a note that arrived the next day!

Let technology help you

Have a system that supports you in taking follow-through action. Use technology to keep things from falling through the cracks. My computer, cell phone, and palm device help to keep me on track with my follow-through activities. I may leave myself a voice mail message to remind myself of what I said I would do. I also make notes in my palm device or on my computer as I go through my day to help me remember to do certain follow-through activities. Obviously, the ideal would be to do the thing right when I think of it, so that I don't even have to make a note to myself or add to my list. But it doesn't always happen that way, because sometimes I have the thought while I'm on a plane, or late at night, or at a time and place where I can't take the action. However, no matter where I am or what time it is, there is almost always a notepad, phone, palm device, or laptop computer available for me to create a reminder for myself. For additional information on how technology can help you with your networking, go to Chapter 15.

Thought prompters

Fine-tuning your focus and awareness helps you identify ways to follow through and thus stay in touch and keep your networking activities flowing. After meeting someone, ask yourself the following questions to help clarify the best follow-through action to take.

✔ What would further this relationship?

✔ What could I possibly do for this person that could be of service?

✔ What could I offer to do for this person?

✔ What did I say that I would do that I must follow through on?

✔ What opportunities have opened up as a result of this conversation?

✔ What's next?

Make a follow-up phone call

Some of the ways follow-through action is handled is via phone, e-mail, and regular mail. A phone call is your best choice if you have something important to discuss, need to have interaction, or want to create an immediate result. Obviously, if you say, "I'll give you a call" you should call.

Prepare for the call

Think about the following before you call so that you will be focused and prepared regarding what you want to say:

✔ Recall where you met the person

✔ Recall what you know or learned about the person

✔ Identify what you can offer to do for the person

✔ Identify what the person can possibly do for you

Create a call outline. Having a call outline helps to make sure you cover everything that you have in mind to talk about. The outline can serve as a checklist. Even if your conversation branches off into new topics, you can review your list and say, "And one other thing I wanted to talk with you about is . . ." in an easy, conversational manner. The other person doesn't need to know you're using a list to prompt yourself.

Make the call

Here's an example of a call outline:

1. **Identify yourself.**

2. **Indicate who referred you or where and when you met the person you are calling. Give your purpose for calling.**

3. **After you state your purpose and make your request:**

    a. Listen and gather information — ask questions.

    b. Make other requests and offer additional support if appropriate.

4. **Identify what you can do with the information and support you are being given**

5. **Summarize the interaction and let the person know the action you will be taking.**

6. **Thank the person for his or her time, willingness to speak with you, support, and assistance.**

7. **Offer your support.**

8. **Say goodbye.**

If you don't reach the person but get voice mail instead, you have to decide whether to leave a message or call back until you get the person. If you think you might leave a message, again it's best to think about what you want to say beforehand. Review the tips on voice mail messages in Chapter 16.

Post-call activity

After the call, your follow-through activity could include any of the following:

✔ Recording in your database system the gist of the conversation, the results, and the action to be taken

✔ Learning from the call by taking a minute to think about what you did that worked well and what you could do differently in the future to be more effective

✔ Sending a letter, e-mail, or note of thanks and appreciation

If the call was to a person whose name you were given by someone else, letting the person who gave you the name know that you made contact and thanking him or her again for the support

Send an e-mail message

E-mail is a great vehicle for communication when the follow-through primarily involves passing along information:

"Here's that phone number that I promised to send you . . . Good luck."

Using e-mail effectively as part of your networking approach is discussed in greater detail in Chapter 15.

Sometimes it's the little things that achieve breakthroughs

Addis Walker is a stockbroker who inherited some clients from a fellow broker who was leaving the firm for which they both worked. He admitted to Addis that these were cases where he had dropped the ball. One couple he passed on to Addis was skeptical of working with another broker because none of their previous brokers had taken care of them or had made an effort to develop a relationship with them.

Although Addis does fee-based work, this couple refused to commit to paying a fee. Addis worked with them for four months for nothing, doing retirement plan reports and helping them get an attorney for estate planning, in an attempt to be of service and establish some trust and a relationship. The couple, however, still seemed reluctant to commit to working with Addis.

One day during a phone conversation with the couple, Addis heard the couple's dog barking in the background. She decided to send the dog (Molly) two dog toys. The wife, who had always been very reserved and quiet in all of their meetings and interactions, was thrilled. She said, "Every time we see Molly playing with those toys, we think of you. That was so thoughtful."

Sending toys to a client's dog may seem simple or even silly. But for this couple, it made all the difference. They had never had a broker show interest in anything other than investing their money. And then they met Addis, who even paid attention to their dog! This couple signed up with Addis and have continued to do business with her.

Send notes as part of follow-through

Even in this day and age of technology and e-mail, the handwritten note is a valuable follow-through tool. A handwritten note is professional and courteous. It's the mark of a first-class networker. It carries a lot of weight because it indicates the sender took the time to put his thoughts down on paper.

Your company may already have notecards with the company logo on the front that are ideal for your business notes. If not, you could recommend having some printed or get some printed for yourself. Remember that your notecards represent you and your business, so make sure you choose a good quality paper stock with a professional design and colors that match your other business literature.

When to send a note

You have many opportunities to send notes. In fact, every time you meet someone at a meeting, conference, or trade show, you could send that person a note letting him or her know that you're glad that you met and that you had a chance to visit.

If you did not give the person a business card at the time that you met, you may want to include a business card with your note. If the person was helpful to you in some way during your initial conversation, be sure to communicate how you were helped and how the advice, suggestion, comment, or lead was helpful and what you have done as a result of the conversation:

> "It was great to meet you at the ABC Conference last week. I'm glad we had a chance to learn about each other's businesses. I look forward to referring some business your way."

> "It was a pleasure to visit with you at the KRC reception last Thursday. Let me know if there is any way that I can be of support with your project."

When you've been to an event or seminar that was valuable to you, send a note to the person or people who were responsible. Let them know of your appreciation and the value that you received. This also applies when you read a book or article that is of value to you. Send a note to the author and express your appreciation and explain how you have used the book's suggestions or ideas and how doing so has led to a certain result or been beneficial in some way.

> "Thanks for the great seminar. I have already implemented your ideas on . . . and have seen great results. Best wishes for continued success."

> "Thanks for organizing a great sales meeting. You clearly put a lot of work into making sure the meeting was valuable and enjoyable. I am reenergized about having a great second quarter."

My favorite story about sending notes is from someone who attended a musical performance and sent the performer a one-word note: "Stunning!" That person's experience and appreciation was so eloquently and beautifully conveyed with that one word!

Don't hide behind the words "I can't tell you how much it means to me." Find the words to say how much something or someone means to you.

Personalizing your note

Personalize the note when possible by mentioning the recipient's business, something that was mentioned in your conversation with him or her, or something about the event or the circumstances under which you met. Your personalized comment can be part of the body of the note or added as a P.S. Here are some examples of personalized comments:

- ✔ It was great to meet you and discover that we have a love of rollerblading in common.

- ✔ I'll think of you the next time I come across any articles on the music industry.

- ✔ P.S. Have fun on your vacation to the Grand Canyon.

Engraved notecards lead to the White House

Brooke Farhood realized while she was in law school at UCLA that she needed more than just good grades to get the type of job she wanted. She had heard it was critical to have a good job between her second and third year of law school. Brooke, therefore, started sending notes as part of her networking approach. She decided that spending some money to get quality cards was worthwhile. She bought engraved cards with her name on the top. Sending the cards paid off when, through her networking, she got a summer job at the Office of Legal Counsel at the White House.

When she was approaching graduation, she decided that she wanted to do business law. So

Brooke started calling people she knew and requesting their support. Two of the people she called were key people she had worked with at the White House who she had stayed in touch with during the year. Sending notes helped Brooke stay in touch with people to start building a powerful career support system while she was still in college.

Brooke says she hasn't stopped sending notes and networking and doesn't expect that she ever will. Sending notes has become a natural and important part of her networking approach. She stills uses her cards to stay in touch with former supervisors and coworkers as well as friends, clients, and business associates.

Thank-you notes as part of follow-through

Another type of follow-through note you can send is the thank-you note. When people give you something tangible or intangible or do something for you, send a note of thanks. This could be a thanks for lunch, a referral, time together, valuable information, business, or whatever.

Your thank-you note can range in length from a few words ("You're the best!") to a few sentences. Keep it simple, but be sure to specifically express what you appreciate.

Here are some examples of when thank-you notes are appropriate:

✔ When someone gives you a lead or referral, thank the person for thinking of you and for trusting you with his or her friend or contact.

- "Thank you for referring me to Matthew Wilson. I have contacted him and look forward to learning more about his manufacturing process. You always seem to know exactly whom I need to meet. Thank you for being a valuable resource."

- "Thank you for giving my name to Barbara Maxwell. We talked this morning and I am sending a packet of information to her this afternoon. Thank you for trusting me with your clients. I assure you that anyone you refer to me will be treated with the utmost care and respect."

✔ When a referral leads to a new client, contract, or business opportunity, send a note of thanks and appreciation letting the person who initially referred you know about the success that has resulted from the referral.

- "Thank you for recommending me to Karen Sommers. I appreciate the opportunity to make a proposal to her regarding ABC's upcoming project. With your help, I got in touch with her just in time to be part of the bidding process."

- "Thank you for referring Jack Marsh to me. We just scheduled Big Percussion to play at their July reception. It's a great opportunity. I appreciate your support. Let me know what I can do for you."

✔ When someone sends you an article or clipping, send the person a thank you letting the person know that you appreciate him or her thinking of you and taking the time to send you the information.

- "Thank you for sending me the magazine article. The information fits right in with the project I'm working on. Thanks for thinking of me and sending it my way."

- "Thanks for sending me the clipping from the paper about our latest business acquisition. This is an exciting time for our business. I appreciate the support that you've been for us over the years."

A really powerful note requires sharing something about yourself. It requires that you reveal your personal thoughts of admiration or appreciation and gratitude. Let people know who they are to you, what they mean to you, and how they have inspired you. For more information on thank-you notes, please see Chapter 16.

Maintain your network by staying in touch

Sometimes circumstances (or life in general) seem to take over and weeks, months, and years can go by before we suddenly realize that we've lost touch with someone. If you're like many people, when that moment of realization hits, you feel guilty, bad, and wrong for having not stayed in touch. Don't go on a negative downward spiral. Simply take the time to reconnect. When someone's name comes to mind, it is a mental reminder that he or she is part of your network and it's time to reconnect and catch up.

How often do you think of people and yet don't tell them they were thought of? If you think of people and never let them know, you are missing out on the opportunity to let your thoughts count. When you put your thoughts into conversation, then networking can happen. If you keep your thoughts to yourself, you are blocking the flow. What if you knew every time someone thought of you? You might be pleasantly surprised to know how often it happens. It would be good if everyone were always expressing to each other "I thought of you."

Staying connected involves keeping the communication lines open. By keeping the communication lines intact, you discover ways to be of support that you could not have anticipated. Don't wait until you have a need to call someone. Maintain your network so that when you have a need, making that phone call for help is easy. Sending notes, e-mails, articles, making phone calls, and spending time together are all part of staying connected and maintaining your network.

When it comes to staying in touch with people, get creative. You know how it is when you fall in love and you want to call that person every few minutes (it seems like). And so you find excuses and reasons to call. You can do the same thing with the people in your support system. Find excuses and reasons to call, e-mail, or send a note. Here are some good reasons for getting in touch with people:

- ✔ You read an article that reminds you of something about them, their businesses, or their interests.
- ✔ You receive an invitation to a conference, workshop, meeting, or event that you think they might be interested in.
- ✔ You haven't talked to them in a long time and their name happens to pop into your head.
- ✔ You are browsing your Rolodex, e-mail address book, or database and come across their name.
- ✔ You see an article about them or by them in a publication.
- ✔ You see something indicating they have been promoted or awarded an honor.
- ✔ You meet someone who would be good for them to meet or know.

Any time someone's name comes to mind, that's a good enough reason to call. Let the person know that you thought of him or her and wondered what the person was doing.

For one week, every time you think of someone give him or her a quick phone call.

Be as good as your word

When you say you're going to call, call. When you say you're going to send someone information, send it. It's pretty simple. Do what you say you will do, and if for some reason you can't, let people know that you can't. Networking involves trusting and respecting one another. One of the greatest ways to develop trust and respect with another person is to do what you say you will do. When people learn that they can count on you, they are more likely to do business with you and refer business to you.

The calendar girl

Every year on December 26th, Lyn Salerno sends a calendar to everyone on her mailing list. The people on her list are clients, previous clients, college contacts, former colleagues, neighbors, friends, and members of the professional groups that she belongs to. Over the years, her list has grown to the point that she now sends about 140 calendars every year.

Lyn says, "It's just a little calendar and it has a small picture of me. It continually amazes me though, how I get comments like 'I think about you all the time because I have your little calendar next to the computer.'" Because people see the calendar all year long, they feel like they've seen Lyn and feel connected with her.

One of the women on her mailing list is someone Lyn worked with for a couple afternoons over three years ago. Yet within the last six to nine months, Lyn has received two referrals from her. Even though Lyn had only worked with her briefly, she had gotten on Lyn's list and has been receiving her calendar for three years. Staying connected and in front of her contacts keeps referrals and new business coming Lyn's way.

Have you ever said any of the following? Did you follow through?

- ✔ "I'll call you."
- ✔ "Let's do lunch."
- ✔ "I'll send you that information."
- ✔ "I'll get back with you."
- ✔ "I'll call her to let her know that you're going to call."
- ✔ "I'll talk with you at next week's meeting."

Okay, so sometimes we say these things as a way of making conversation. But if you say things without meaning them, then how do people know when you mean what you say? Small talk is an important and valuable networking skill. But don't confuse small talk with shallow talk that has no substance. Idle promises and agreements erode your reputation.

Stop yourself before you say automatic words or phrases that have no meaning to yourself or others. If you don't mean it, don't say it. Say something that you do mean instead. Think of it as a variation on an old saying you may have heard from your mother, "If you can't say anything nice, don't say anything at all." In this case, *if you can't say anything sincere and with commitment and conviction, don't say anything at all.*

Insincerity shows through no matter how simple or minute the situation. Be genuine. Be sincere. Be honest with your words and actions.

Of course, there may be times when you say you're going to do something and then you realize you won't be able to fulfill the obligation. Don't run away, hide, or berate yourself. Notice what happened that got in your way. Communicate to the people that you are aware that you're not able to do what you said and, if possible, let them know that you're willing to make a new commitment. Here are some examples of ways to tell others that you need to renegotiate a commitment:

✔ "Mike, I said that I would get a demo video in the mail to you by today and I just got word that the duplication process was delayed by an equipment failure and the videos will probably arrive in my office by Friday. Sorry for the delay. I will put one in the mail to you as soon as possible. If it's any later than Saturday afternoon, I'll let you know."

✔ "Jill, I wanted to let you know that I called Gerry as I said I would. However, he's currently out of town so I did not talk to him personally. However, I did leave him a message telling him that you would be sending him a resume and following up next week with a phone call."

✔ "Oops, I goofed. I just came across your card and my reminder to myself to call to give you Mark's phone number. You can reach Mark at xxx-xxx-xxxx. Sorry for not getting back with you more promptly. Good luck and let me know how things go."

For at least one week, only say that you'll do what you're absolutely committed to doing. Think before you speak. Replace those idle promises with sincere statements of commitment.

Part III
Using Your Network: Networking Opportunities

The 5th Wave   By Rich Tennant

INTERROGATION ROOM

"He's a new breed of Cop, Captain — smooth, cocky, a real networker. He's getting names, addresses, contributions to the Police Benevolence Fund ... it's incredible."

In this part . . .

Whether your looking for a job, running your own business, climbing the corporate ladder, or taking your first steps into retirement, this part shows you how to best utilize your network. I include information on how to find a mentor and be a mentor, as well as how to create a name for yourself and become visible in your community. Career management information that I've put in this section also includes a job search assessment and tips on what to do with your resume.

Chapter 9

Networking Your Way to the Perfect Job

*I*n days past, people went to work for a company, found themselves a nice niche there, stayed for a lifetime, and enjoyed a sense of job security. Well, things have changed.

Today, you are responsible for your own job security. No matter what your position is, you can't assume that because your company is stable, your job is safe. Your job security has to come from the sense that no matter what happens, you are employable and can quickly find another good job. You develop your security by building your skills and your network.

Creating, building, and maintaining your career network are vital career-management tools. Don't wait until you need a job to focus on building your network. And when you get that perfect job, don't think the networking is over. Always be building and maintaining your network so that whenever you desire a promotion or need a job, you already have your support system in place, working for you.

Statistics show that more than 70 percent of jobs are found and filled through networking. Someone you know knows someone who knows someone who has what you're looking for.

Finding the perfect job isn't easy, whether you're currently out of work or have a job but feel you can do better. In order to make a positive change, you need

> ✔ **Focus.** An opportunity may show up at the most unexpected moment or from the most unexpected person. Without focus, you miss out on these opportunities. They will simply pass you by.
>
> ✔ **Persistence.** Finding a great job is important and worth some effort. You must find or create something great and wonderful — that doesn't happen immediately.
>
> ✔ **Confidence.** More about this later in the chapter!

Your Current Job is to Find a New Job

When you're between jobs, your "job" is to find a job. Therefore, the first thing to do is create a job description that lists your duties as a *job seeker*. What are your duties and responsibilities, goals, working hours, and benefits, while you're looking for a job?

Note: This isn't a description of what kind of job you want to have — it's a description of what you have to do while searching for a job.

Identifying how you're going to go about finding a job helps you stay focused and on track and helps you maintain a sense of accomplishment while you progress towards your goal.

Write a job-search job description for yourself. Here's an example:

Job Title: Job Seeker

Job Description: Finding a position that allows me to fully utilize my public relations experience and abilities to enhance the image, visibility, reputation, and success of a company that fully appreciates my abilities and actions.

Job Responsibilities and Duties:

- Review the list of the top public relations firms from the Princeton Business Journal's annual list of top companies.

- Update my resume.

- Have someone review my resume who knows me and my career expertise.

- Have business cards printed that I can use during my job search.

- Make a list of key people from my career network that I want to notify and keep informed about my job search.

- Order or purchase notecards that I can use for sending thank-you notes to people who assist me during my job search.

- Organize my database and schedule calls to people who can help me.

- Review the Web site of the industry association to get information on conventions, meetings, job chat rooms, career newsletters, and so on.

- Make a list or draw a chart of my career net (see Figure 9-1) and include people I want to meet as well as people I already know.

Compensation: Golf on Friday afternoon, taking my kids to the park.

Hours: Six hours a day, four days a week

Benefits: Restrategizing my life, taking time to review my options to see at this point in my life what I really want to do next, using this opportunity to reconnect with friends, using this time to spend some quality time with spouse and family, finding the perfect job.

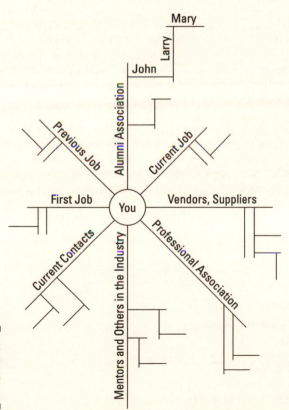

Figure 9-1:
A sample
network
diagram.

As you can see from the job-search job description above, there are things you can and must do (including building and maintaining your career network, discussed in the following section) if you're to "finish the project" — meaning "get the job!" The following section provides a self-assessment test you can take, as well as some tips and activities for improving your effectiveness.

Assessing Your Effectiveness as a Job Seeker

The value of a self-assessment comes from the opportunity to objectively review what you're currently doing, what more you could be doing, tasks that you need to perform, and habits that you could develop.

Fill out the assessment (see the following figure) according to the scale of 1 = no way, Jose to 5 = as regular as a sunrise. Once you complete the form, tally the numbers to see how you rated yourself. Then look back through the assessment and notice the sections and items where you scored yourself well and accept that as a validation and acknowledgement of what you are already doing. Notice the sections and items where you want to rate yourself higher and identify what actions you will take. Some of the items represent action while others actually represent a shift in one's attitude or approach.

With this information in mind, develop a networking action plan for your job search. And remember that even when you find your job, it's important to continue to focus on and develop your network as a means of continued success and satisfaction, both personally and professionally. By retaking the assessment every three months, you will progress very quickly in building a powerful network of support.

Are You an Effective Job Seeker?

Rating System:
1 = No way, Jose
2 = If I wake up on the right side of the bed
3 = Fifty-fifty chance
4 = Every chance I get
5 = As regular as a sunrise

Getting yourself focused and ready

____ I know how to speak about my expertise and accomplishments to best position myself for career advancement.

____ I know what I need in my job and workplace environment in order to satisfy the values and principles that are important to me.

____ I have thoroughly researched the companies I want to work for.

____ I have business cards that represent the work that I do and who I am as a businessperson.

Asking for contacts versus passing out resumes

____ I consistently utilize opportunities to ask, "Who do you recommend I contact given that I am interested in a job in XYZ industry (ABC company)?"

____ I realize that every conversation I have presents the opportunity to mention my job search and possibly acquire some valuable information.

____ I follow up on job leads promptly.

Maximizing your conversations and interviews

____ I introduce myself in a way that clearly communicates my expertise and generates career opportunities.

____ I approach each contact and interview with an open mind.

____ I gain value from every contact and interview through well-prepared questions and active listening.

____ I give acknowledgement daily to those who have given me support, encouragement, or ideas for my job search.

Building and maintaining a career network

____ I have a network diagram of my career network with the names highlighted of the people who I plan to contact about my job search.

____ I have established an effective system for organizing and contacting my career net.

____ When my confidence, enthusiasm, and clarity start to wane, I call a friend or associate who can give me a boost.

____ Networking is a lifelong, valuable career-management tool for me!

61 to 75	Enjoying the perfect job
56 to 60	Multiple choices
41 to 55	Suiting up and showing up
26 to 40	Expecting a miracle
15 to 25	Still pouting

Becoming an Effective Job Seeker

Based on the self-evaluation, how do you stack up as a job seeker? Did the statements describe you? If on some statements you thought, "Yeah, that's me," you're already doing some things right. If you gave yourself a low score on some items, you need to change what you're doing in those areas so that you can be more effective. This section covers areas presented in the self-evaluation and gives you tips and suggested actions.

Getting yourself focused and ready

To best identify the job that is perfect for you, you must first figure out what your strengths and skills are. You have to *think* with clarity. After you think with clarity, you can *speak* with clarity to enhance the way people hear you and respond to you. Being focused and feeling prepared can go a long way in helping you come across with confidence.

- ✔ **I know how to speak about my expertise and accomplishments to best position myself for career advancement.** Don't expect people to be able to read your resume and figure out how talented you are. Make sure that you've figured it out ahead of time so that in interviews and other appropriate situations, you can speak confidently about your skills and expertise and the value that you provide. Be able to explain how your expertise can help a company succeed. Your accomplishments illustrate the skills and expertise that you have. When on a job search, be prepared to explain your major accomplishments.

  List five accomplishments that you are proud of and what it is about those accomplishments that makes you proud.

- ✔ **I know what I need in my job and workplace environment to best satisfy the values and principles that are important to me.** Identify the things that are important to you — expressing your creativity, being a part of a strong work team, corporate ethics, flexible work hours, training and development opportunities, prestige, autonomy, and so on. Be realistic about what you need in order to thrive and find out which of your values and principles are supported at the companies that you are considering.

- ✔ **I have thoroughly researched the companies that I want to work for.** Find out everything there is to know about the companies that you are pursuing and considering. Look up their Web sites and get their promotional materials and annual reviews. Talk to people who work there or have worked there. Talk to people in the industry. Conduct informational interviews to gather information.

✔ **I have business cards that represent the work that I do and who I am as a businessperson.** Business cards are just as important when you're looking for a job as they are when you have a job. When you are in job transition, your card lets people know how to be in contact with you. Ideally, your card should include your name, industry or job title, address, phone number, fax number, and e-mail. If you don't want to use your home address, consider getting a postal box on a temporary basis.

Asking for contacts versus passing out resumes

People do it all the time. Pass out resumes to anyone and everyone. Now really, where do you think most of those resumes go? Yeah, the trash bin. People have enough papers to deal with. They don't need one more piece of information to keep track of.

How one job seeker networked his way into a job

Michael Alexander is a lawyer friend of mine, and he's a masterful networker. Here are a few examples of how Mike's networking skills have helped him in his career and what he does to keep his network thriving.

When Mike left a job in Cooper Industries' legal department, he decided he wanted to go into the legal headhunting business. As part of his job search, he sent letters and resumes to attorneys with whom he had previously worked and followed up with phone calls to get names of people the attorneys recommended that he contact. As a result, he received leads from all across the country about great jobs. He followed up and sent handwritten notes to thank people for their help. He also called his contacts to let them know the results of their leads.

It turned out that a friend from law school ended up referring Mike to the firm that hired him. For Mike, networking means keeping "my name in people's minds" and remaining visible and easily accessible. He makes it a point to be in touch with people at least every three to four months. In order to do this, he has developed some great networking habits.

One of Mike's habits is to review weekly what decisions the Texas Supreme Court has handed down. He then writes a short memo to other lawyers who would be interested in the information. Likewise, he reads a weekly publication on decisions from lower courts and then passes some of that information on to other attorneys. Mike also belongs to professional organizations.

Mike realizes that although he has a great job that he loves, continuing to network is important. He markets himself constantly. He's learned the power of keeping his network alive and active rather than waiting until he needs a job to focus on his network.

This is *your* network and *your* job search. You are the driver. Even though you may ask for directions, you are the one who must stay focused on where you're going and make sure you get there. Don't just toss resumes into the wind and hope that a job offer comes back.

Gather information that keeps you moving in the right direction to create or find your perfect job. Ask people for suggestions on whom to contact. When they give you a name and number, then you are in the driver's seat to stay in action and on the right road.

The following list provides a discussion of the questions in the self-assessment test you just took, as well as some tips and activities for improving your effectiveness in the area of asking for contacts:

✔ **I consistently utilize opportunities to ask, "Who do you recommend I contact given that I'm interested in a job in XYZ industry (ABC company)?"** Ask questions that prompt people to give you information right then and there. Doing so gives people a chance to contribute to you on the spot. And because they had to think in order to respond to your request, they are more likely to continue to think about you and your job search and other ways that they can be of help. When you hand people a resume, they don't have to think and they are less likely to think of you even when they do hear about a perfect opportunity for you.

When making requests for contacts for your job search, be specific. The more specific you are with your requests, the easier it is for people to think of a response. When your request is specific, it is more likely to trigger a thought in the other person's mental computer that leads them to information that can be of value to you.

Instead of:

> "I'm looking for an engineering job. Who do you recommend that I contact?"

Be specific:

> "I'm interested in an environmental engineering position with a company in Seattle. Who do you know that would be good for me to contact?"

The second example may seem like it narrows the chances that a person will be able to help you. Yet, the truth is that the more specific request is more likely to generate a response and is definitely more likely to generate a useful response. With the second request, you give people three pieces of data to use in their mental search: the environment, engineering, and Seattle.

When I heard someone make a similar request to a group of about thirty other people who were looking for jobs, he immediately got two responses that were exact fits with what he was looking for. If he had not been specific with his request, he may not have gotten either response, even though the information was out there in his network.

✔ **I realize that every conversation I have presents the opportunity to mention my job search and possibly acquire some valuable information.** In every conversation, be aware of the opportunity to mention your job search. You can steer the conversation in a way that will create opportunities for you. Ask people about their work. Ask where they are from. Ask them how long they have lived in your city. Just by asking these types of questions, you are likely to find information that you can segue into a conversation about employment. If the person has lived in the same city you're in for a number of years, you can comment, "Having lived here ten years and doing what you do, you must know some people in the . . . industry. I'm interested in making some contacts."

When someone asks you what you do, respond with "I'm an . . . and I'm currently conducting a job search for a new position with a company either here or in . . ." Consider initiating or generating a certain number of conversations each day regarding your job search. Doing so keeps you in practice and ensures that you don't let anything pass you by.

✔ **I follow up on job leads promptly.** When someone says, "You know, I think they may be hiring over at XYZ Company," take action. Get the information you need to check it out! Stay on top of things. Job opportunities can come and go very quickly. Responding promptly to leads speaks highly of your character, discipline, and focus.

Maximizing your conversations and interviews

Every conversation and interview has the potential to lead to another interview, a job offer, a referral to a prospective employer, and so on. Utilizing your listening, asking, and conversation skills helps you gather valuable information and generate career opportunities.

Here are some examples of how you can positively present yourself when you are either researching job opportunities or actively looking for a job:

"Hi. My name is Emily Smith. Mike Sanburn recommended that I call you. As a result of a recent corporate merger, I am in a position to be exploring new job opportunities in environmental law. Mark suggested that I call you because of your vast expertise and knowledge of people in this industry. Would you be willing to spend about 10 minutes on the phone with me?"

"My name is Iftekar Ahmed. Sharon Miller gave me your name and number when I was talking with her today at the Chicago Business Alliance. She recommended that I call you because I'm conducting a job search for a marketing position with an accounting firm. She thought you could be a valuable resource for me in making some contacts with some of the local firms. Is this a good time or could we schedule a time to talk?"

"Mr. Kelly, my name is Wayne Thomas and I understand we have a mutual friend in James Roster. (Pause, response.) While talking with James yesterday, I was telling him about a career decision that I've made to leave the legal industry and pursue my lifelong desire to teach. Your success and contribution to the education industry with your charter school is very inspiring and I would greatly appreciate an opportunity to talk with you."

Of course, speaking with confidence becomes even harder when you're talking with a representative of a company you'd like to be hired by. Here's a model to follow when you're on the phone in that situation:

"Hello, my name is Jerry Bomback. I'm conducting a job search for a research position and have identified BioTech Energies as one of the companies I would like to get to know better. I have over 12 years experience with R&B Technology and would like to provide you with information about my expertise for current and future opportunities that may arise. How about a brief meeting next Wednesday or Thursday at your office?"

Always speak with pride and confidence regarding your strengths, skills, expertise, and accomplishments.

To project confidence over the phone, take a deep breath before dialing, smile, and sit up straight or stand. Focus on your strengths and skills and imagine yourself in that perfect job.

Seeing eye to eye

Throughout her 29 years of teaching marketing and career skills to high school students, Patricia Tyler was always helping and encouraging her students to find the perfect job. One of her students went on a number of interviews but could never seem to get a job. He was a good kid and Patricia couldn't figure out why he never got a job offer. He was nice looking, dressed well, had a good vocabulary, and was easy to talk with. Patricia was so confused by the situation that she decided to go on one of the job interviews with this particular student. She immediately saw the problem. The student never made eye contact with the person interviewing him. He would look around, look down, and look off to the side. He would look everywhere but at the person across from him.

Patricia came back to the classroom with her student and immediately developed a class exercise to help not only this student but also everyone else in the class in developing the ability to make a connection with the people they meet. She had them sit knee to knee and just look at each other for one minute without saying anything. Soon after that, the same student went out for an interview. This time he got a job!

When you're in job transition and people ask you what you do, tell them what it is that you do in your career life rather than immediately responding with "I'm out of work" or "I don't have a job." You can respond, "I'm an accountant. Although I was with a public accounting firm for seven years, I'm now interested in acquiring a position as chief financial officer for a manufacturing firm."

The following list provides a discussion of the questions in the self-assessment test you just took, as well as some tips for improving your effectiveness in the area of contacting prospective employers and interviewing:

✔ **I introduce myself in a way that clearly communicates my expertise and generates career opportunities.** Develop an introduction that generates interest and opportunity (for more information on introductions, see Chapter 5). Even when you don't have a job, you still have expertise, a title, and skills that you've worked hard to acquire. You don't need to use a company name in your introduction to proudly and effectively introduce yourself in a professional manner:

> "My name is Jim Greer; I'm an electrical engineer. I have been in the industry for 12 years and am currently looking for a position in . . ."

✔ **I approach each contact and interview with an open mind.** You may go in to interview for a particular job, and during the interview you discover that another opening is ideal for you. You may discover that the company doesn't have any job openings, but that you can create a whole new position and fill it for the company. You may discover that the job the company has isn't a perfect fit for you, but would be great for someone you know. Or you may create an opportunity for contract work or a consulting engagement with the company. Explore and ask questions that give you the information that you need to create and generate new possibilities.

✔ **I gain value from every contact and interview through well-prepared questions and active listening.** Ask questions that will give you the information you need to know to determine if the company is a good fit for you. They are interviewing you, but you are also interviewing them.

Make a list of all the things you want and need to know about a company: work policies, benefits, mission, expectations, and so on. Make sure that you gather all this information so that you can make a wise decision.

✔ **I give acknowledgement daily to those who have given me support, encouragement, or ideas for my job search.** Sprinkle the word *thanks* throughout all your conversations. Thank people for their emotional support and encouragement. When you call them or go in for either an informational interview or an actual job interview, thank the interviewers for their time. Thank the people who give you ideas, names, and encouragement. Thank them for making calls for you or setting up lunch meetings or interviews for you. Thank the people who review your resume for you.

Every day, you have the opportunity to thank people. Making gratitude a daily habit keeps you aware of the support that's all around you so that you won't feel isolated and like you're doing it all on your own. Thanking people also keeps you in the right frame of mind to keep calling people and pursuing leads.

Send a note to anyone who helps you get an interview or who interviews you. I write a personal note at the bottom of each follow-up letter I send after an interview. Research indicates that even if people don't read the letters they receive, they will read the P.S. at the bottom or a personal note handwritten at the bottom.

Building and maintaining a career network

Your career network is a subset of your whole network. It consists of the people who are most influential in your success. Although anyone in your network has the potential to be a great resource for a job or career opportunity, certain people are important professional contacts.

✔ **I have a network diagram of my career net with the names highlighted of the people who I plan to contact about my job search.** Your career network would likely include employers, former employers, some coworkers, mentors, leaders in your industry, and so on. Highlight the names of the people who have influence in your industry, the business community, or with companies that you desire to interview with. Although you could potentially contact everyone you have listed in your career network, the highlights help to give you focus as you start your job search.

Draw a diagram of the people you know who can be valuable resources for you during your job search. Include

- Contacts in the industry and with companies you're interested in working for
- Friends and associates who can provide valuable emotional support and encouragement
- Former coworkers, employers, and employees
- Leaders in the industry
- Current coworkers, employers, and employees
- Suppliers, vendors, and affiliates of your industry
- People in related industries
- Mentors

✔ **I have established an effective system for organizing and contacting my career net.** Make sure that you have a way to keep track of the information you're gathering as you meet people and interview with potential employers. You can use index cards or a notebook; however, I recommend a contact management system on your computer. (See Chapter 15 for technology tips.) A computer database program allows you to access people by company name, last name, or industry. You can keep a record of all their contact information as well as information about how you can be a resource for them and how you plan to follow up with them. List your follow-up calls and activities so that every day you have a clear list of what's next in your job search.

✔ **When my confidence, enthusiasm, and clarity start to wane, I call a friend or associate who can give me a boost.** Utilize your support system for encouragement. In this day and age, most everyone has gone through downsizing, reengineering, losing a job, changing jobs, or changing careers, and have had family members and friends go through the same challenges. People know what it's like and are typically willing and ready to be of support.

✔ **Networking is a lifelong career-management tool for me!** Networking is not just a good idea; it is a vital career-management tool. It is an ongoing building process that requires constant attention. Maintain, strengthen, and expand your career net so that you always have, at your fingertips, the best resources available for your career growth and fulfillment.

The most important time to be networking is all the time. Don't wait until you need a job to start building your network. Always be building and maintaining your network so that it is already strong and in place anytime you have a career challenge or are looking for a career opportunity.

Understanding that Transition Can Be Positive

If you are in transition and didn't choose to be, seeing the positive side of the change can be difficult. Nevertheless, many people are able to look back later and see that a forced change was a blessing because of the new opportunities they discovered by having to make tough career choices, reidentify their career goals, and use the job transition as an opportunity to move forward in their careers.

A woman I met at a seminar told me how difficult it was being laid off at her last job. She spoke with a lot of emotion about feeling unappreciated, how she had wasted all the hard work she'd put into her position, and on and on.

Mile-high networking

Vicki Barber is an insurance agent with clients all over the country. About four years ago, her youngest daughter, Alicia, moved to Denver after taking a ski trip with her two best friends and falling in love with the city. After a couple of months, she landed a job as a phone rep for a major independent call center company. It seemed like a good fit, in that Alicia had her securities license and the company had clients in the securities industry. However, after about a year, she began to realize this was not going to be the road to the type of success that she anticipated and desired.

One day, Vicki was talking to a client from Tulsa who happened to mention that he had a former boss who was now in Denver working with Merrill Lynch. That got Vicki's attention and she said, "That's interesting. I have a daughter who lives in Denver and is looking for another opportunity." As a result of that conversation, Vicki's client called his friend, who requested Alicia give him a call. She did and he hired her — she is now a senior supervisor in the Denver call center for Merrill Lynch and has a fantastic career! And when people ask her how she got her job, she tells them that her Mom in Sugar Land, Texas got her the job!

I started asking her questions about her new job and what she liked about it. She very clearly was in a great position that utilized her skills and talents beautifully. She was pleased with the management of the new firm and couldn't seem happier about her new job — yet she was still holding on to resentment about being let go at her previous job. When I asked her if her previous job had utilized her talents fully, without hesitation she said that it had not and even admitted that she had been thinking about leaving for something better for over a year and just hadn't had the guts to leave.

Through our discussion, she was able to see that everything had really worked out for her. Any meaning she had attached to how things happened was useless and counterproductive. I saw her whole face light up and her body relax when she finally let go of her past and chose to be grateful for her new job and wonderful employer.

Don't take a job transition personally and don't let it change the confidence, self-esteem, and self-respect that you have for yourself and your skills.

All that's changed is where you hang your hat

If you're currently out of work, remember that who you are as a person has not changed, even if your work status has. Being out of work means nothing more than that you're in a transition phase. Don't make it mean something that it doesn't, don't lose your sense of self, and don't apologize for it or over-explain the situation.

Maintain your professional confidence and strength. Companies merge, downsize, are bought, close, and reorganize every day. When that happens and you end up out of work, it's not personal. And it's not necessarily bad. Being temporarily out of work does not say anything negative about you.

Chapter 10

Networking in the Corporate World

Graduating from college and getting a job with a big corporation was pretty exciting. My thinking was "I'll go in and do a good job and they'll take good care of me." Now, looking back, I see that my thinking was pretty naive!

I learned quickly that going in and doing a good job was not sufficient and that I couldn't count on a company to take good care of me. I came to realize that I was responsible for creating visibility for myself within the company. I needed to build a network, work that network, and honor that network. I needed to focus on building relationships and becoming known within the departments and divisions where I wanted to work and further my career. I needed to find out who I needed to know and be known by. I needed to find a mentor and get a career strategy in place. I needed to take charge of my career and my career net.

Networking Benefits You, Your Coworkers, and Your Company

Your company consists of a network of people. That network includes everyone who works as an employee, everyone on the board, all the vendors and suppliers, and your customers. When these people contribute to one another, they generate a positive, productive energy that leads to results, success, and satisfaction.

A strong corporate network provides valuable links for solving problems, conveying information, and sharing resources. Your network also helps you advance in your career. It channels information to you regarding new positions and opportunities. As you take advantage of these opportunities, you build your network further because you meet new people, learn new skills, and expand your visibility even more.

Imagine what it could be like if everyone in your company related to each other as networking resources. If this were the case, people would interact with respect and dignity while expressing an interest in being of mutual value and benefit. Great opportunity exists in the corporate environment to learn from and with one another.

The power of your network grows to the same degree that your visibility, expertise, experience, and skills grow. When you're networking and you grow, it is just natural that your network grows simultaneously.

A networked corporate environment creates camaraderie, creativity, innovation, and efficiency. People share resources and ideas rather than hoarding information or feeling threatened by the success of others. With networking, everyone is served by the success of everyone else. Being focused on your own goals is important; however, you expand your power when you look beyond your goals to the goals of others and the overall goals of your department, division, and company.

Every time a valuable piece of information comes across your desk, take a moment to ask yourself, "Who else could get value from this? Who else could make good use of this information?" Networking is like recycling. You pass along information so that it can be fully utilized in additional situations and by other people.

An organization is a network of networks

You may think of your company's structure as a top-down hierarchy, but there is another way to look at it. A company can also be viewed as a series of interconnected networks. Each person in the company is the center of his or her own network, which interconnects with countless other networks. The company president is the center of his or her network, with links to company officers, department heads, customers, vendors, and others. When you put all these networks together, you have a very intricate system of links and relationships across all levels, positions, and departments.

Everyone within a company is a valuable part of the networking links that combine and connect to make the company successful — or not. The resources available throughout your corporate network provide effective ways to address issues, solve problems, create new initiatives, and network with others within the company. When people are willing to relate to each other as part of the same network working for the good of everyone, then people are more likely to get together to talk through ideas, build positive relationships, share certain skills and resources, and produce powerful results.

Networking isn't just for sales folks

Networking is a people skill that is important for anyone within a company who wants to be efficient, productive, and successful. So many people think of networking as a sales tool that it's easy to think the only people who need to know how to network are the sales and marketing folks. However, everyone from a clerk to an executive can utilize networking to further his effectiveness and contribution to the company. Corporate networking involves being a valuable resource for others.

And as for sales, everyone in a company has the potential to meet or know people who could be clients and prospects for your company. Everyone in the company also has the opportunity to be a source of positive public relations for the company. Think about how you speak about your job and the company that you work for. Do you speak with pride or do you complain and downplay your importance? Speak with pride and confidence. You represent the company in everything you do and say. You and your fellow coworkers are all PR reps of the company and influence the morale of others within the company and the reputation of the company to the public.

Making an office networking friendly

Here are the traits of an office in which networking can flourish:

✔ Management provides a safe environment for learning, which means that employees are able to admit to mistakes and ask for assistance.

✔ People ask for help as an expression of their strength and commitment to accomplishing their tasks efficiently.

✔ Management encourages networking as an important core value that supports the flow of information within the company and increases cooperation.

✔ The corporate culture acknowledges people for their contribution to others in the corporate network and the overall success of the company.

✔ Executives, managers, and supervisors make themselves accessible and model networking behaviors.

✔ People take responsibility for developing trust and confidence in themselves and their corporate network.

✔ People can say no graciously, say yes sincerely, and offer resourceful options.

Everyone within a company has the opportunity to network. Everyone has the potential to meet people who can become customers. Everyone has the potential to be a resource for business growth.

Knowing Who You Are

Networking effectively within the corporate environment requires that you be clear about your own career goals. By knowing what you want to accomplish with your career, you can then choose what skills to learn, how to best position yourself with the projects you take on, and how to find a great mentor.

Your career success is up to you. Networking is about creating visibility for yourself throughout your company and your industry. It is your responsibility and no one else's. When you're clear about your strengths, talents, and abilities, you are more likely to find the jobs that best suit your expertise.

Keeping your career goals on track

The clearer you are about what you want in your job and your career, the easier it is to fulfill your career goals. Without clarity, you are more likely to veer off in various directions rather than stay true to your career track. Your goals can actually help you make decisions about job and career opportunities. When opportunities come your way, you can compare what the opportunity offers with what you have identified as your values and goals.

Answering the following questions requires that you make yourself aware of what is important to you. This awareness allows you to better express what you want and make requests for opportunities that best serve you. You have some goals that relate to your current job and employer. You also have goals that express what you want to accomplish throughout your career.

- ✔ What are the core values that define what is important to you in a job?
- ✔ What are your long-term career goals?
- ✔ What type of person are you that you would have these career goals?
- ✔ What is it about this particular career path that is most appealing to you?
- ✔ What are the qualities and characteristics that make you valuable as an employee?
- ✔ What are the skills and strengths that make you perfect for your profession or position?

Know who you really are, instead of letting your career define you.

Goals give you direction and focus. When you reach a goal, you feel satisfied and valuable.

- ✔ What are your goals for yourself with the company that you currently work for?
- ✔ What are your goals for yourself in your industry?
- ✔ What are your goals for your department/division/team?
- ✔ How is what you do important to the overall goal of the company?

Making yourself visible within your company and your industry

Create an identity for yourself that supports you and the company that you work for. And learn how to have your identity be visible and known throughout your company

Visibility means being known by the people of influence in your company and industry. If someone says, "We've got a new position opening up on our management team," then someone who knows you should respond with, "Gregory could be perfect for that position. Here's his extension. Give him a call!"

Create visibility by getting to know people and letting others get to know you. Ask for opportunities to participate on projects and committees that give you exposure to more people. When attending company meetings and events, make sure you get around to meet the people who are there. Be willing to walk up and introduce yourself to people. Be active in company events and industry associations.

Maybe you aren't where you want to be in the company or the industry . . . yet. However, you can be on the path to the position that you want. No matter what your current role is within the company, realize the value of what you are doing while creating a pathway to your ideal job. Find the place where you fit and where you can be yourself and excel. The title of the position, or even the size of the paycheck, may not matter as much as having a place to shine!

Every job within a company has value. Otherwise, the company wouldn't pay someone to fill that position. If you don't have the job that you want, you still need to maintain a strong sense that you contribute to the company and are important.

Being and Having a Mentor

Mentoring is a form of networking. It can be either a formal or informal relationship in which the mentor helps the protégé advance in his or her career.

People can achieve the success they desire much more quickly and easily with the help, support, and encouragement of someone who has already attained that same or similar success. Your mentor can help you succeed faster and with fewer mistakes.

A mentor combines attributes of a teacher, coach, and guide. A mentor can point the way. A mentor can provide shortcuts. But he or she isn't a means of bypassing the work that's necessary on your part to succeed.

I recommend both having and being a mentor. By having a mentor you help yourself learn and grow. Working with a mentor helps you create and maintain a momentum of success. Your mentor can introduce you to people you wouldn't normally have access to. He or she can open doors for you and create opportunities that may have taken years to get to on your own. A mentor can also help you take your vision (or the vision of the company you work for) and break it down into manageable action steps. This, combined with all the benefits you glean from your mentor's experience and advice, puts you on the fast track and can catapult your career.

Having a mentor also helps you feel more connected and less like you are out there on your own. By knowing you have someone you can call on and count on, you can more easily maintain your emotional balance and mental focus.

Being a mentor is also beneficial. It keeps you humble, honest, and on track. It indicates that you have attained a certain level of success and gives you the opportunity to continue to move your career forward. Being a mentor also keeps you at your best. In mentoring others, you are reminded to heed your own advice. When you focus your attention on someone else, you often gain new perspectives on things that are of value to you and unleash creativity that has been stifled by your routine. You deepen your own experience, understanding, and enthusiasm.

Mentoring also helps you develop your skills as a leader, trainer, and coach. Mentoring can add to your skill set an ability to effectively teach and train others. And don't forget that you get the satisfaction of knowing that you're helping someone else succeed. What goes around comes around, and the energy that you spend helping someone else will certainly come back and benefit you.

Establishing the type of mentoring relationship you want

A mentoring relationship can be formal or informal. You may have a formal, agreed-upon arrangement in which you meet with your mentor or protégé on a regular basis for a specific period of time. On the other hand, you may have several informal mentors or protégés whom you call or meet with occasionally, as the need or opportunity arises. Whether you've thought about them as mentors or not, you probably already have people in your company and industry who you call on for advice, wisdom, and expertise. Table 10-1 compares formal and informal mentoring from the perspective of the protégé.

Table 10-1	Formal versus Informal Mentoring
Formal Mentoring	*Informal Mentoring*
You and your mentor meet at regularly scheduled times.	You call or get together occasionally.
You have a fixed list of things to do with your mentor.	You pick up pearls of wisdom here and there.
You have a list of things to do.	You occasionally run ideas by the mentor.
Guidelines and timeframes exist that govern your relationship with the mentor.	The relationship is fluid and changes as your needs change and your mentor's availability changes.

Both formal and informal styles of mentoring are effective. Both can be important in furthering one's success. They simply are based on two different arrangements and styles of relating.

Give your mentor feedback regarding the action you take based on his or her ideas: what worked, what was difficult. Ask for additional advice if you need to. It is very important that you let your mentor know that you are making good use of his or her time and ideas and are taking action based upon what he or she suggests.

Choosing a mentor

Before you set out to find a mentor and set up a formal mentoring relationship, think about why you want a mentor. Identify what goals you want your mentor to help you reach. Clearly identify your expectations and motives. This clarity will help you identify the perfect person to be your mentor. It will also assist you in communicating with your mentor so that you can have clear goals and guidelines for your mentoring relationship.

JPMorganChase Bank's mentoring program

Debby Selke, Vice President of Human Resources at JPMorganChase & Co., has been in a leadership position with the bank's Texas-based mentoring initiative since it started in 1995. Debby attributes the success of the program to the fact that senior management not only advocates mentoring, they participate as mentors. In addition, the culture understands the importance of employee development, formal training is required for mentors and protégés, significant resources are provided to oversee the program, and the program brings people together who might not normally meet.

Whereas many mentoring programs focus on matching people who have similar focuses and career paths, the Diversity Mentoring program combines mentors and protégés from various business lines within the bank. The program intentionally mixes people of different race, gender, age, education, tenure, and level within the bank. According to Debbie, "Mixing it up accelerates the learning for both parties."

Currently the JPMorganChase organization offers nine mentoring programs to its Texas-based employees, each with a different goal and target audience. Here is a success story from the Diversity Mentoring Program, which is open to all levels of employees across all business lines:

After eight years in the same position, Barbara Joe was feeling stagnant and unhappy. She wanted another opportunity within the bank but had no idea how to find the right opportunity. Then she heard about the JPMorganChase Diversity Mentoring program and decided to apply as a protégé, hoping that she would be matched up with a mentor who would have some answers.

In only a few weeks, she was notified that she was accepted into the program and was told who her mentor would be. Barbara was thrilled.

Detria Mitchell — her mentor — seemed to be just what she needed. Detria had a wealth of experience and knowledge about the bank and showed Barbara a different way of looking at things. Through Detria, Barbara was introduced to opportunities at the bank that she would never have bothered to check out or become involved in on her own. Barbara's stagnation transformed into aliveness and she knew that she had someone in her corner whom she could rely on and count on.

At their Diversity Mentoring kickoff, Barbara identified the competencies that she needed to work on and developed a plan for her future at the bank. It was in this kickoff session that Barbara also had the awareness that even if her mentor did have all the answers, Detria would make Barbara work for them. Nothing would be given to her. As Barbara said, "My mentor kept me on track by pointing me in the right direction and encouraging me to work on the competencies I needed to develop."

The Diversity Mentoring program helped Barbara gain confidence, develop her interpersonal and professional skills, become involved in bank-sponsored activities, and expand her network of friends and associates. Within six months of joining the Diversity Mentoring program, Barbara accepted a new position within the bank.

Here's what Barbara said afterwards: "My participation in the Diversity Mentoring program was the best thing that has happened to me throughout my twelve years at the bank. The positive energy that emanated from working together, learning from each other, and supporting one another . . . was a life-changing experience for me."

Another Diversity Mentoring success story involves a back-office worker who was unhappy in her job. Her goal was to become a trainer in another area of the bank. She knew the exact position that she wanted; she just didn't know how to get it. She had confidence that she could do the job and she knew in her heart that training was what she was meant to be doing, but her educational background and previous job experience would not have her show up on paper as a top candidate. Sure enough, she applied but was turned down. And then her mentor made a phone call to the right person: "I know that on paper this doesn't look like what you're looking for; however, I recommend that you take time to get to know her." She was given a chance and she turned out to be the perfect person for the job. That chance may have never happened had that mentor not gotten to know her well enough to know her capabilities.

In a recent follow-up survey of all formal mentoring program participants, 87 percent of the protégés surveyed said something significant (promotion, new job, or expanded job responsibilities) happened with their career that they can attribute to the mentoring experience. At the graduation ceremony in one of the formal programs (just 12 months after the kickoff), 60 percent of the protégés reported that they had already seen significant career results. Further evidence of the power and success of the program is that many of the participants continue to stay in touch after completing the formal program.

Your mentor should be someone you like, respect, and enjoy. The mentor should have accomplished something you aspire to for yourself. Your mentor should have values that are similar to yours regarding what's important in life and business. He or she should have a positive reputation in your industry and clearly have something to give that would greatly enhance your growth and success.

Many corporations have mentoring programs. Check to see if your company has a program or has plans to start a program. If there is a program, talk with some of the people who have been through the program to see if they were pleased. Find out what you need to do to be part of the program.

People who care about their company and the people in the company usually make very good mentors. A good resource for mentors is the list of retirees from the company. Retirees often have a wealth of knowledge that they are happy to share.

If you don't personally know someone who fits the bill or if your company doesn't have its own mentoring program, then ask the people in your network if they know anyone who fits your criteria. You can conduct your own research, if necessary, by using the Internet, the library, and trade association magazines.

Your mentor need not be in the same geographical area as you. You can have mentors around the world and use phone calls and e-mails to communicate, convey information, and stay in touch with one another. If you do have a mentor who is not in the same geographical area, consider having a local mentor as well.

Network your way to your mentor. The people in your network have links to the people who can be your best mentors. Ask: "I'm looking for a mentor who can help me . . .? Who would you recommend?"

You may be able to join a professional association that has a mentoring program. I'm a member of The National Speakers Association, for instance, which has a mentoring program. We have found that many people hear about our program and actually join the association because they want to be a participant in our mentoring program.

Sort your list of mentor candidates according to your preference. There will be certain things about each one that make them appealing (or unappealing) to work with. Think about which person would be the best possible match for you based on your personality and goals and what you know about that person.

Don't rule out possible mentors just because you think they're too busy or that they wouldn't be interested. Give people a chance to say no for themselves. They may surprise you and say yes.

Initial contact with your mentor

Contact the person you desire to have as your mentor. You may decide to make your initial contact in person, by phone, or by letter with a follow-up phone call. Or you may know a friend or colleague of the potential mentor who would be willing to call or write on your behalf or set up a meeting between that person and you. If you attend the same association meetings or events as your potential mentor, you might make the initial contact at one of those occasions.

Initially you would ask for a chance to meet with the person to talk about the possibility of developing a mentoring relationship. Let him or her know why you're looking for a mentor. Communicate that you have a vision and a purpose for your mentoring relationship. Also, explain what it is about the potential mentor that caused you to seek out him or her — what you admire or appreciate about the person.

> Example: "I'm calling to ask a favor of you. I would like a chance to visit with you for about 30 minutes sometime over the next couple of weeks. What I'd like to talk about is the possibility of establishing a mentoring relationship with you. I am growing my business by adding new product lines and you have been so successful with . . . (be as specific as you can) that I wanted to see if you would advise me on some things."

The person who you would like to develop a mentoring relationship with may not be available. Pat yourself on the back for having asked and don't take it personally. In fact, if the person you ask is not available, consider asking for the name of a person who would be available. (That's networking!) Be gracious and thank the person for considering the possibility. The individual may already have too many protégés.

You never know what might open up as a future possibility with the individual you approached. The fact that you approached the person will make him or her more aware of you and has enhanced your visibility.

Conversations with your mentor may take place over the phone or in person, depending on schedules, locations, and preferences. Prepare for your initial meeting with your mentor by considering the following questions:

✔ Do you prefer a formal or informal mentoring relationship? Do you want to have a regularly scheduled time to meet or talk? Do you prefer to know that you have permission to call your mentor on an as-needed basis and to check in periodically?

✔ If you develop a formal relationship with regular meetings, how often would you like to meet and for what length of time?

Find out if your mentor prefers being contacted by phone or e-mail to either talk or schedule a time to get together. Find out if there is a best (and worst) time to call.

You may want to request that your mentor observe you in action by accompanying you on a sales call, sitting in on your speaking engagement, observing a typical day at your place of business, and so on.

You need to think through what you want in a mentoring relationship and then present your ideas to your prospective mentor. The two of you will then identify the guidelines, parameters, schedule, and objectives of your mentoring relationship.

Typically the protégés will initiate and arrange for the meetings with their mentors unless they are in a mentoring program organized by the company (or an organization) and the meetings are planned as part of the program.

Types of questions to ask your mentor

Prepare for your meetings with your mentor. You want to be respectful of your mentor's time and be prepared to make the best use of your meetings. Make a list of the questions you want to ask. Here are some questions for you to consider asking your mentor at the beginning of your mentoring relationship:

✔ What one piece of advice would you give to someone striving for success in your industry?

✔ If you had your career to do over again, what would you do differently?

> ✔ What characteristics have you developed that have been most influential to your success?
>
> ✔ In your opinion, what skill is most important for being successful today?
>
> ✔ What words of caution would you offer someone just starting in your industry?

Pay close attention to what your mentor tells you. Document ideas, suggestions, and agreements so that you can follow through and refer back to them.

Not all mentoring matches will be wonderful. Keep in mind, however, that almost everyone has something of value to offer. And know that you can find someone who will be a good match for you.

Mentoring commitments

A mentoring relationship requires commitment from both parties. Just like any relationship, it's important that each person participates equally in the give and take of mentoring. Here are some of the commitments that are a part of mentoring:

✔ **Time:** Both parties must be willing to give their time.

✔ **Commitment to success:** Mentors want to succeed just as much as anyone does. They may consider their success as a mentor to be based on whether their protégé succeeds. In that case, they are very much counting on the protégé to be committed to success.

✔ **Sincerity:** The mentor will want to know that the protégé is sincere about his or her goals and is committed to doing what it takes to reach the goals. Successful people want to be around people who are successful.

✔ **Support:** The protégé trusts that the mentor will be supportive and is willing to have the protégé accomplish great things.

✔ **Openness:** Mentors give of themselves, which may include sharing ideas, tips, and information about their successes and failures. Being a mentor involves giving of oneself, one's ideas, and one's emotion.

There is a risk involved for the mentor. If the mentor sincerely makes a commitment to the protégé and thus gives time, support, and ideas, and the protégé doesn't apply himself or herself, then the mentor may feel used, taken advantage of, and frustrated. The mentor may end up feeling like he or she opened up in vain. The mentor must communicate honestly with the protégé if the mentoring relationship is not fulfilling to the mentor.

Role of a mentor

The role of a mentor is to empower and encourage others. Here are some specific roles in which you, as a mentor, can help your protégés:

- **Listener.** Many protégés actually have great answers to their own questions. Sometimes all they need is a trusted, respected person to listen to them. Having a valued sounding board may be all they need to come up with their own clarity and direction. By listening, mentors can help protégés discover their own brilliance.

- **Inquirer.** By asking the right questions, mentors help their protégés think through things and create new understandings and new possibilities. Asking questions helps people discover new perspectives and uncover potential pitfalls. Objective questions help protégés discover their blind spots and personal attachments that may hinder their progress. Strategic questioning can also unleash their passion and direct their energy toward the most effective action items.

- **Provider of opportunities.** Mentors can open doors for their protégés by giving them access to people and opportunities that they would not normally have access to at this point in their careers. It's like providing a free pass in a board game to advance a certain number of game squares. With the help of a mentor, the protégé can jump forward rather than take the normal route.

- **Teacher/coach/advisor.** A mentor teaches things that can't be learned in a classroom, workshop, or seminar. As a coach, the mentor works with the protégés to continually improve their performance. As an advisor, the mentor can tell the protégés if their goals are too small or are off track. A mentor can advise and help develop plans for protégés to reach their goals in the quickest and most efficient way.

- **Encourager.** A mentor provides information and encouragement that helps protégés take the action and risks necessary to fulfill their dreams and goals. Even in the midst of difficulties, the mentor can help the protégé stay focused on the light at the end of the tunnel and on the long-term vision. The mentor also provides encouragement by celebrating and acknowledging the growth and successes of the protégé.

- **Accountability figure.** A mentor gives the protégé someone to be accountable to. Accountability assists people in staying true to their commitments, agreements, goals, and dreams.

It is not the mentor's place to discipline, punish, dictate to, or find fault with the protégé. A mentor is not meant to be a disciplinarian. By being accountable to the mentor, protégés begin to see the consequences of all their actions and non-actions.

Role of a protégé

The role of the protégé is to take the value provided by the mentor and utilize it to enhance his or her efficiency and success. Ideally, the protégé will inspire and honor the mentor by being a great student and wonderful success. Here are some specific tips for how to be a protégé:

- ✔ **Listen respectfully to and value the feedback and advice of your mentor.** If every time your mentor recommends something, you say, "Yeah, but . . ." your mentoring relationship will lose effectiveness quickly.

  You are never required to act on your mentor's advice, but showing respect for and considering the value in what your mentor says is important.

- ✔ **Be appreciative.** Express your appreciation and thanks for your mentor's time, support, advice, and ideas. Let your mentor know that you appreciate his or her willingness to be your mentor — to be generous with you and share his or her success — and what an honor you consider that to be.

- ✔ **Communicate your goals clearly.** Have clearly defined goals so that you and your mentor can get to work and measure and celebrate your progress and success based on those goals.

- ✔ **Respect your mentor's time.** The monetary value of your mentor's time is bound to be more than the monetary value of your time at the beginning of the mentoring relationship. If your mentor could be out booking a $4,000 deal or selling a $50,000 project during the time that your mentor is spending with you, then treat the time as being that valuable and generate that much value from your time with him or her.

  If a mentoring relationship begins to fizzle, find a way to bow out of the relationship gracefully. That same mentor may be a valuable source in the future if you respect him or her in the present.

- ✔ **Ask for what you want.** Your role as a protégé is to create the most value from your mentoring relationship and make it easy for your mentor to contribute to you. You are the one who knows best what you want and need, so ask for it.

- ✔ **Be willing to take action and be accountable for what you say you will do.** Mentoring is not all about great conversations and wonderful ideas. Show your mentor through your actions that you mean business and that you have the discipline and commitment to follow through on what you say. The more you respond to your mentor with action and results, the more information and support your mentor is likely to provide.

Be responsible for your own career growth and development. Your mentor can serve as a guide, but your growth and success is really all up to you.

> ✔ **Make your mentor proud.** Present yourself to your mentor and to others in a way that is suitable and appropriate. Present yourself as the success that you aspire to be.

All relationships have conflicts at times and differences to work through. However, if you get into a mentoring relationship that simply does not work, move on and find someone that you can work with effectively for the good of yourself and the other person.

Lifetime versus short-term mentors

Lifetime mentors are like lifelong friends. They are always there. The relationship continues to grow, even though there may be times when you connect infrequently. However, you always know that you can call them and count on them. They have influenced your life in a way that creates a domino effect of ongoing value. They are continually growing personally and professionally and thus stay far enough ahead of you to always have additional value to pass along.

 When you're mentoring with someone whom you want a long-term connection with, do everything that you can to make it a meaningful mentoring relationship and you will be giving it a chance to become a lifetime relationship.

On the other hand, there are people who influence you through one interaction, one comment, or one piece of advice and then they go on their way. They are mentors for the moment. No formal relationship or agreement exists. Yet their momentary generosity contributes in some way. You may have a life full of momentary mentors. Be aware of them and appreciate them. Taken together, they can be just as much of a jewel as a long-term mentor.

Some mentors are there to teach, coach, and guide you through a specific project, whether at work or in your personal life. You might have a mentor for your hobby or favorite sport. You could have a mentor for parenting or spiritual growth. You could have a mentor for any project that you take on in life. (See Chapter 2 for more information on these sorts of mentors.)

Today, we need multiple mentors

Susan RoAne, best-selling author and speaker on Savvy Networking, says, "The days of having only one mentor for life are gone. In your network you must have people with different interests and talents so they can help you in the different phases of your life or career. And because there is reciprocity of the process, we must mentor others as well."

Whenever you're faced with a challenge or a new situation, remember that many other people have been through the same experience. You can find a mentor to help you get through your medical issues, or to give you advice on balancing children and a career, or to help you transition through a divorce, or whatever it is that you need help with.

List some of the people who have been mentors for you throughout your life. With each person, list the difference they made in your life or how they helped you. Take a moment to give each one a call to let them know, once again, how much you appreciate what they have done for you.

Mentoring as a legacy

Mentoring is a way of guaranteeing that knowledge is preserved and passed along. Mentors have a strong passion for their industry and want to further the industry by sharing what they've learned with the people following in their footsteps.

Successful people typically understand that they did not achieve their success on their own. They acknowledge that there are many people who have contributed to their success. They realize that success comes from a blend of their own vision, hard work, and the wisdom, ideas, encouragement, and support of others. Being a mentor is a way of acknowledging the debt that you owe to those who helped you. It is also a way of passing on the wisdom that was passed on to you.

Chapter 11

Networking for Entrepreneurs and Business Owners

When I first considered starting my own business, what immediately came to mind were all the reasons why not. The most prominent thought was "I don't know how!" I grew up in a family of corporate workers; my dad worked for Borden Foods for 30 years and my mom with Celanese (a textile company) for 17 years. There were no immediate entrepreneurial role models for me to follow. Yet during my soul searching about my career, I heard a voice say, "You don't have to know all there is to know. You simply have to have people you can call on." Something clicked for me at that moment. It was like a light bulb went on. I thought, "Okay, I can do that. So maybe I *can* have my own business." A small window of opportunity and possibility opened up in my mind. That started me on a journey that has been touching, challenging, inspiring, and ever expanding.

Since the path to fulfilling my dreams involved having people I could call on and count on, I decided it was time to build my support system. I know a lot of people (just like everyone does) just from going through life — people from school, church, my neighborhood, jobs, and so on. But had I really focused on building long-lasting connections with those people? No! Had I stayed focused on staying in touch with people? No! Had I called people for help in times of need? No! Had I been willing to take my focus off of me and be truly interested in them so that I could be a valued friend to them? No! I saw that I had some major work to do to revamp my attitude and behaviors in order to foster a powerful support system.

As an entrepreneur or business owner, you want to create a name for yourself and your business that has people choosing you over anyone else who does what you do. You can have the best product in the world, but if people don't know about you, the product is worthless. This chapter is about how to get the word out so that the people who want and need you can find you. Develop your brand — create a name for yourself. Create a reputation that speaks so loudly that it draws people to you. Provide so much value to people that they become loyal clients and send referrals to you on a regular basis. Initiate a word-of-mouth marketing grapevine that keeps people talking about how you're the one — and only one — they should consider for the product or service you offer.

The principles of networking outlined throughout this book apply to any type of business, entrepreneurial endeavor, home-based business, and network marketing endeavor.

Making Your Name a Household Word

There are certain names that automatically pop into your mind when someone mentions baseball, architects, or authors. Check it out. Who comes to mind for the following?

- ✔ Leader in the automobile industry
- ✔ Baseball icon
- ✔ Famous tap dancer
- ✔ Top-notch architect
- ✔ Famous children's author
- ✔ Authority on men and women and their differences

(*Note:* I give some possible answers at the end of this chapter.) The people who came to your mind are great examples of people who have definitely created names for themselves. Through their talent, expertise, marketing savvy, or extraordinary accomplishment, or a combination thereof, they have become the person that you think of when you think of their field, industry, or career.

What about you? When your field, industry, or career is mentioned, do people think of you? Have you become the known expert in your field? If not, now is the time to start taking steps to make that happen. Use this chapter to identify what name you want to create for yourself and in what arena and in what magnitude.

Successful businesses have a great product or service that people want or need, and then they make sure people know about it. It's your job as an entrepreneur or business owner to become known — to create a name for yourself so that the people who want and need what you have can find you.

Branding your to way to being known

Branding involves creating a word, phrase, or image that has people immediately thinking of you, your product, or your business. Branding is what makes you stand out from everyone else. My friend Jeff Tobe is a corporate trainer and speaker on the topic of creativity. Jeff has created *Coloring Outside the Lines* as his brand. People refer to him as "that coloring guy." Jeff's brand helps him stand out and be remembered even though there are many other speakers on the same topic. His promotional package includes various crayon-related packaging. Everything he does (his Web site, brochure, handouts, and so on) reinforces his brand and thus strengthens his name recognition.

Be a brand worthy of notice and recognition. Make your name stand out and make a statement.

Branding is your opportunity to create a distinctive name for yourself. What makes you unique? What makes you stand out from everyone else? What are you noteworthy for? Nordstrom created a name for itself as the department store that provides exceptional customer service. That is their brand. That is what people think of when they think of Nordstrom. That is what people expect when they go to Nordstrom. Nordstrom now has to live up to that brand in order to maintain it.

Whether you want to be branded as an expert, guru, authority, advocate, icon, or leader, as a person who is respected, well known, or famous is up to you.

When I started my speaking/training business I was encouraged to pick a niche. I admit I wasn't initially sold on the idea of being focused on one topic and creating a name for myself in that way. I thought it would be too confining, or that I might get bored with that topic, or that people might get bored with the topic. I also thought that I wanted and needed the freedom and variety that would come with speaking about a multitude of topics. I wanted to keep my options open and have a smorgasbord of things I could speak on depending on what I felt like doing.

Well, I listened to my mentors and advisors and chose to focus my speaking on networking, relationship marketing, and building powerful connections. It turns out I haven't gotten bored with the topic at all as my topic encompasses the things that I am passionate about — communicating effectively, connecting with people, creating a sense of belonging, honoring and valuing one another. I continually find that people are hungry to learn how to connect with others and create a powerful support system. I have actually become more fascinated with the way opportunities develop as people connect with one another. Rather than being limiting, specializing has turned out be a great way to develop an expertise and generate valuable exposure and name recognition. That exposure led to the contact that led to me writing this book. My topic continues to deepen as I relate the people skills involved with networking into marketing, sales, relationship marketing, building powerful connections, generating business through word-of-mouth marketing, dealing with change, and career management. Focusing on connections and the power and importance of human interactions has contributed to my ability to deliver an inspirational message about the power of connecting through the spirit and heart.

Ideally, the name that you create for yourself will reflect the core of who you are and what you are about. It represents something important to you in life, a cause, an expression, a belief, and a commitment.

In some ways your brand represents your reputation, your image. Individuals, Martha Stewart, Oprah, Michael Jordan, Barbara Streisand, Madonna, and so on, develop a brand image the same way that businesses do.

Creating a name for yourself is not about diminishing anyone else's worth. It is a way to set yourself apart by distinguishing yourself. For example, one computer consultant may brand himself as the one who's available around the clock and another may create a name for being the quickest to respond to clients' phone calls. A third may become known as the expert in dealing with computer viruses. All of the consultants can have very successful businesses and actually do a lot of the same things; however, each has decided to create a brand — something in particular that they become known for.

The value of branding is the visibility that's created that leads to results for you and your business. Branding can be so powerful that you become the only option people consider for your particular product or service. You can become their only acceptable resource. Build your name and your reputation to the point to where they wouldn't even think of calling on or using someone else. You are it for them!

If you don't create and promote a brand for yourself, your customers and clients will begin to do so for you. You can find out what brand is getting created for you by asking your customers what word or phrase they would use to describe your business. This will give you an idea of what type of name you have already created for yourself and what you need to do to create the brand recognition you desire.

Writing articles to make your name known

By writing articles and getting them published in magazines, newsletters, newspapers, and online, you get your name in front of hundreds of thousands of people. This gives you instant credibility and you are immediately viewed as an authority because you wrote an article.

Once your article is published, you can further increase the value it provides to you and others by having reprints made and sending them to the people in your network. This way they get the value of the information in the article and you enhance your credibility, exposure, visibility, and name recognition.

Do not write your articles in a way that is self-promotional. Articles are not advertisements. The focus of your articles must be to give value to your readers. However, you do want to be sure to include information about you in a byline that lets people know how to contact you (phone, address, Web address). Published articles can be sued as public relations, positioning, and marketing tools.

Think about your industry, your expertise, and the value that you have to offer people. You have a great deal of information and knowledge about your products, services, and industry that can be of value to others. Begin to think about how you can educate people regarding things that are happening in your industry that may affect them. You don't have to be a great writer to come up with a list of "The Ten Most Common . . ." Here are some examples:

- **Realtor:** You could write articles on how to best work with a realtor, ten things to check out before making an offer on a new home, how to choose the best time to sell, or seven easy steps for increasing the value of your home.

- **Optometrist:** Articles on taking care of your eyes, new options for enhancing your eyesight, and the pros and cons of the latest treatment of certain eye conditions.

- **Chiropractor:** Articles that give information on exercise, vitamins, supplements, and preventive care tips.

- **Job recruiter:** Articles on interviewing, resume writing, and business etiquette.

- **Accountant:** Articles on money management, tax-planning tips, organizing your financial data, and how to apply for a business loan.

If you are concerned about your writing ability, you might consider taking a class at the local community college or hiring a freelance writer or editor to review and edit your aticles before submitting them for publication.

You are the expert and thus you have information that is of value to others. Think of ways to organize that information for publication in magazines, newsletters, newspapers, e-zines, and on Web sites.

There are, obviously, other forms of media available for getting yourself positioned in front of people as an expert, such as the radio or TV. The important thing is that you make a name for yourself, not how you do it.

Position yourself as the authority, the expert, and the best in your field. Take on the role of educating people regarding the things that you know that would be of value to others.

Benchmarking your industry

Your success can raise the bar for your whole industry. You may be the one who sets a new benchmark for what is expected of everyone in your industry. In that way, you actually become an advocate for your industry and for others in your industry. Get involved in the associations that represent your industry. Position yourself as a leader and get to know the other leaders. Have your articles published in trade journals for your industry's associations.

Identify what it would take for you to be considered one of the best in your field. List the things that you can do to make that happen.

Being visible in your community

Your customers, clients, and prospects have certain places that they frequent based on their hobbies, interests, and careers. Find the existing networks that your customers are a part of and make yourself a prominent part of that community or organization.

The scope and type of visibility you create in your community is up to you. You may define your community as a certain geographical area that is in close proximity to your place of business or as a certain group of people who utilize your products and services. You may even define your community as your market — the people to whom you target your services.

Your community involvement could include joining organizations that you enjoy being a member of and have things in common with the other members. This could be a charitable organization where you volunteer in some capacity and, as a result, become known in your community as a civic leader, a concerned citizen, and as an advocate for a particular cause. See Chapter 13 for more information on community and charitable activities.

You can become known as a business leader in your community, a spokesperson for small businesses, a role model for minority-owned or women-owned businesses, or an example of a business that is committed to giving back to its communities.

Attracting Loyal Clients

Honey attracts bees. An accident attracts curious stares. Music and bright lights attract attention. The color red attracts hummingbirds. Ideally, as an entrepreneur and business owner, you want to attract loyal clients. People are attracted to that which they are curious about, interested in, or desire. In business, therefore, you want to offer people something that creates interest, curiosity, or fulfills a desire. Here are some questions to consider in determining what that would be for your clients and customers:

- What are your clients interested in and curious about?
- What are the desires, wants, and tastes of the people who are your prospects and clients?
- What characteristics and qualities are most important for your clients and prospects?
- How can you best exemplify the qualities and characteristics that will attract prospects and new clients to you?

According to Stacey Hall, cofounder of PerfectCustomers Unlimited, every business is designed to serve a particular group of customers and employees who are a perfect fit for that business. She regards "a perfect customer" as one "whose needs are a perfect fit for the company's mission."

When the relationship between need and service are perfectly aligned," Stacey says, "positive results occur with amazing velocity and synergy . . . almost without effort." She maintains that business owners can recognize perfect customers by "first identifying a prototype of what that customer would look like, how they would behave, the qualities and talents they would possess, the products and services they would purchase from you, and the perfect amount they would pay you."

Identify who you would pick as your favorite clients and customers. Write down their names and by each name list why they are your favorites. It could be things such as they pay on time, are easy to work with, refer their friends, or buy a lot of product. Talk with them and let them know what you like about having them as clients and customers and find out what they like about doing business with you.

Part of what would constitute a perfect client is loyalty. Your customer's satisfaction with you, your product, and your service is important; however, satisfaction by itself does not guarantee that they will return. Loyalty is based on a relationship and is created by treating people so that they feel honored, included, respected, valued, and taken care of. Loyalty is a type of unswerving or faithful allegiance. Loyalty is what makes the difference in clients staying with you for the long term.

Identify the reasons that you stay loyal to certain vendors and suppliers. List the reasons that you feel this loyalty and identify ways that you can make sure you are providing the same things to help create loyalty with your clients and customers.

Obviously, you know that treating your customers well is important and everybody's always heard the customer comes first. Still, I recommend that you define exactly what "treating the customer well" means to you and your business.

✔ Do you have a customer service policy? Do you have clear standards and guidelines for how customers are to be taken care of and treated? If not, then chances are your customers are not getting the level of attention and service that you could be giving them. Provide a clear mandate on how your customers are to be treated.

✔ What is the norm in your industry? What is expected and are you delivering it? Ask yourself what you can do that is beyond the norm. What can you do that would be an unexpected treat for your customers?

✔ What are the determining factors for you when you are deciding where to buy a product or service? Convenience? That you know the company or person? That the company or person has a particular reputation? That someone has recommended or referred that company or person to you? That they offer their product or service at a lower fee than anyone else you know of? Or that they offer better guarantees and customer services than anyone else you know of?

By answering these questions and applying the answers to your business, you begin to create a customer service plan that generates not just customer satisfaction but customer loyalty, customer goodwill, customer referrals, customer repeat business, and more profit with less emotional and financial effort.

People make buying decisions on factors other than just price, convenience, and quality. They also consider the level of relationship and respect they experience. I may even be willing to pay more and go out of my way for the same quality of product in order to do business with someone I admire, appreciate, and have a connection with.

Beware of the tendency to always focus on finding new customers and thus forget to continue to give attention to already existing customers. Your already existing customers are the best source of future and referral business. Be sure to continue to nurture and develop your relationships with current customers to create loyal, lifelong customers. Getting customers and then losing them because of a lack of attention and service is a financial drain on your business.

Some ways to foster loyalty include

- Being interested in your customers as people, not just selling to them.
- Educating your customers as well as selling to them.
- Calling your clients and customers to give them updates on new products, services, specials, and so on.
- Being friendly, fun, and easy to do business with, making it a pleasure for people to buy from you.
- Providing a personal touch.

Stay on top of your customers' needs. Be aware of how often they need your product or service and make sure you are in touch with them right before or close to the time that their need arises. If you're in the automobile industry, you probably know the average length of time someone keeps a car before they buy a new one. If you keep good records of your clients, then all you have to do is be in touch with them so that when they get that urge for a new car, you're the one they're already talking with. Don't leave it up to the consumers to have to call or find you. You know your industry and product well enough to know their needs. Use that information to be there for them without them having to even think about how or where to fulfill their need.

The result of creating loyal clients is happy clients who buy more from you and continue to buy over the long term. Also loyal, happy clients tend to consistently refer business to you. When you are doing an exceptional job, referrals come to you automatically — from your happy clients.

The same things we appreciate in any type of friendship we appreciate in business relationships. People tend to want to do business with people they like, enjoy, trust, and respect.

You earn business, repeat business, and referrals by providing a quality product, excellent customer service, and referrals. Even if you do a great job of networking, your networking efforts will be short lived if you are not providing excellent products and services.

Utilizing Word-of-Mouth Marketing

People talk. They tend to talk readily about unsatisfactory service. What you want is to have them talking about your great service.

Statistics indicate that the average unsatisfied customer tells at least eight people about an unpleasant experience. But imagine if every person who came to your business told eight people about how you are enhancing his or her life. The people you serve are your best vehicle for positive word-of-mouth marketing.

A word-of-mouth endorsement influences people to use your products and services. Your job is to create such a great experience for your clients and customers that they tell others how great you are. You want people recommending you and talking about you in a positive way.

When Sally is not treated well at the local cleaners, she not only doesn't go back there, she tells others of her unpleasant experience. People talk! They tell each other about their frustrations, disappointments, poor service, and inadequate products.

Benefits of word-of-mouth marketing

Word-of-mouth marketing is not only the most effective marketing tool for attracting clients and business, it is the most cost effective. Very little financial resources are needed to get a word-of-mouth campaign going. Large companies commonly have huge budgets for their advertising and marketing campaigns. Yet word-of-mouth marketing campaigns can produce even greater results and financial benefits than traditional campaigns and cost only a fraction of the typical marketing/advertising budget.

Strong personal endorsements can make it impossible for people to resist doing business with you. Your business becomes compelling. They have heard so much about you they have to check it out for themselves. They become so curious and intrigued and interested that it doesn't matter anymore to them what it takes or how much it costs. They want to be part of what everyone is talking about. Be irresistible. Be in demand. Be the service everyone wants or the product everyone just has to have.

Tips for generating word-of-mouth marketing

A certain amount of word-of-mouth marketing may just happen automatically. However, there are some things that you can do to get more people talking and spreading the good news about your business.

✔ **Create a memorable, easily repeatable brand value statement.** Decide what it is that you want people to say about your business. Make it easy for people to talk about you by giving them the words to say. Mike Henry, owner of Houston Percussion has created the brand statement "Everybody's a drummer." His slogans include "You want percussion, we've got it!" and "We build custom drums to your specifications." He and his employees are consistently including these phrases in their conversations as they talk with customers and tell people about their store.

✔ **Provide quality service, and — most of all — treat people with respect.** Make sure respect is present in everything you do and say. Respect creates a feeling of honor, which nourishes people's souls.Communicate your commitment to respect by the way that you speak:

- "We respect the difficulty you must face when . . ."

- "We respect your need to . . ."

- "We want you to feel like you've been treated with respect."

✔ **Give people something great to talk about.** Do something extraordinary that makes people want to talk. Think about what can you do that will just naturally get people talking (in a positive way). It could be a community project, a new service, or an in-house program. Be willing to be creative and do something extraordinary that gets people's attention. Attempt to exceed people's expectations.

Be great! Create a WOW experience. Identify and implement actions, behaviors, and standards that have your customers saying WOW about you.

✔ **Ask people to spread the word.** Ask people to help you reach others who can benefit from the services you provide. With a little encouragement, individuals will help you spread the word to others in the community.

✔ **Stay in touch with people.** By staying in touch with people, you increase the chance that they will mention and recommend your business to others. There are always plenty of reasons for being in touch with people. Make sure you don't get too busy to ignore those nudges to call people and send notes. Be aware and alert to opportunities to be in touch.

Stay in touch with people even when you are not attempting to sell them anything or get anything from them.

✔ **Acknowledge people.** Acknowledge people for being clients, contributors, vendors, and community supporters. Make sure that the people in your life realize they contribute to the work that you do. Include people in celebrations and acknowledge them.

✔ **Ask people for their input.** Solicit feedback and let people know you have used their feedback to improve your product or service. When people get involved, they feel a sense of ownership. If they have given you ideas for your business and you implement those ideas, they have an investment in wanting you to succeed.

Get the word out to people about the value and benefit of your services. Initiate a word-of-mouth grapevine that creates positive visibility and exposure. Creating this type of visibility is critical — it's the way that the people who want and need what you have can find you.

Creating a word-of-mouth marketing plan

Create a plan by making a list of all the actions that will help you get your name in front of people (and keep your name in front of people). Include the goals that you want to accomplish via word-of-mouth marketing. Identify all the activities that will get your grapevine talking about you. Put your ideas into a plan and put your plan into action.

Here is what my word-of-mouth marketing plan looks like:

- **Slogan/brand identification:** Drumming Up Business
- **Target market:** Corporations and associations who conduct corporate meetings, trainings, conferences, and conventions
- **Activities:**

  - Send thank-you gift to client after engagement

  - Request testimonials after every engagement

  - Offer follow-up e-mail support to all attendees after engagement

  - Phone calls to new contacts every week (50 per week)

  - Handwritten notes included in all packets that are sent to prospects

  - Follow-up phone calls made to prospects within 10 to 14 days

  - Books personally autographed

  - E-mail response to people placing orders thanking them for their order and giving them an update on the status of their order

  - Notify people of events, book signings, and programs in their city

  - Let people know when an engagement has been scheduled as a result of their recommendation

  - Call current clients and prospects to stay in touch (10 per week)

  - Send a monthly mailing, in the form of a postcard, article, survey, or tip sheet

  - Write an article every month and submit for publication

- Send e-mail announcements when new articles or other information is placed on Web site

- Request referrals from clients, prospects, and other people in my network

- Give referrals as often as possible

- Turn referrals into clients as often as possible

If you find yourself thinking, "Oh, I don't need to write it down. I know what to do!," get out your pen and get your plan down on paper. Give it form and substance. It has been documented that you are much more likely to achieve the goals that you have written down as part of a plan than goals that are just in your head.

Tracking results and progress

Create some kind of form, report, or chart that tracks your results. Give yourself a way to see your progress and celebrate the results. This helps to keep your plan in action. Most plans get created with great intentions but are soon forgotten. Keep your attention on your plan and watch your success grow. Giving something your attention generates energy and growth. When you ignore or do not give attention to something, it withers and dies. This is true of goals, projects, relationships — pretty much anything. Here's what my tracking form looks like:

Marketing Plan Action and Progress

- **Contacts who became prospects:** Executive Women's Golf Association, Medical Alliance, and so on

- **Prospects who became clients:** Chase Bank, Texas Education Agency, and so on

- **Activities that helped create visibility:** Article written for American Business Women's Association monthly magazine, postcard mailing sent to everyone in database

- **Notes or gifts sent:** Notes sent to people in Lilly training class, gift sent to meeting planner

- **Referrals given:** Referred Cameron to Ed Connolly, referred Ann to Trish Strangmeyer and Kenan Branam

- **Referrals requested:** Joanne who called in with book order for contact at bank, Cheryl for contact with their national convention

- **Follow-through after a speaking engagement:** Testimonial received from Business Travel Association, e-mail tip sent for distribution to entire training group

Making a Difference to Your Business through Referrals

Referrals create a win-win situation for everyone involved. An existing client refers a person to you. One of two things happens: The referral becomes a new client — who then gets served because you offer a great product or service — or the referral does not become a client but now knows about you and your service and has information that could be of value to him or her in the future. The existing client has won by serving both you and the person referred to you.

The terms *lead* and *referral* are often used interchangeably, although some people would say that a lead is simply the passing along of information, while a referral includes an endorsement or recommendation of whatever is being passed along.

Referrals are a way to generate new business from existing clients and customers. See Chapter 6 on how to make requests for referrals.

Benefits of generating business through referrals

As a business owner or entrepreneur some of the sweetest words you'll ever hear are "Jane sent me" or "Markus recommended that I give you a call." Referrals are gifts from your customers, clients, and friends. They can warm your heart and fill your business.

Referrals are a good way to generate business because:

✔ **There is no financial cost or overhead.** Marketing expenses, if any, are minimal. You do need to have business cards to give to your clients and contacts so that they have your information to pass along to others, but you need to have business cards anyway. You do have to spend time with your clients, but you would be spending that time with them anyway. You also have to spend time with the referral, but you would be spending time with prospects no matter what and spending time with a referred prospect is much more likely to produce a sale than spending time with a cold prospect.

✔ **Referrals can create a stream of new business as one referral leads to another and to another.** If I refer a friend to you and then that friend comes back to tell me how happy and pleased she is, I am likely to want to send more people to you. And every referral can give you access to a whole new group of people.

✔ **You are able to develop trust and a close relationship more quickly with clients who are referred to you than with those who simply stumble upon your business.** You're more inclined to trust referrals if you trust the person that referred them. Likewise, because someone they know already has a relationship with you and has told them about you, referrals feel that they know you and can trust you. You start off with an experience of relatedness. Remember the last time that you met a friend of a friend or a friend of a family member and that person said, "I feel like I already know you"? We get to know people through association.

✔ **You get to experience the satisfaction of knowing that your clients are pleased with you.** When you get referrals, you are consistently provided with evidence that your clients are happy. If they weren't pleased, they very likely would not refer anyone to you. The catch is that you have to do a good job for your clients in order to get referrals.

✔ **Working with referrals requires less energy and effort on your part and the sales cycle is typically shorter.** The referred person already has some of his needs met and his concerns addressed by the person who made the referral. You have the person's attention already. He or she will at least be ready and willing to hear what you have to say and give you consideration. There is less resistance on the person's part.

✔ **You develop a base of clients who know each other and are therefore more likely to stay related and loyal to your business.** If Susie and I both go to the same hair designer and we see each other sometimes and we comment on each other's haircut, there is a camaraderie and sense of community related to the salon. We feel a greater sense of community knowing that the people we know are walking in the same circles and being served by the same vendors. It breeds familiarity and comfort. And as humans, we tend to move towards what is familiar and comforting.

Your current clients are the people most likely to know who would be a good fit to do business with you. You are likely to get great clients from referrals.

How to encourage people to give referrals

You encourage people to give you referrals by asking them to do so. Invite them to support you. Give them permission to support you. Let them know that they can help you. Let them know that you value their support and contacts. Develop a comfortable, natural way of talking about your business and asking for help.

You have to ask. Even be willing to ask the people who are close to you and love you and think you have the best product in the world. Review the criteria in Chapter 6 for making requests.

You may get referrals from unexpected sources

During her career as a financial planner, Genie Fuller got involved in networking and was one of the officers of a networking club in Dallas. One of the things the group did to get its members networking with each other was to fill a basket with one business card from each member. Then the members would each pull a card from the basket and have lunch with the person whose card it was.

Genie once drew the card of a young man who Genie thought would probably not be a beneficial resource for her and her financial planning business. He was, in fact, one of the last people from the group that Genie would have chosen if it had been up to her.

However, she called and scheduled lunch with him. At the lunch, she listened and learned about his business. She began writing down the names of people she would refer to him and ended up handing him a list of about 15 people to contact. She recommended that he use her name when calling them.

Then the conversation switched and Genie started explaining her business. As she spoke, she noticed the puzzled look on his face and decided to get very specific by telling him that she was looking for people who fit the basic criteria: married, 42 years of age, 1½ children, and an income of $107,000 per year. He responded by saying that he couldn't think of anyone at the moment who fit the description, but that he would get back to her when he did.

Genie didn't really expect to hear back from him, and she was okay with that. She felt good about

meeting him and giving her contacts to him. To her surprise, a few days later she received an envelope from him with a sheet of paper listing the names of five people and a paragraph about each one — people who fit the basic criteria of her clients. She called each of them and ended up with a new client!

The things she noticed and learned from that experience were

- Not to write people off based on assumptions and judgments.

- Once she got specific, rather than speaking in generalities about her business, he was able to respond.

- People feel inclined to respond when they have been given to freely — what Genie calls "the rule of equal exchange." In other words, Genie gave from her heart generously and felt good about it and was comfortable with not getting anything back in return.

This experience became the basis for Genie's networking and her business success. Years later, she started a company of networking clubs, gathering business people together to teach them about networking and provide them with a supportive environment for their networking. Today she is known as "America's Referral Coach" and she coaches individuals on how to apply a networking philosophy to their lives and their businesses in order to generate consistent referrals.

Thank them. No matter what happens, thank the people who give you the referrals. If they give you a referral and the person is unresponsive and doesn't become a client, still be grateful for the referral because they did their part and were willing to give you the name of someone they knew.

If you're not succeeding with referrals

If you have not been successful with referrals, check out both your attitude and your approach. Shift your attitude so that you experience referrals as an opportunity to serve rather than as an opportunity to grab a new client. Approach each referral with a positive networking approach and look for an opportunity to be a resource for them as well as exploring how you can fulfill their needs with your product or service.

If they appear to want to give you some referrals but can't seem to think of anyone, thank them for considering it, thinking about it, and attempting to be of help. At this point, you can possibly help them by prompting them with questions or ideas about the people they know who you would like to be of service to. If they don't respond to your request or say no to giving any referrals, thank them for their business and the opportunity to be of service and let them know that you would be pleased to respond appropriately if they change their mind about referring or run into someone who needs what you offer.

If a person doesn't want to give you referrals now, that doesn't mean the person won't ever want to give you referrals. A no is always a no in the moment. It means nothing more than at that moment the person chooses no.

When clients give you a referral, reward them in some way. Rewards, appreciation, thanks, and acknowledgement reinforce positive and desired behavior so that the behavior is repeated. It is a natural and sometimes automatic, unconscious response for people to give more of what they are rewarded for giving.

Sometimes you can reward them with a free product or surprise them with a discount the next time they buy from you. When they have been instrumental in a referral that led to a major piece of business or have given you a large number of referrals over a certain period of time, give them something special like tickets to the theater or a sporting event, flowers, a coupon to their favorite store, or a donation in their name to their favorite charity.

Start keeping track of the referrals you are given. Make note of who gives you referrals, the result of the referral, and they way that you rewarded or thanked the person who gave you the referral. This will help to keep you conscious of the value of referrals and make you more aware of opportunities to ask. It will also make you remember to give appropriate thanks for your referrals.

Here are some other things you can do to encourage people to give you referrals:

- ✔ **Refer business to people.** Give them leads and referrals without them even having to ask. You can get them thinking about referrals simply by giving them a referral. This can automatically trigger them to think, "Wow, this is great. Let's see. I wonder what I can do in return."

  Make a list of people for whom you can be a good source of referrals. Develop a reminder system so that you consistently pass referrals to them.

- ✔ **Stay in touch with people and keep yourself in the forefront of their thoughts.** Send them articles, newsletters, postcards, or promotional items that remind them of you. Remind people of your existence, otherwise people simply forget to think of you and send people your way. Give them gentle reminders on a consistent basis. Some of these reminders should include information that they find useful.

- ✔ **Join and participate in a group that is designed for the purpose of networking and encourages people to recommend and refer one another.** Networking clubs, networking focus groups, and chambers of commerce bring people together for the purpose of doing business with each other and referring business to each other. See Chapter 3 for more information on networking clubs and events.

- ✔ **Set goals for business growth and let staff, clients, family, and friends know what your plans are for growing your business.** People tend to rally behind goals. Your goal serves to spark other people's enthusiasm and direction.

- ✔ **Remember that businesses in your same industry can be a source of referrals.** As a speaker, I often refer business to other speakers when either I am not available for the date the client wants or I do not present on the topic the client wants. A dentist may refer to an orthodontist. A printer who specializes in business forms may refer a client to a printer who specializes in annual reports or books. A commercial photographer may refer people to a portrait photographer.

Do you know how much of your business is from networking, word-of-mouth marketing, and referrals? Whatever the percentage is, calculate what the results would be if you increased your referrals by even 25 percent, 30 percent, or 50 percent.

Running a Home-based Business

By using today's technology, you can conduct business efficiently from your home, your car, your golf cart, the airport, your hotel room, or your vacation retreat. With a cell phone and laptop computer, you have access to nearly all the resources that you would have in a normal office. This convenience has led to a proliferation of successful home-based businesses. Even corporate employees are choosing to have home offices that allow them more freedom and flexibility with their time and their lifestyle.

Running a home-based business has its challenges, however. Working at home requires focus, discipline, and motivation. Typically you have your computer, office equipment, files, phone, and lots of time. The key, obviously, is what you do with your time. It may seem like staying focused would be easy when you don't have the distractions of people dropping by your cubicle. There's a downside, however — rather than going into an office where you see other people all day and have people readily available for interaction, support, ideas, and encouragement, you have to generate your own enthusiasm and energy all day long. Moreover, there are no businesses down the hall to provide you with the products and services that you require, and no company sign on the office building, the front door, or the building register.

It is up to you to make sure people know about you and think of you when they need your product or service. You must develop ways to stay connected and keep your name in front of customers and prospects. Computer networking has made it more feasible for you to have an office in your home. At the same time, having a home office makes networking more important than ever.

How to create visibility and avoid isolation

With a home-based business, you don't have the visibility that naturally comes with being in a business location. People will not happen upon your place of business by accident. Therefore, it is up to you to create visibility for yourself and your business so that those clients and customers find you. Here are some suggestions:

- ✔ Join a professional networking organization of business owners that meets on a regular basis to do business with each other and support each other in the growth and success of everyone's businesses. See Chapter 3 for more information on these organizations.

- ✔ Create an advisory board that meets with you once a month to review your progress and goals and actions for your business.

- ✔ Be active in the association of your industry as a way to stay connected with others and abreast of the latest happenings and trends in the industry.

- ✔ Be in phone contact with certain people on a regular basis who are advocates and supporters of you and your success.

- ✔ Consider hiring a business coach to help provide direction, encouragement, and accountability for your business success.

> ✔ Use a contact management system to make regular calls to prospects and clients, keep current information on all your contacts, and send out periodic mailings to keep your name in front of people. See Chapter 15 for more information on contact management systems.
>
> ✔ Have a Web presence. Maintain a Web site that gives you visibility to a global network and a link with others who can help direct potential resources to your site. Make sure that your Web address is on all your marketing material. Make sure people can find you through search engines and that you link with other sites. See Chapter 15 for more information on having and maintaining a Web site.

Leveraging your way to network marketing success

Instead of using the traditional means of marketing products (retail stores and catalogs), network marketing companies distribute and market their products through a network of independent distributors who bring in customers and distributors for the distribution of products and services. Typically people receive compensation for a percentage of the sale of products three to four levels deep within their downline (distributors they have brought in). The strength and power of the network marketing system is based on the multiplier effect of leveraging and duplicating. For much more information on network marketing, see *Network Marketing For Dummies* by Zig Ziglar (Hungry Minds, Inc.).

Answers to household names quiz

Here are some names you may have thought of in the earlier section, "Making Your Name a Household Word." You may have thought of some other names to add to this list as well. There is obviously no one right answer. Whoever you thought of is someone who has done a good job of creating name recognition.

✔ Leader in the automobile industry — Lee Iaccoca

✔ Baseball icon — Mickey Mantle, Babe Ruth

✔ Famous tap dancer — Fred Astaire or Gene Kelly

✔ Top-notch architect — Frank Lloyd Wright

✔ Famous children's author — J. K. Rowling or Dr. Seuss

Network marketing is in some ways like having your own business at home, while at the same time being part of a large, supportive family business. You are your own boss and yet you have an upline sponsor and a large organization of people available to train, encourage, and support you. You have proven products, quality supplies and marketing materials, and proven success through many role models in the company. In some cases, there is a corporate history of success. Network marketing can be like having your own business because it is up to you to provide your own office space and equipment, build the business, manage your finances, make wise business decisions, organize yourself, and be efficient with your time. You have the freedom and potential to work as much as you choose and create an income based on what you produce and what the people you bring into the business produce.

People in the network marketing field work in an environment that's based on the concept of networking. If you're a network marketer, your success is based on the success of the people who you bring into the business and who you mentor. Network marketing exemplifies the idea that what goes around comes around. You give to others and commit to supporting them in whatever way possible. This is the basis of networking in any industry — the idea of working for the greater good of everyone and that what you give to others will come back to you tenfold.

Network marketing requires discipline, focus, and persistence. It is not a get-rich-quick scheme. It is a well-defined path of success that, over the long-term, can generate generous financial rewards. It is, obviously, important to choose a network marketing company that is solid and reputable and that offers quality products that you believe in.

If you are involved in a network marketing business, the following suggestions can be helpful:

- ✔ **Listen to what people say that they want in life.** People are always saying what they want in idle conversation and without any idea of how they can have what they want. Let people know how network marketing could be a vehicle for their particular goals in life.

- ✔ **Be a trainer, encourager, advocate, cheerleader, and coach — all in one!** Give people everything you can possibly give them in terms of your experiences and your knowledge. The more information people have, the more likely they are to assimilate that information in a way that enables them to make decisions and take action.

- ✔ **Help the people in your downline see that they are on path and making progress even when things don't go exactly as they desire.** Continue to build up the commitment that people have even when they are discouraged. Be a mirror for people, always reflecting back to them the greatness that they possess. Let them know that they're not the only ones who have discouraging and frustrating days. Help them to stay true to their goals and dreams.

✔ **Speak clearly about what it is that you do and what you offer to people.** There tend to be a lot of misperceptions about network marketing that scare some people off. Be as clear as you can about the value and benefit that you offer to people. Don't be mysterious or evasive.

✔ **Create community with people in your upline in order to provide yourself and your downline with inspiration, encouragement, and support.** In network marketing, people typically have home-based offices and are required to be self-motivating. Even though there is a whole corporation and a large upline out there to support them, they can sometimes feel like they're out there all alone.

Because your success is ultimately up to you, staying connected to your upline can make the difference in staying persistent, committed, and on track with your goals.

Chapter 12

Networking throughout Life

As I explain throughout this book, networking is a universal principle of giving and receiving — a lifestyle rather than a technique. Although you may think of networking primarily as a means to further yourself professionally, it can benefit you in all aspects and circumstances of life. Whether you're moving from college to a career, from a career to retirement, or from one city to another, your network can be your greatest source of support and encouragement.

You can meet someone who influences your life dramatically at any point in your life. And you can likewise influence that person's life and be a source of help to him or her. Networking doesn't end when you retire any more than it ends when you find that perfect job. In this chapter, I show you how to utilize your network in the various stages and circumstances of life.

Networking from College to Career

Your college years are a rich time for building your network. You meet people from various parts of the country, possibly from around the world. Building relationships is relatively easy because you are all thrown into an environment where you live, study, and socialize together.

It's not what you know; it's who you know. Make sure that while you are educating yourself, you are also building your network. Pay attention to the people around you. Get to know the students, professors, and leaders at your school. Get involved in campus activities that relate to your interests. The people you know can make a big difference in your success. You never know which one of your classmates or professors might be a resource for a perfect job, become your biggest and best client, or develop a talent that makes him or her a valuable partner or associate for your business. If you don't connect and stay in touch with these people, the opportunities that could develop may never be accessible to you.

Although these contacts are easy to develop and maintain while you're in college, the challenge is maintaining the contacts after everyone leaves college to pursue their careers and get on with their lives. After you graduate, make efforts to stay connected with the school and the people from the school. For example:

- Be active in the school's alumni association.
- Attend school reunions.
- Consider writing an article for the school newsletter or publications.

Even if you haven't been diligent about keeping up with those college connections, you can reach out to reconnect. Review the section on staying in touch in Chapter 10.

Everything you want and need is available and around you. Accessing the multitude of resources in your network is your responsibility.

Following your passion

Growing up in sunny California, Ashley Porter developed a love of the ocean. When the time came to choose a college, she chose Texas A&M because of its Institute of Nautical Archaeology (INA). Although attending school in the middle of Texas took her away from the water, she was impressed with the program and wanted to learn all she could about nautical archaeology.

After her freshman year, she became interested in working with INA and thus began to introduce herself to "every teacher in the nautical department." Ashley was determined. But she still struggled. She says, "I felt inferior to the PhD professors. I was only a measly undergraduate, what did I know. I usually received a haughty attitude from many of the staff. I was

not deterred. I knew that I had to start somewhere and work my way into the department. I sat in on classes that I wasn't even registered for just to get to know the teachers."

Ashley continues her story: "One day while walking through the halls of the anthropology building, I came upon a flyer about a field school to teach graduate students the discipline of nautical engineering. I was beside myself with joy. I was not undaunted by the fact that the course was for graduate students, but I read the fine print and noticed that it said, 'Graduate students will be accepted on a primary basis, but undergraduates are encouraged to apply.' The excitement I felt was overpowering. I had to tell someone. I didn't want to tell my parents. I was afraid they would think it impossible for me to be accepted to such a program. I did what any dreamer like myself would do. I applied and got accepted!"

Over the following months, Ashley talked with the individuals at the University of Hawaii, where the course was to be conducted. She realized that she needed a base contact, someone at Texas A&M who could help her with information and a letter of recommendation. Bill, the diving safety officer for INA, became her "angel." He helped Ashley purchase dive gear, get signed up for her dive physical, and communicate with the dive officer at the University of Hawaii. On top of everything, he wrote her a letter of recommendation. Bill gradually introduced her to people throughout the department of nautical archaeology.

According to Ashley, her summer in Hawaii was wonderful. "I learned about everything from underwater photography and cinematography to underwater navigation to underwater artifact drawing. I made contacts in Hawaii with a girl who was on the project with me. It turned out that she might be coming to Texas A&M in the fall and we might have a chance to work together there."

Ashley returned to Texas with a sense of pride. She had accomplished her goal of working on an actual nautical survey. She thought life couldn't get any better — and then it did. One of her water polo teammates knew of her diving interests and sent her an e-mail with information about how students could apply for a summer excavation project with INA. Ashley said, "I jumped out of my chair when I read the e-mail, thinking that I might actually be able to work with the program of my dreams. I went to Bill to find out more, and he immediately introduced me to Mr. Arnold, the man heading up the project. I graciously shook Mr. Arnold's hand

and introduced myself. He in turn introduced me to his graduate assistant, who gave me all the forms necessary for applying to the project crew." Ashley quickly updated her resume to include information from the Hawaii project, got a letter of recommendation from Bill, and turned in her application. Within two months, she had gotten word that she was accepted and she began to meet the graduate students with whom she would be working in the summer.

Once again, Ashley had a great summer learning experience. She had a chance to meet and work with engineers, a computer specialist from Colorado, and much of the staff and members of the Institute of Nautical Archaeology.

The day after school started in the fall, Ashley entered the nautical office and was greeted with open arms from her former crewmembers. She was immediately offered a job in the nautical office and realized that she now had the recognition in the department that she had always wanted. She was thrilled. "People knew who I was and I was receiving a paycheck. Over the next month, I would get to know the new president of INA and discover that we share the love of surfing. I am now able to talk easily with the office staff and students, and some of them have become dear friends thanks to a summer of hard work."

Ashley has applied to go to Turkey next summer. She says, "If I am accepted, I will be working with Dr. George F. Bass, the founder of INA and one of my former teachers. It sometimes amazes me that I have been able to accomplish this much with my life at only 21. I apply in a month to attend the masters program of nautical archaeology at Texas A&M. I hope I get accepted. I guess one of the things that I won't have to worry about is who will write me a letter of recommendation!"

Moving to a New City

You may think that when you're moving to a new city, you need to build a whole new network. But you don't. Instead, you need to expand your existing network. You're not starting over; you're adding to the contacts you already have.

When you move to a new city, your network is your most valuable source of information to help you with your move. People in your network have likely lived in that city or know people who live there now. People in your network may travel there on business or have clients there. People in your network may work for a company that has an office in the city you're moving to. All those people can be resources for you to learn more about the city, the work environment, and the people to contact. Network with the support system that you already have in order to expand your network. Ask your friends, coworkers, and acquaintances who they suggest you make contact with in the city to which you're moving. By doing so, you can quickly and efficiently bridge the gap from where you live to where you're moving with a network of resources that makes your move much less stressful and challenging. Rather than having a network that's limited to one city or area, you can create a global network.

Find out if the organizations that you currently belong to have chapters in the city that you are moving to. Join community and professional groups as soon as you can to make new contacts.

Surviving Life's Challenges

A crisis, challenge, or traumatic circumstance can make you reach out to your network in a whole new way — to move beyond your comfort zone and discover the generosity and goodness of the people around you. When you're going through a stressful situation, your network can be a source of nurturing and encouragement, as well as information on how to best move through the situation. No matter what you're dealing with in life, other people have been through the same or a very similar situation. And people want to help and contribute, to be there for you. It's up to you to let people know what's going on in your life and give them a chance to be of support.

When life gets tough is the perfect time to reach out to your network. At every turn, opportunities exist for people to help one another. And that's what networking is all about.

Figuring out who in your network you can turn to

Identify the people in your network who are good at handling difficult situations. Include the people you are close to who would want to know when you are in a time of need.

Think about all the people you know who may have dealt with a similar issue or problem. Also think about people you know who are experts or resources regarding the issues you're dealing with. Anyone who has experienced something similar to what you're going through will have knowledge and resources that could support and be of value to you.

Keeping in touch with your network during the tough times

Your core network consists of the people who you are closest to who are most vital to your personal and professional success. These are people who care about you and your success. They want to know how you're doing. They want to know how they can be of help. They want to know when you are going through difficult times so that they can be of support. In fact, these are the people who will likely be offended or disappointed if you don't give them an opportunity to be of support to you during challenging times.

Don't be a fair-weather networker who only lets people know when things are going great. Networking is about being there for each other during the ups and downs of life. Rather than isolating yourself during difficult times, you should be calling on your network to rally around you to help you get through the difficulties more quickly and easily. By calling on your network during the tough times, you are also giving other people permission to reach out during their tough times.

People may, in fact, be disappointed if you don't reach out to them during your tough times. They may feel this way because:

✔ You have been there for them and they value the opportunity to return the favor.

✔ They find out too late that they could have been of help.

✔ They find out from someone else that they could have been of help, and they feel that they should be closer to you than the person who knew what was going on.

✔ They have expertise in dealing with what you're dealing with and didn't have the opportunity to pass along what they have learned through their own experiences.

Leaning on your network when caring for aging parents

Many people today take care of their aging parents. Learning what resources are available and how best to address your parents' needs can be difficult emotionally. In this situation, networking can be a lifesaver.

Stan's mother had passed on, and his dad's health was worsening. Stan knew that his dad's living situation was going to have to change. His dad had been living in the same home for 40-plus years. After Stan's mom passed on, his dad was having more trouble taking care of himself and Stan was concerned for his well-being.

Stan began checking into nursing home options. Since his dad thought he could continue to live on his own, he was obviously not pleased or interested in following Stan's advice to move from his home into a nursing home. Three people in different conversations (and in the middle of what started out as casual conversations) shared with Stan their experiences of moving a parent into a nursing home. They all provided emotional support, information, and encouragement to help Stan get through one of the most difficult decisions he ever had to make.

While talking to the phone company about setting up a phone for his dad, he discovered that the woman who was helping him was a member of the church his family attended. She offered to pick Stan's dad up at the nursing home and take him to church on Wednesday nights for a church dinner and on Sunday mornings for the church service.

Stan felt like everywhere he turned, he found support. He had never been aware of these people or resources before, but as soon as he had a need, the resources started to appear.

An opportunity typically creates a time of need because within the opportunity, you are called on to stretch, grow, or reach out in a new way to respond to the opportunity.

Helping someone else deal with sensitive circumstances

Remember the difficult times during which people have been there for you. Recall how much it meant to you and how it assisted you in maintaining your sense of self. With the help of others, you were able to move through the situation in a healthy and productive manner. You can be as helpful to others who are experiencing tough times as other people have been to you.

Networking even in illness

Sue Pistone was getting ready to lead a seminar when all of a sudden she doubled over in pain. She tried to brush it off because she felt like she couldn't let her clients down by not showing up. But the pain was excruciating! After being rushed to the hospital and going through days of testing, she was diagnosed with a large cancerous tumor on her kidney and was told that she needed to undergo surgery immediately. To make matters worse, she developed a slight case of pneumonia while in the hospital, and the doctors said that they couldn't perform surgery until she was better.

Even though her focus was on getting the medical help she needed, she noticed that the doctors needed her help as much she needed theirs. At some point in their conversations, the doctors asked Sue what she did. She told them how she made a difference in other people's lives through enhancing their organization, time management, and personal and professional development. This always piqued the doctors' interest and prompted them to ask more questions. After every appointment, the doctor would ask Sue to send more information and Sue would walk out of the office with the doctor's business card.

After three weeks, Sue was well enough for surgery. The surgery was a success! During the three hours in the recovery unit, as she began to come out from under the anesthesia, she could vaguely hear the nurses talking about a seminar they had attended. Even though work was the furthest thing from her mind, she couldn't help but respond. She mumbled to one of nurses, asking who the speaker was for the seminar they were discussing. This led to the nurses asking what Sue did. When they found out, their response was, "Boy, could we use your talents in our unit!" Sue said that she would be happy to send information, and this time she left the recovery room with a nurse's business card, a new lease on life, and a new opportunity.

Later that day, Sue's children and close family members came to see her. Her daughters (who work with her) came in first, and as they approached, they noticed the business card in Sue's hand. She handed the card to them and asked them to make sure a packet was sent to the nurse that week. They couldn't believe that Sue was actually mumbling about business right after a major surgery. But according to Sue, "It proves that you never know when and where the perfect networking opportunities will arise." And Sue has proven that she's not going to miss out on any of those opportunities.

You may tend to back off from networking with people who are having difficult times because you feel uncomfortable and don't know what to say. When someone is dealing with the loss of a loved one or an illness, for example, you may feel awkward and not make contact with that person because of the awkwardness. Don't fall into this trap. Networking is about being there for people and making a human connection. In some situations, all you have to do is show up for people to let them know that you're there for them. Your presence may be the connection they need to remind them that they are not alone and that people care.

In these situations, don't try to fix everything or even make people feel better; just be with them in their sorrow, grief, fear, or pain. What you say may not make as much of a difference as the fact that you are there. Your words can be as simple as:

- ✔ "I care about you."
- ✔ "I'm so sorry."
- ✔ "I've been thinking about you."
- ✔ "I wish I could be of help."
- ✔ "I'm here for you, whatever you need."
- ✔ "My thoughts and prayers are with you."

When in an emotionally draining situation, people may not be able to think clearly about what they need. You, however, may be able to observe the situation and offer support and assistance.

- ✔ "I know you've got a lot to handle right now. What I would like to do is call and reschedule your appointments for you so you don't have to worry about that right now."
- ✔ "I went through a similar situation recently and learned a lot as a result. I will put together a packet of information that was helpful to me and drop by your office."

Networking during the Holidays

Holidays are meant to be a time to count your blessings, visit your family, and be of good cheer. Yet the holidays can also be a time of stress, anxiety, and depression.

Everyone deserves a holiday season of fun rather than stress, enthusiasm rather than anxiety, and gratefulness rather than depression.

Generating interesting conversations

Approach holiday gatherings with the intention of generating new and interesting conversations rather than the same old interactions. See what you can discover by asking open-ended questions. However, be more specific than just the typical "How are you doing?" or "What's new?" Instead, ask questions such as:

- ✔ "I know your work has something to do with . . . tell me more about that."

> ✔ "How did you and Uncle Harry meet?"
>
> ✔ "What's been your most satisfying accomplishment this past year?"
>
> ✔ "How did you decide to become a . . .?"
>
> ✔ "What kind of fun plans do you have for the New Year?"

No matter how long you've known someone or how much you think you know about that person, you can almost always learn something new.

In turn, think about how you will respond when people ask "What's new?" or "How's life treating you?" Instead of responding with a general statement, respond with something specific that can lead to an interesting conversation..

You have the ability to keep the conversation interesting. Think about all the things that have happened in your life that could be of interest to the people you talk with and share those stories in an interesting way.

Keep your conversations relatively light. Generate conversations about positive times and good memories. Holiday gatherings are not the time or place to preach, teach, impress, or show off; they are a time to reconnect. And the best way to reconnect is to focus on others by listening, paying attention, and putting others at ease.

When you talk, pay attention to the other person's attention span; don't talk on and on if he or she isn't showing some interest in what you're saying. Explore to see if you can find a topic that's of interest to both of you.

Base your communication on an attitude of giving, listening, serving, and being a resource for your family and friends. Listen for the words "I want," "I need," "I'm looking for," or "I'm involved in" and then think about your network to see if you can offer a name, idea, or information. Also listen for the opportunity to ask others for information, ideas, and contacts for yourself.

Reaching out to people outside your normal circle

Mix and mingle at holiday parties, whether it's a corporate party or a family gathering. Notice if you have a tendency to gravitate to and stay with the relatives or coworkers you already know well. Use this opportunity to reach out to people you don't have a chance to talk to or see regularly.

Be sure to spend some time listening to family or company elders. Hearing about the family or company history and learning from others can be interesting and valuable. Also, spend some time playing with the young children. Bonding with the young is rewarding and valuable because of the young spirit in all of us.

If you have a new spouse or guest attending a gathering with you, make sure that you know how to help the person feel comfortable and have a good time. Be sure to introduce him or her to the hosts and to several relatives or coworkers. Include the person in your conversations. Touch base periodically to see how your guest is doing.

If you are a guest or a new family or office member, you will probably meet many new people while most everyone else already knows most of the people at the gathering. Think about how you can put yourself at ease to feel like a part of the group. Gather information ahead of time from the person who invited you. Find out if any conversation topic or information is taboo. Learn about the family and who will be there. Find out if you should be aware of or alert to anything in particular, or if there is anyone in particular you should meet.

You may notice how easy it is to fall into family roles and familiar patterns when you attend family gatherings. Gossip, regrets, and the rekindling of family arguments can all characterize holiday get-togethers. If you approach your family as a network of contacts and explore with the purpose of discovering new ways to share information, and ideas, however, I guarantee that you can find ways to network with one another that will develop new behaviors that are more pleasant and satisfying.

Expressing your gratitude

Expressing gratitude and appreciation to the people in your life is an essential part of building strong relationships throughout your network. Since holiday gatherings are a time of celebration and appreciation, they are a perfect place to say thanks and express appreciation to your relatives, friends, and coworkers.

- ✔ "Grandma, I appreciate the way you helped take care of me when I was little."

- ✔ "Thanks, Karen for a great year. I'm really looking forward to strategizing with the team on next year's projects."

- ✔ "Uncle Harry, I went fishing last weekend and I thought of you and how you were the one who took me fishing all those years."

- ✔ "Jerry, I'm really glad you got assigned to our project this year. It's a pleasure working with you."

- ✔ "Mom, thanks for the support you've been to me over this past year. I really appreciate the friendship we've developed."

Other holiday tips

Take good care of yourself. Pamper yourself during the holidays by getting plenty of rest and doing something nice for yourself. The more relaxed, rested, and at ease you are, the easier it will be for you to be pleasant, courteous, and have fun with the people you meet during the holidays. Pace yourself. Schedule a nap if you can prior to your family gathering. Give yourself plenty of time to get ready so that you can arrive feeling refreshed and at ease. Do whatever you can to look and feel your best!

Expanding Your Network into Retirement

Your network shifts dramatically when you retire because the people with whom you have been spending 40-plus hours a week are no longer automatically a part of your day. In retirement, the responsibility of building, expanding, and strengthening your network to support your lifestyle is up to you. You must be more conscious about choosing who you spend your time with and taking action to keep in touch with your network. When you're working, your primary networking needs likely have to do with success, security, and fulfillment in your career. After you retire, your needs may be geared more toward hobbies, community service, travel, or something else that's not related to work. In the same way that your network served you while working, your network continues to serve you in retirement. In fact, it's even more important after you retire to focus on building your network to continue a full and rewarding life.

My mother has been retired for over ten years, and in some ways her life hasn't slowed down. She has volunteer work at the church, yard work that she still loves to do, doctor visits, church classes, grandmotherly and motherly activities, and regular outings with her friends. My mom has a powerful local support system that consists of my brother and his family, church friends, neighbors, and lifetime friends who stay in close contact and would be there in a heartbeat if my mom needed them.

She has developed friendships with people who offer to go to the airport with her every time I fly into town (I live in Houston, Texas, and she lives in Charlotte, North Carolina) or she flies out to see me. If the weather is bad, they check on her. If she's going to the doctor, she always gets more than one offer of someone to go with her. She and her friend Willie Mae have breakfast together every Saturday morning. The Stubbs, a family she is close to, expect her for lunch after church every Sunday, and she is referred to and treated like just another member of the family!. My brother talks with her daily. And her grandchildren, Valerie and Leslea, are in regular contact through calls, visits, and e-mails from school. Her life is very rich as a result of her friendships and her support system.

Moving from success to significance in retirement

For 33 years, Jim Matson had a successful video production company. Relationship marketing and networking was a natural part of his business approach. Although Jim feels that he was always low key and never too obvious about his business, he received a lot of referrals. He noticed that even people who had never done business with him would refer others to him.

When he sold his business after 33 years, he began to think about what he wanted to do with the rest of his life. Although he had some ideas, he wasn't sure where to direct his time and energy. So he reached out to his network. He went to lunch with the publisher of the city's business journal and mentioned that he really didn't feel suited to a retirement of "sitting around," and they began to discuss his possibilities. Jim's focus in life has always been to recognize the excellence in others. He considers himself a talent scout, always looking for people with leadership skills and encouraging them to fulfill those skills. He likes to put people to work doing the things they're good at. As a result of the lunch discussion, Jim began to think about being a consultant in the areas of employee retention and employee satisfaction.

To continue to explore the idea and develop his courage, he called some friends and invited them to lunch. He was actually creating his own focus group (see Chapter 3), which consisted of the president of a chamber of commerce, the owner of a financial services agency, an attorney, and other successful business people. His invitation to them was "I will feed you for your feedback. I have ideas about what I want to do with my time and I would like to get your feedback." He wanted to run some ideas by them, and yet he started the lunch meeting by telling each person why he chose to call them and what he admired in their lives. The participants enjoyed the meeting so much that they wanted to get together again and did so the following month.

Jim believes that continuing to invest in the future is important. He is still active in his community, his new consulting business, and many organizations throughout the city.

His attitude about retirement is that there's more to life than measuring the passage of time. Retirement can be a time for moving from *success* to *significance*. He seeks out people for his network who are looking to the future rather than talking about their ailments and their past. To keep himself mentally stimulated and alert, he chooses a variety of venues for networking: one-on-one lunch meetings, small group breakfast meetings, association monthly meetings, and so on.

Jim is 75 and networking strong. He is masterful at building connections that keep him and his support system alert, active, and contributing to the world.

List the hobbies and interests that you have now that you are retired (or the hobbies and interests you plan to have in retirement). Next to each hobby and interest, list the people you know (or want to get to know) who share the hobby or interest. Also, list the needs that you have based on your retirement plans and identify the people you want in your network who can assist you with handling future needs that may arise.

Your needs will depend on what you plan to do with your retirement. You may plan to buy a new home and therefore you would need a good Realtor. You may plan to buy an RV and travel around the country, which means you would want to learn about RVs and RV parks around the country. You may plan to get involved in volunteer activities and need information about the various volunteer opportunities available in your community. Whatever your plans and goals are in life, there are certain needs associated with fulfilling those goals. Your network is your greatest source of information and resources regarding all of your needs and goals.

Paring Down Your Network

Although, theoretically, everyone you've ever met can be considered part of your network, you always have the choice of who to maintain contact with in your network. Just as it's important to maintain focus by regularly reflecting on and updating your business plan, marketing plan, and your goals in life, it is also important to periodically review which people are the main sources of influence in your life. Don't let your mind, files, database, or Rolodex get so cluttered that you lose sight of where your focus should be. You want to give your attention to the sources that are most important for your own fulfillment, happiness, and success.

Cleaning out your Rolodex is not about discarding people; it is about creating focus for yourself. Think of it in the same way as you do your lifetime "to do" list. Although you may have a huge list of things that you eventually want to accomplish in your lifetime, you should cull that list to create your focus for your current year. Items can be reinserted on the list as opportunities present themselves or when the time seems right. Do the same thing for your network. Although you have a vast and unlimited network, you may choose to focus on nurturing, building, or reinforcing a certain segment of your network during certain times of your life. For example, if your focus this year is to sell your business and retire, you would focus on your circles of influence that can help you make those business and lifestyle changes.

Some people in your network come and go, and sometimes relationships come back around full circle when you least expect it. Someone you haven't talked with in a long time may be the perfect connection for what's going on in your life at this moment. You can reconnect with people after a few months or a number of years and recreate your relationships in ways that generate mutual value and benefit.

It is important to eliminate persons from your network who are negative, time wasters, or energy drainers, even if it seems they've been part of your network for a long time. Instead, you are wise to choose people you enjoy, love, appreciate, and respect. Surround yourself with people who you feel great being with — the people who make your spirit soar, your heart sing, and your dreams come true.

You are the one who chooses who you want to keep in the center and active part of your network, and who you want to attract and draw into your network.

Chapter 13

Networking in a Charity or in Your Community

• •

In This Chapter

▶ Doing good for others while making contacts that may help you later

▶ Finding the right volunteering opportunity

▶ Becoming involved in your community

• •

I learned to network in the not-for-profit industry. In that environment, you have to be resourceful. As the director of a charitable organization, I had to ask for funds, volunteers, and donations of products and services. One of the things I noticed was that when people got involved, they received tremendous benefits back from giving of themselves. And I noticed that the people who got involved developed heart-warming, and often lifelong, relationships with other people who participated. I began to see and experience the value of networking every day as I watched people giving with no expectations of receiving anything in return, but receiving so much value for themselves. It was a time I will never forget — a lesson in the nature of the human spirit.

People want to give and contribute. Many people are simply waiting to be asked. And some people don't even realize that they're waiting to be asked. Some people don't realize the value of giving until trauma in their lives creates an opportunity to give, and then they experience the power of giving, and ultimately the power of networking.

The easiest way to build relationships with people is to do something together for a cause or for the good of the community. To give in a selfless way creates bonds that extend deep and long. When you are there for truly unselfish reasons, you discover yourself and your spirit in a way that enhances your capacity for networking.

Creating Networking Opportunities by Doing Work for Charitable Organizations

Networking happens naturally when you volunteer with a charitable organization. Networking is easy when you're focused on giving instead of receiving. You get to know people with whom you have a common interest because you are volunteering together and supporting the same organization and cause. Whether you work on a single project or long-term committee, you learn about and get to know other volunteers just in the process of talking with each other and working together. Your relationships develop to the point where sharing resources and ideas and doing business with each other is natural and automatic.

Getting involved with a worthy cause can be a powerful benefit to your life. You establish a name for yourself as someone who is interested in the community or dedicated to a particular cause. You expand your sense of self-worth by giving of yourself and taking on something bigger than yourself. You expand your network by becoming part of that organization's network.

Typically, many levels of participation are available in charitable organizations. For example:

✔ Committee chair or committee member

✔ Board of directors or advisory board

✔ Event chair

✔ Project volunteer

✔ Office assistant

Every volunteer organization has its own list of volunteer opportunities and duties. Organizations that rely on the support of volunteers include hospitals, churches, chambers of commerce, community service associations, and so on.

You want to find the role that best suits your desires and availability. If your purpose is to meet people and network, choose to get involved on a team, committee, or project so that you will be working with people rather than doing a task on your own. Certain committees or projects may have special appeal because they need your skills and talents or because of the opportunities they offer to you. Or maybe you want to get involved with something totally different from anything you've ever done so as to develop new talents and skills or simply because a change would be enjoyable.

Lending your talents to a board of directors

If you're already well established with your business and in the community, you might consider participating on an organization's board of directors. If you have the time and interest in serving in a leadership role, board involvement can be a great way to get to know other business professionals. Typically, a board commitment is for a certain number of years and involves participation and decision making that is vital to the organization's success. If you pursue this type of volunteer position, make sure that you're ready to assume the responsibility and accountability that goes with the opportunity.

Get involved in a cause that you can be committed to. If everything in your life were taken care of, what would you choose to give your time and energy to? If you had no need to work for a living, and instead could live a life of service to some cause, what cause would you choose? Think about what you want to support and how you want to be involved.

Be sure to handle your volunteer duties with the same commitment and professionalism with which you handle your business tasks. People you volunteer with will notice how you handle your volunteer responsibilities and will figure that you handle your business responsibilities the same way. You show your character whether you're doing work for hire or work for service.

If you are a natural leader or want to develop your leadership skills, consider taking on a leadership role in a charitable organization. Your volunteer activities can help you develop skills for yourself while you help others — a win-win combination! Or you can choose to use the skills, strengths, and expertise that you have already developed in your career to be of value to a not-for-profit organization. For example, if your business is information technology, you could help a charity set up or maintain its Web site.

Participating in Community Events — and Networking Along the Way

You may think that business opportunities and leads are more likely to come from a business conference than a neighborhood association meeting . . . but why?

Ropin' up business at the rodeo

Terri Scott, who owned a printing business with her husband, signed up to volunteer with the Houston Livestock Show and Rodeo as something fun to do. The rodeo raises money for scholarships, and she saw this as "two weeks away from the office." Although she knew that a lot of people volunteered for the purpose of networking for their businesses, she didn't want to mix business with pleasure and consciously chose a volunteer activity strictly for the fun she expected to gain from it.

When the printing industry went through a downslide because more and more people were printing their business forms on their own computers, Terri did two things that led to major results for her business: She opened an additional business, Best Specialties and Printing, which enabled her to promote the advertising specialties side of the business better. And she decided that she might as well let her rodeo friends know what she did in the business world.

After six years of volunteering at the rodeo, she casually began to let people know that she would be glad to help them if they ever needed advertising specialty items for their companies. If someone showed an interest, she would take their card and call them later. She still didn't like mixing business with pleasure, so she made sure that the business conversations happened during business hours rather than at rodeo committee meetings or social events.

Her rodeo friends have become her greatest source of business. One of the volunteers started working with Terri's company right away and ordered more than $300,000 worth of items over a period of a year and a half.

Another piece of business came from a friend of one of the volunteers who attended a Christmas party for Terri's rodeo committee. Terri figures that she never would have met this person in any other way, and if she had tried to reach her without knowing her first, she never would have been able to get beyond the receptionist.

Terri says, "Now it seems like every time I turn around, someone calls who knows someone from the rodeo and wants to order some products or printing." Terri believes that the business came to her so quickly once she was willing to tell people what she did because she had already built relationships with these people.

Terri is on a committee of more than 300 people broken down into teams of 30. Becoming friends with the team of 30 and getting to know many of the others through various meetings, parties, and volunteer duties was easy. When her business experienced a slump, Terri had to make some major decisions. She decided that she didn't want to join new networking groups. Instead, she wanted to make good use of her participation in the community, and it paid off big time!

Community events are a great place to expand your professional network. You expand your circle of influence by getting involved in something that's outside your normal routine. These networking opportunities include everything from school activities to church meetings to spring festivals. The types of networking gatherings that happen in communities include the following:

✔ Informal gatherings, such as bridge clubs, parents' groups, and book clubs

✔ Professional networking groups, such as Business Networks International (www.bni.com), LeTip International, Inc. (www.letip.com), and Network Professionals, Inc. (www.npinet.com)

✔ Industry and trade associations, such as the National Speakers Association, the Association of Authors and Publishers, the Women's Council of Realtors, and the National Association of Catering Executives

✔ Civic groups, such as Kiwanis (www.kiwanis.org), Rotary (www.rotary.org), Exchange (www.nationalexchangeclub.com), and Optimists (www.optimist.org)

✔ Community groups, such as local theatre groups and concerned citizens groups

✔ Charity groups, such as the American Heart Association, Women Helping Women, and Covenant House (see more information on volunteering with charitable organizations in the first part of this chapter)

✔ Religious groups, such as prayer groups, choirs, and the Association of Christian Athletes

✔ Hobby, sports, and special interest groups, such as ski clubs, calligraphy guilds, and exercise groups

✔ Company clubs and groups, such as corporate Toastmasters clubs, corporate women's initiatives, and corporate golf clubs

✔ Alumni groups

✔ Neighborhood associations

You may choose to get involved with organizations where you have a natural interest in the focus, purpose, or activities of that group. When you've developed your people skills, your attitude, and your awareness, the networking happens naturally. You don't have to do anything in particular to network; every activity is an opportunity to connect and contribute.

List the various parts of your life in which you have goals and specific interests. Identify the support systems you have for each of these aspects of your life. Determine in which areas in your life you would like to have more support and begin to network to find the appropriate groups and organizations.

For example, if your goal is to speak to teenagers about your experience growing up with a handicap, consider groups like the Toastmasters or the National Speakers Association, as well as church youth groups.

You don't know where that next job or client or big opportunity is going to come from. You don't have to know. All you have to do is be aware, be considerate, and be available. Your next opportunity could show up with someone you've known your whole life or with someone you have a ten-minute conversation with in the bleachers of your child's first band concert. Do your part, and the spirit of networking will take care of the rest.

Networking on the dance floor

One of my hobbies is dancing. I have always loved dancing and music and movement. Before my first worlds competition, I was talking with a friend about how I should be using that time to work, that this was a bad time of year to take five days off for a dance competition. As my thoughts raged on, my friend calmly responded, "You know, it's possible that you could meet someone there who wants to hire you for their company or conference." I was tired and nervous and had gotten into a negative spiral of thoughts, and I needed my friend to remind me of the philosophy I teach.

Two weeks after returning to Houston from the competition in Canada, I got an e-mail from Tami Augustyn, girlfriend and dance partner of my dance instructor, saying that she had given my name to the people she worked with and recommended me as a speaker for one of their meetings.

I had never approached Tami about doing business with her company. I had never even initiated a conversation about what I do. But in being around each other during dance practice and during the competition in Canada, we got to know each other and chatted about our careers. She took the initiative to mention me at her office. Tami took a simple conversation and added awareness, initiative, and action. She is a great example of a powerful networker, with her interest in creating connections and opportunities.

Networking can happen anytime, anywhere, with anyone. You never know. The universe doesn't go on hold just because you aren't in your normal environment or the "business" environment where you think you will discover opportunities. Even I forget this sometimes. Trust the process. Set up systems and reminders in your life and develop habits that keep you interacting with people. Even when you forget that you're networking, your network will be growing all around you.

Volunteering enables you to give and receive

Jason was on the board of the nonprofit agency where I was the executive director. Jason is a very successful businessman and is always giving to the community through his participation in various organizations and activities. As a volunteer coach of his child's soccer team, he got to know a lot of the parents well. Although their conversations were mainly about soccer, school, kids, grades, and so on, they also learned about each other's lives and careers.

Without Jason's ever asking for business or even being the one to bring it up, many of those parents became clients of Jason's CPA firm. Jason was simply doing what made sense for him as a parent: being involved with his son's life and activities. He certainly didn't sign up to be a coach to get more business. However, his participation and involvement led to new business — not to mention new friends and a deeper relationship with his son.

Part IV
Networking Challenges

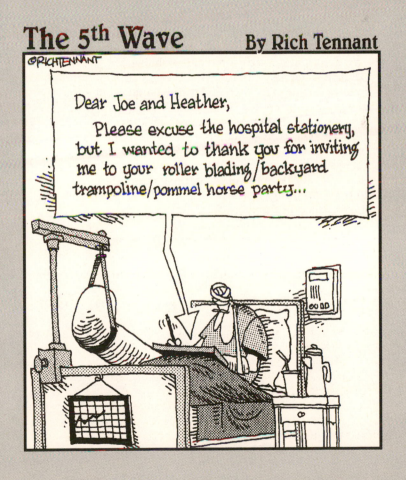

The 5th Wave — By Rich Tennant

In this part . . .

This part addresses some of the challenges you may face when networking. Whether you consider yourself an introvert or extrovert, review the common networking traits of each personality type! And then there's always that age-old question about men and women and how they communicate — and network — with one another! You also find out how to maintain a personal touch through the use of voice mail, e-mail, and the Internet. And I write about the ins and outs of networking etiquette — how to do the right thing at the right time and lessen the risk of offending anybody.

Chapter 14

Personality and Style Differences

• •

In This Chapter

▶ Understanding introverts and extroverts

▶ Making the most of your natural strengths when networking

▶ Networking with the opposite sex and with people from other cultures

• •

On every personality test I ever took, I tested introvert — not borderline, but full-fledged introvert. After working hard to develop my people skills, I decided to take one of those assessments again, thinking that my score may have changed. However, the results showed the same high score on the introvert side of the scale.

Although I have developed my ability to network comfortably and effectively and to enjoy being around other people, my inherent need to have solitude and time to process my thoughts and get rejuvenated by getting away hasn't changed. I have learned that you can be a powerful networker no matter what your personality — extrovert or introvert, shy or outgoing. And you don't have to network a certain way. You have to learn to network in a way that fits your personality, personal style, and lifestyle.

SUCCESS STORY #1

Even Mouseketeers can be shy

In the 1960s, Annette Funicello was one of the biggest and brightest young stars on TV, due to her role on *The Mickey Mouse Club.* Yet, despite her bubbly personality and outgoing persona, she worried about what she refers to as her "extreme shyness." According to her autobiography, she was so concerned that she asked Walt Disney if she could see a psychologist to help her get over her shyness. He promptly refused and explained to her that her charm and charisma were linked to her shyness. She thought that she should go to a psychologist to change herself, but Walt Disney's response was "Why do you want to change?" He saw the shyness as an important piece of what was endearing and appealing about Annette. He helped her to accept her shyness as one of her strengths, rather than as something that needed to be changed.

In this chapter, I write about introverts and extroverts and how both types can tailor their networking efforts to their personalities. I also talk about the differences in male and female networking styles and about interacting with people from other generations and cultures.

Understanding the Strengths and Challenges of Introverts and Extroverts

Are you an introvert or an extrovert, a feeler or a thinker, a perceiver or a judger, a director or a follower? You can place many labels on yourself and others. It's human nature to want to identify characteristics that explain who you are and why you choose to act the way you do. Doing so can be useful, but be careful how you label yourself (and others). Labels can be limiting.

Self-awareness is a powerful aid in understanding and accepting yourself. And self-acceptance is critical for living up to your potential. However, make sure that you don't use a label, like *introvert*, as an excuse. Whether your style is introverted, extroverted, shy, outgoing, or whatever, don't use it as the excuse for not having what you want or not being able to network effectively. Some of the most powerful networkers I know are introverts who have not let their introversion be a weakness. I also know extroverts who have not yet mastered the art of networking because they assume that their outgoing style is sufficient to build a network, and they haven't bothered to deepen other aspects of themselves or their networking.

Introversion and extroversion are two different styles or preferences for how one functions. Where introverts prefer to deal with things internally, extroverts prefer to work through things externally. While introverts don't feel a need for a lot of interaction, extroverts need interaction. Whereas extroverts get energy from people, introverts get energy from their own ideas and thoughts. Being around people tends to make introverts feel drained.

 No matter what your personality or style, you have strengths, weaknesses, challenges, and talents. You have the same opportunity as anyone else to know yourself and to grow. Be willing to uncover new qualities. Be willing to reinvent yourself as you continually grow into who you desire to be.

We tend to support and appreciate extroverts over introverts. Yet, people who can combine and balance both qualities have the greatest value and wisdom in today's society. No matter what your personal style is, you can adapt to incorporate some of the qualities of the opposite style into your way of interacting with yourself and other people. The ideal is to know, accept, and utilize your strengths, and then to work on your weaknesses and improve your ability to relate to people, no matter what their personal style.

SUCCESS STORY #1

Conquering shyness by attracting people to you

When Jan Brogniez was 18 and attending the University of Houston, she couldn't even walk in front of the glass windows of the student center because of the fear that people would laugh at her. She worked hard over the years to get over that shyness, and feels that after 20 years in sales she has gotten over most of it.

Even at 40 and as vice president of sales, she had a chance to see whether the shyness was still there. She was attending an industry-related conference and as soon as she walked into the grand ballroom on the first evening, she froze in her tracks. Jan says, "All I could see were suits and ties. My fear caused my stomach to churn. My boss expected me to network with these people and bring back contacts and leads! I was almost sick."

Jan walked to the side of the room where there was an open space and planted her feet on the floor. She decided that she would let influential people come to her because she was too scared to approach them. It seemed like only a matter of minutes before some of the "suits" started to walk over and introduce themselves to her. One man, who was the president of a well-known company in the industry, stood with her for over an hour. As they talked, others came over to say hello to him and as a result were introduced to Jan. When he introduced Jan, he referred to her company as "one of the best companies in the industry." Jan was thrilled! She had a successful evening of meeting people and making valuable contacts.

Jan learned the importance of being approachable and available. Even though she was scared, she didn't run away. Instead, she decided to be visible and ready to respond when approached. As a result of this experience, Jan became aware of the power of staying clear, centered, and focused. When she is able to stay calm and centered she generates more confidence and seems to attract people to her.

All this has led to Jan's current career. She and her partner, Stacey Hall, teach others how to attract customers. Jan believes that "learning to attract is an effective networking tool, as well as a helpful way for shy people to overcome their fear of approaching people they don't know."

Your attitude and behavior can either turn people off or attract people to you. Think about who you are drawn to talk with when you attend an event. Notice what it is about them that makes you want to meet or talk with them. And identify what can you do that will make people want to meet and talk with you.

Networking strengths of the introvert

Introverts have many natural strengths that contribute to their effectiveness as networkers:

> ✔ They tend to like to think things through before speaking, which means that they have a strong ability to come across as thoughtful, prepared, and focused.

✔ They tend to dislike too much stimulation and are drawn to their inner nature, so they often exhibit a highly developed ability to concentrate and focus on one thing at a time. When they use this ability to concentrate and focus on the people they meet — thus conveying courtesy, interest, and respect — introverts develop immediate rapport and trust.

✔ They can tap into their intuition in order to know how to best respond to people and circumstances.

✔ They tend to be good listeners because they don't feel like they have to talk in order to connect with other people. Their quiet nature enables them to relate to others in a considerate, loyal, and reflective manner. They are seldom perceived as pushy or as coming across too strongly. People find them approachable rather than intimidating. They may therefore attract others who desire to connect.

✔ Their modesty ensures that they never need worry about coming across as arrogant.

✔ They tend to observe people and situations prior to making decisions and thus they gather valuable information.

✔ They're interested in having a congruent inner and outer life. Because of their strong drive to go within, they can be great sources of well thought-out and intuitive ideas.

✔ Their sensitivity to outer stimuli becomes a strength in their ability to pick up on and relate to others' needs, desires, and feelings. They convey a concern for others. This enhances their natural ability to be interested and empathetic.

✔ They have no need to be overly gregarious and therefore are less likely to be too energetic or enthusiastic.

✔ They're able to be present to people because they don't like to have a lot of things going on at once. They give thought to what people tell them, which shows up as attentiveness and interest.

Networking challenges of the introvert

Introverts have some challenges in networking. Here are some examples:

✔ Because they generate energy from within, introverts at times withdraw from people in order to have time to themselves. Introverts actually *need* time to themselves. Too much interaction, activity, or noise can be overly stimulating, draining their energy and making them tired, quiet, and withdrawn. As a result, they may miss out on opportunities to be around people because they have already had all the interaction they can handle.

✔ The tendency to be reflective, if taken to the extreme, leads introverts to be so focused on themselves that they miss opportunities to connect with others. Sometimes introverts appear hard to get to know. They may even appear aloof because they monitor their involvement and become protective of their energy. All this can contribute to their being private to the point that others don't really know them.

✔ Because they like to think through decisions rather than jump on opportunities, they may be too late with their responses. When opportunities are happening all around them, they appear to be one step behind.

✔ They're stimulated by their inner world rather than the outer world of people and things — all the things that are part of the business culture. American culture tends to be geared to the extrovert with lots of outer stimuli and encouragement to respond to that stimuli. People are seldom encouraged to slow down, stay home, and be quiet.

✔ Introverts tend to gravitate to the people they already know because it's comfortable and doesn't require as much energy as meeting and interacting with new people.

✔ They often appear shy and quiet because they sometimes take a backseat to others during a conversation. Introverts may have a lot of valuable information that never gets shared because getting heard appears to take to much effort. Also, they often don't acknowledge the value of what they have to offer.

✔ Because they are sensitive to outer stimuli, they may respond strongly to interruptions and distractions.

Although introverts don't need to talk a lot and don't like to bother with people a lot, they can be powerful networkers by utilizing their strengths to make powerful connections. They can learn to balance their need for solitude with their ability to be social. They can learn to conserve their energy and choose when and where to engage with others. They can be masterful networkers.

Ways for introverts to develop their networking effectiveness

If you are an introvert, you may have second thoughts about whether you even want to enter that crowded room as you stand in the doorway. Yet the truth is that people want to connect with one other. The only way to make friends is by talking to strangers, and the only way to expand your network is by talking with strangers.

After you have the experience of making a connection in a room full of strangers, you have a greater awareness of what's possible with networking and how important and valuable it can be. Introverts can't become extroverts; however, introverts must learn how to succeed in a people-oriented world.

Business is all about people, and life is about people relating to one another. There are different ways to connect. There is no one right way. You need to find a way that works for you.

If you are an introvert, here are some specific areas to focus on to improve your effectiveness as a networker:

- ✔ **Develop a willingness to include others in your life.** Even if you are very comfortable on your own, don't be afraid to ask others for help, support, and information, and give people a chance to get involved in your life. You must also expand your willingness to speak up and give input to others. Realize that your ideas are valuable and find ways to share them with others.

- ✔ **Prepare for interactions.** The more prepared you are, the more likely you will be to feel comfortable and confident when talking with people. Learn as much as you can about an individual before you call on him or her. Research the situations you will be in so that you have plenty of information ahead of time.

- ✔ **Interact with people in a one-on-one environment.** Get to know people individually so that when you see them at a group meeting or event, you already have a relationship that makes it easier to go over and talk with them.

- ✔ **Ask questions.** Asking questions enables you to learn about the other person while taking the attention off of yourself. Questions give you time to warm up to the other person. Get other people talking and then use easy prompters, such as "How interesting" or "Tell me more," to stay in the conversation

- ✔ **Realize that it's understandable to feel awkward at times and that you can choose to participate even you feel awkward.** Don't wait for your feelings to change before you venture outward with your networking. Remind yourself that feeling what you feel is okay — you can still choose to network. Your feelings do not need to dictate your actions. Feelings are often based on misinterpreted information and ideas.

- ✔ **Develop a methodology for connecting with people.** Create a conversation initiator that you're comfortable with and that always works for you. Say hi to the host of a party as soon as you get there so that you can warm up your social skills. Find someone to approach who is standing alone. Invite someone to attend networking events with you so that you can network in tandem.

- ✔ **Do something to help you relax.** You may take a deep breath before you enter the room or picture yourself effortlessly and graciously speaking to anyone who comes over to you. Or maybe you have an affirmation or mantra that you repeat to yourself.

✔ **Self-affirm.** Remind yourself that you are important, your ideas are valuable, what you have to say is important, and networking is important. Remind yourself that networking is an acceptable and natural activity that people do all the time, everywhere.

✔ **Be willing to make your ideas known and your resources shared.** Practice speaking up so that doing so becomes easier and easier. Realize that networking is more important than minimizing your discomfort regarding speaking to people.

✔ **Remember that events are moments in time.** If you are panicking at the thought of attending a business or social event and having to network, remind yourself that the event will not go on indefinitely — you can retreat to your home later. Knowing that you'll have quiet and comfort later can help you come out of your shell for periods of time. Develop some guidelines for yourself that support you in stepping out of your comfort zone one little step at a time. Example: I will attend this event and talk with at least three people. I will go the event, stay for at least 30 minutes, and then give myself permission to leave, or stay if I so choose.

✔ **Change your thought patterns.** Instead of thinking about interactions as you typically do, ask yourself "How would I approach this person if I felt confident?" or "What would I say to this person if I weren't concerned about how I was going to come across?"

✔ **Learn to take networking gradually.** Sometimes a simple hello is all you need to invite someone to connect with you. Talk directly to one person at a time, look the person in his or her eyes, and say the person's name. Go at your own pace. Don't think that you have to keep up with the pace of others if their pace doesn't work for you.

✔ **Observe how others interact and learn from them.** Introverts learn well by watching and observing others. Based on what you observe, you can practice networking by planning what you're going to say and do.

Networking strengths of the extrovert

Extroverts typically have the following qualities that make them good networkers:

✔ They can initiate and carry on conversations with people in any situation. They are at ease with small talk and chitchat. Being engaged in conversations is easy and natural for them because they process information through conversations. They think things through by talking.

✔ They are social creatures who enjoy being around people. They are drawn to activity and noise. They're able to handle a lot of outer stimuli and don't require a lot of solitude or quiet. Their focus is outward. They actually need interactions with others or they begin to feel out of sorts.

✔ They tend to think out loud, which means that people know what's going on with them and thus have a greater ability to support their needs and desires.

✔ They tend to be assertive, which means that they usually speak up and ask for what they want and need and expect people to respond. They tend to speak freely about their accomplishments, goals, and projects as a natural and expected form of self-expression.

✔ Because they think out loud and respond positively to noise and activity, extroverts can be very effective brainstormers. They don't have to think ideas through before expressing them. Plus, they tend to make quick decisions, which allows them to respond quickly to opportunities that come to them via their network.

✔ Because they are energized by outer stimuli, they have the energy to be around people and stay involved in activities for a long period.

Networking challenges of the extrovert

Although the extrovert personality style is a naturally outgoing one, extroverts do have some challenges in networking:

✔ Their tendency to speak without thinking sometimes leads them to say things that they obviously haven't thought through. This can make them come across as too forthright and cause them to be inconsiderate of others.

✔ They can be so stimulated by interactions that they may ramble or take over a conversation. By doing so, extroverts can come across as cold, self-centered, and impersonal. They may so enjoy being social that they don't really use the social opportunities to network. They need to learn how to switch gears and listen sometimes.

✔ Because they make quick decisions, extroverts at times forget to include others in the decision-making process. It can appear that they don't consider others' thoughts, ideas, and feelings.

✔ They may come across as intimidating and aggressive to people who are quiet, shy, and less assertive. Because they tend to take action before they think, they sometimes miss out on making the best use of conversations and networking opportunities.

Ways for extroverts to develop their networking effectiveness

If you are an extrovert, here are some ways to ensure that you are being as effective as possible as you network:

Unexpected resources in unexpected places

Ryan and his wife went to a party at the home of one of her coworkers. Not knowing anyone there other than his wife, Ryan felt awkward and uncomfortable, kind of on the fringe. In fact, he was standing off by himself at one point when he noticed another guy standing off by himself. They both seemed to be in the same situation, so he said hi and initiated a conversation.

In the process of having a casual conversation with this man, Ryan found out that he was a bricklayer and that he was currently looking for work. Ryan and his wife had recently decided to sell their house and had already found a new home. They had, however, just found out that in order to continue on with the contract to sell their home (which was built in 1925), they needed to have some work done on their chimney right away. So Ryan told this guy about his 75-year-old home with the chimney. The guy offered to do the chimney work that Ryan needed done at half the price that others were asking. Because of a simple conversation, Ryan got exactly what he needed, in a timely manner, and at half the price.

✔ **Learn how to give your attention to others.** Rather than being the conversationalist all the time, give people your attention Make sure that your words are not falling on deaf ears and that people are engaged in conversation with you. Create more dialogues than monologues.

✔ **Find out what others want to talk about.** Don't race off to talk about your favorite topics or stories. Remember that your purpose is not just to converse, but also to discover common interests and experiences and to find ways to be a resource for others.

✔ **Follow through on your conversations.** Don't just enjoy the conversation for conversation's sake. Don't get so carried away with how fun conversations are that you forget to create value and be there for people after the event.

✔ **Show an interest by asking questions.** Get curious and be really interested in learning about others.

✔ **Be aware of others' wants and needs.** Be conscious of when people are feeling uncomfortable or trapped in a conversation. Learn how to put people at ease. Be in control of yourself so that you can control your enthusiasm and excitement and interact appropriately for the event and the conversation.

Understanding and tolerating personality differences

Laura notices the difference between her introversion and her husband's extroversion when they go camping. At the end of the day, she wants to relax and read. However, her husband wanders around the campsite and talks with everyone. When he starts doing that, she becomes concerned that he'll have everyone stopping by their campsite to chat when all she wants is peace and quiet. Laura isn't shy; she just enjoys her downtime. However, if people approach her and attempt to engage her in conversation when she's trying to maintain her personal space, she may come across as shy, aloof, and unfriendly. This is an example of why it's important for extroverts to be aware of and willing to honor the introvert's inner needs rather than expecting introverts to be talkative and social all the time.

Looking at the Differences between Men and Women

Just as each personality style has strengths and weaknesses, each gender has strengths and weaknesses regarding their natural style of networking. The principles of networking are the same whether you're male or female, though. And the process of connecting, communicating, and sharing resources is universal, whether you choose a typically male networking environment, such as the golf course or a college football game, or a typically female one, such as a professional women's conference or a church meeting.

Note: The differences that I talk about are based on stereotypes and generalities. Women may be perceived as being better listeners, and men may be perceived as being more assertive. However, men can be great listeners and women can be assertive. Everyone is served when you take steps to erase the stereotypes and be a unique and powerful individual.

Today, some gender stereotypes are dissolving as both men and women are networking in business and social environments to further their personal and professional lives.

For both genders, the goal is to network in a professional, courteous, and respectful manner with people of the same gender and across gender lines — to reach out to one another in the workplace, in the community, and in social settings.

Women's strengths

Some of the strengths that we attribute to women are important parts of what it takes to be a masterful networker:

- ✔ Relationship building
- ✔ Listening
- ✔ Caring
- ✔ Focusing on others
- ✔ Multitasking

Although many women are naturally talented at networking, many women hold back because they confuse assertiveness with aggressiveness. Once you give yourself permission, as a woman, to ask for what you want and to be a powerful resource for others, you can utilize your strengths as a woman to be a naturally powerful networker.

Whether it is to find a job, a babysitter, a trusted investment advisor, a good hairdresser, a reliable auto mechanic, or a source for a business loan, women often tap into each other's networks easily and naturally to enhance their lives. What's shifting today is that women are enjoying and expanding their networking and taking pride in their ability to network effectively.

Women are coming together to share, contribute, and create new opportunities for themselves, their companies, and our world. A gathering of women tends to be very open and generate lots of leads, ideas, support, and information for everyone in the group.

Corporations are responding to the influx of women into executive roles in the workplace by corporate initiatives that encourage and support networking and mentoring among their professional women. But women aren't by any means waiting for organizations and corporations to create networking opportunities for them. Women are creating networks on their own.

Women sometimes feel disadvantaged when men get together for golf or for a drink after work. But plenty of men spend time with the guys and still don't have the same networking success as women who know how to position themselves as powerful resources in the business world. Women have gained momentum and made their own mark by networking over breakfast, dinner, or coffee, at corporate meetings and conferences, on the boards of nonprofit organizations, and on the golf course. Women realize that their business success is due to more than good ideas and solid business skills; it lies in their ability to network effectively.

Women need to take care that they don't get so immersed in the social atmosphere of a group event that they lose focus of the business goals and opportunities that they can share with each other. Women can get so into enjoying companionship and friendships that they neglect to provide the direction to produce major results. It is as if they think at times that doing business will dilute fun and friendship. However, supporting the success and growth of other women's businesses *deepens* friendships.

Men's strengths

The strengths that enhance one's networking effectiveness that are commonly considered masculine include

- Being assertive.
- Speaking up.
- Being a resource for others.
- Being a valued team player.
- Being action oriented.

While many men are blessed with these networking strengths, men sometimes focus too much on producing results and miss out on making connections and developing the relatedness that leads to long-term repeat results.

A gathering of men tends to lead to lots of interesting and valuable conversations. At the same time, there may be less open sharing of information and ideas than in a gathering of women (unless the group is small and has already developed a lot of trust and closeness). Men tend to play their cards close to their chests.

Networking with Various Cultures and Generations

Baby Boomers grew up in a different environment than Generation Xers. People in the United States have a different way of networking and conducting business than people in other countries, and there are regional differences within the United States. And different companies have different cultures, policies, and guidelines for the way people are expected to relate and interact with one another.

Every day, you deal with the differences of the people in the world. Companies are comprised of a mix of people from various countries, cultures, religions, and races. More companies are conducting business internationally than ever before.

All of this can make it difficult to know how to communicate and connect with others in an effective and appropriate manner. Yet the basics of networking — treating people with respect and dignity and graciously supporting each other's successes — are universal and cross all cultural and generational barriers.

At the same time, learning about other cultures is important in order to honor others in your interactions. Here are a couple of tips:

✔ When you know that you're going to be meeting people from another country, another company, or a different area of the country, do your research. Learn everything you can about their spoken and unspoken ways of relating, networking, and doing business with one other.

✔ Don't expect others to accommodate you. Be gracious and willing to expand your own horizons by knowing how to include and honor others.

You don't have to change your style, although your networking will be more powerful and effective if you're willing to expand your style to make it better suited for interacting with others.

For more information on cross-cultural etiquette, please see *Business Etiquette For Dummies* by Sue Fox (Hungry Minds, Inc.).

This Is the Way I Am: Choosing What to Accept and What to Work On

You are a growing, evolving human being. You have certain traits and needs that are basic to who you are, and at the same time you have the opportunity to expand your abilities and develop capacities that are currently untapped.

Accept everything about yourself and then identify areas where you would be pleased to experience growth. You can set goals for yourself to support your growth and development. However, you need to follow some guidelines as you set your goals and take steps to achieve them:

✔ **Set goals that relate to actions you will take, but don't set goals to change your natural inclinations.** You may continue to feel hesitant about some social situations, and at the same time discover that you can behave differently. It's the same thing as anger management. People learn how to behave differently when they feel angry rather than to unrealistically think that they will never feel anger. However, as you begin to take different actions and make different choices, you may discover that your thoughts and feelings adjust accordingly.

When attending a networking event, you may decide to introduce yourself to at least two new people even if you feel nervous about being there. Or you could decide to make eye contact with people you meet as you shake their hands. Giving yourself something to do may help to take your focus off your feelings and your discomfort. Even though I enjoy social activities and interactions, I don't expect myself to be the first to arrive and the last to leave. And I always monitor my participation to some degree.

✔ **Stretch yourself, but don't think that you have to run a marathon before you've run a 10K.** For example, rather than thinking that you need to go to a networking event and mingle for the whole two hours, go for 45 minutes and actively network during that time. Then pat yourself on the back, say job well done, and leave if you've had enough for one event.

✔ **Don't assert to yourself in vague terms that you are going to become "more friendly" or "more talkative" or "more outgoing" or "more approachable."** Instead, give yourself specific parameters of things that you will do that help you be more friendly, talkative, outgoing, or approachable. Examples include:

- "I will talk to at least five people tonight for at least five minutes each."

- "I will say hi to people that I don't know."

- "I will invite someone from the chamber to meet me for lunch once a month."

✔ **Realize that the feelings of fear, discomfort, or awkwardness you have are felt by a majority of the people you will meet when you network.** Also, notice that the feelings you're having are a result of thoughts that you're having. Notice the thoughts, challenge the thoughts, and try focusing on thoughts that generate more supportive feelings. Simply by choosing new thoughts, you will start generating feelings of assurance, confidence, ease, relief, and comfort.

Set a few goals (new actions and behaviors) that will be steppingstones to expand your comfort zone and develop new aspects of your personality and networking style. Remember that this is not about changing your personality. You want to honor your personality and strengths and expand yourself.

Here's an example: Angela typically attends conventions with great intentions but then gets overwhelmed and nervous by the crowds of people and withdraws. Her goals could include the following:

✔ Initiate conversations with the people sitting next to me at the seminar sessions.

✔ At least once during the conference, at the end of the session, introduce myself to the seminar leader and say thanks.

✔ Review the roster of conference attendees to identify who I know or want to meet there, and then make a point to look for those people in order to say hello.

Interpreting Others' Behavior with an Attitude of Curiosity

People interpret others' behavior in many ways. For example, an outspoken person may interpret a quiet person's silence as meaning that the silent person is not interested, is angry, is silently thinking badly of him or her, or is silently agreeing with him or her. Be aware of your interpretations, and realize that they are interpretations and not necessarily the truth.

Developing your ability to be interested in people will diminish any tendency to be judgmental. From a mindset of curiosity, your response to people's actions and behaviors is "I wonder why they think that way?" or "I wonder why they did that?" Curiosity generates an interest in knowing what's behind their actions and thoughts rather than thinking that you already know. The only way you can judge and blame is when you think you know. You think you know everything that there is to know about the situation, which gives you the right to judge.

Be curious not from a place of being nosy, but from a place of understanding and developing a bond. Interest implies value, and a masterful networker treats people with value and therefore creates value.

Finding role models

You may know people who have developed the types of behaviors that you would like to exhibit in networking situations. Notice what they say, what facial expressions and body language they use. You don't need to mimic them or try to become like them. However, certain aspects of their behavior could serve as a good model for what would work for you. You can even keep a particular person in mind as you approach an interaction and think, "Now what might Bill say in this situation?" or "I wonder how Jane would handle this?"

Honoring Yourself and Others

You have your own mix of strengths, skills, and character traits. Your uniqueness sets you apart from everyone else. At the same time, you have many things in common with everyone in your network. Being aware of the differences helps you understand the needs and wants of people with different personalities, upbringings, backgrounds, and so on. However, it also helps to know the similarities so that you can relate to and include others and stay connected rather than isolating yourself or thinking that you are the only one with certain needs.

There are basic human needs and desires, such as a need for connection, love, safety, comfort, success, validation, health, and well-being. People may fulfill those needs differently, yet everyone can relate to these similar needs and desires and help each other lead fulfilling lives.

There is no surefire rule that that you can follow to make yourself a success. For every person who became a success by doing X, someone else became a success by doing Z. Whatever your style, personality, background, or gender, you have access to success through the utilization of your strengths. Although there is no specific personality style that is required, some basic guidelines apply to everyone:

✔ To be an effective networker requires discovering your strengths and accepting and building on those strengths, while at the same time expanding your comfort zone to explore and develop new skills and characteristics. You don't change your personality; you honor and expand your awareness of who you are as a being beyond the core personality that defines you.

✔ To be effective with others, you must accept them and accept that your differences can be an opportunity to expand your awareness. Being around people who have different strengths and personalities than yours can help you bring out an undeveloped side or characteristic within yourself. Other people can show you that there's more than one way to get things done and be successful. A diverse network will provide you with ideas beyond what you would normally have. Diversity and differences add depth and breadth to your network.

Chapter 15

The High-Tech Connection

Because technology influences our lives in major ways every day, it's easy to think that being an effective and successful person in today's world is all about using technology. And to a certain extent that's true: Today's technology is providing quicker, easier access to volumes of information. Just as the advent of trains, planes, radio, and television influenced our culture and how we live, computers, voice mail, and other types of technology are giving us new ways to spend our time. Because of the computers and the Internet, people are restructuring their lives, sometimes spending hours every day surfing the Web, checking out Web sites, and sending and answering e-mails.

Technology won't ever replace the human need to connect, relate, and be social creatures. However, technology is providing numerous ways for people to network by staying in touch and exchanging information via the Internet.

Technology provides you with an opportunity to maintain strong and lasting relationships with others when you can't be with them in person.

Notice whether you use voice mail as a means for connection or as something to hide behind to avoid real conversations. Also, be aware of any tendency to use e-mail to avoid personal interactions. Voice mail and e-mail are meant to be useful communication tools for staying in touch and conveying valuable information. However, these are not the best communication tools for every situation. You must choose whether voice mail, e-mail, over the phone, or face-to-face communication is your best option in a particular situation.

Success in this high-tech age requires mastering the art of effective communication via voice mail and e-mail, knowing how to connect with people quickly when people are on the go, and understanding how to build relationships across modems, cables, and communication lines. In other words, what is needed to harness technology's power is the ability to actively combine your human skills with your tech skills. Combining the human with the technical is what this chapter is all about.

People you access through the Web are real people just like you, your friends, your customers, and your neighbors. Technology will never replace the human desire for face-to-face communication with these people.

Technology is serving its purpose when you are using it to serve, contribute to, and enhance your relationships. How you, as an individual, use the tool of technology is what's important.

I've Got that Phone Number Here Somewhere!

You will meet a lot of people throughout your life; however, to be effective with your networking, you need a way to keep track of the phone numbers and addresses of the people in your network.

I use a contact management software program (a database program) to keep me on track while at the same time helping me keep track of my network. This program allows me to access contact information by last name, company name, industry, and a multitude of other categories.

So if I meet you at a networking event and I want to contact you a couple weeks later but can't quite remember your name, I can do a search on industry, or company name, or the date when I met you, or even the event where I met you. There is a strong likelihood that one of those searches will help me find you and your contact information.

Through the use of this system, I can also easily send e-mails to groups of people (my breakfast club, family, a group of girlfriends, and so on). I can remind myself to follow up with you, stay in touch with you, and send you certain information. My database management system is the safety vault of my network. It's where all the valuable information is stored. As a bonus, the information is organized for easy access and use.

Remember to back up your data on a regular basis so that you don't lose all that valuable information about your contacts.

You can synchronize the data in your computer onto a palm device so that you can have those names and phone numbers at your fingertips.

You can be a great networker, but if you're not organized and don't have a system for keeping track of contacts, then much of the value of your network can be lost.

Networking through the Web

Networking used to revolve around those activities in which you meet and greet people in a room of strangers. Now, technology gives you access to strangers around the world through cyberspace. Online networking gives you a virtual room of strangers where you can mix and mingle to find the connections you desire. You may then choose to make phone calls and even have face-to-face encounters in order to add the human connection to the cyber interaction.

The Internet is a powerful tool for connecting with others, finding information, and exchanging information. It can be a valuable vehicle for communicating with individuals and groups of people. Just as there are many ways of being in communication off of the Web (letters, memos, meetings, voice mails, and fax), there are various ways to be in communication via the Web.

Web communication can occur through e-mail, discussion groups, chatrooms, bulletin boards, Web links, and more. Each of these vehicles can be used to research information, plan events, collaborate on projects, and announce new products. Still, the core of all this activity is building and maintaining connections. The best benefit of technology is more ways to cultivate strong connections with other people.

Using the Internet to find information

You can use the Internet to conduct research that will help you grow your business. You may want to learn more about a particular company that you plan to call on as a prospective client. By going to that company's Web site and reviewing its information, you will be much better prepared to know how who to call on and how to be of service to the company.

You can also research your industry and related industries that affect your business. Some of this research can be done through e-zines or electronic newsletters. Find out what e-zines, newsletters, and magazines your clients tend to read and you can stay up to date on their needs and interests by reading the same literature. The Internet can help you stay current, up to date, and in the know.

Almost any information you could hope to find is available through the Internet. You may have to surf, search, and learn how to best use some of the directories and search engines. However, you shouldn't have to spend much time practicing before you can quickly locate the information you want.

Be sure to validate and verify information that you find on the Internet or receive via e-mail. Realize that some information is opinion rather than fact. Consider checking with the source of the information and reviewing other sites and sources to verify accuracy.

Making yourself visible and helping others do the same

Your Web site exposes you to more individuals than you could ever contact on your own. It enables you to market yourself, making it easy for people to find you, learn all about your products and services, and express an interest with the just the click of a mouse.

Consider partnering with other businesses to put reciprocal links on each other's sites. Choose to link to sites as a way of networking and passing along information to others.

Promoting your business

The Web gives you a place to present, showcase, advertise, and sell your wares to people all over the world. One of the ways to promote your business over the Web and to give value to your clients, customers, and Web site visitors is with an electronic magazine, newsletter, or tip of the day. Make sure that the information you provide is valuable and not purely promotional. Send it only to people who have requested it and yet give people plenty of ways to find out about it in order to subscribe. Also be sure to give people an easy way to unsubscribe from the list if they so choose. You may choose to have your electronic publication come out daily, weekly, monthly, bimonthly, quarterly, or just whenever you feel the urge. Choose a frequency that you know you will be able to maintain.

Making contacts and finding old friends

The Web can be instrumental in helping you stay in touch with people, maintain connections, and even reconnect with people that you lost touch with somewhere over the years. The Web has left us with very little reason to ever say we can't find someone or don't know how to reach someone.

One of my best high school buddies tracked me down years after we lost touch and went our separate ways. He found my Web site and called my office and left a voice mail for me. We left several messages on each other's voice mail until we connected in person. As a result, I visited with him and his family on my next business trip to Atlanta. We then exchanged e-mail addresses as a way to stay in touch with each other. The Internet, voice mail, and e-mail all played a role in reconnecting and finding ways to maintain that connection.

Contacts can be made through the Web by accessing online networks of alumni associations and industry trade groups. You can search the database on some of these sites by graduation year, place of residency, industry, and other helpful criteria. This allows you to do your own searching to find people with whom you have something in common and a good reason to make a connection.

The Internet can help you find people with similar interests through search engines and lists. If you are looking for associations and organizations of people in your industry, you can find them by typing the industry name into a search engine. Most associations have Web sites that are typically the name or acronym of their name followed by `.org`. Typically, their Web sites give you valuable information about the industry, a list of chapters of the association around the country, a listing of members, association activities, and conferences and conventions. You also have access to individuals and companies in your industry that have their own Web sites.

An alumni group can be an excellent and rewarding networking group. If your alumni association is not online, suggest the use of the Web to your alumni office as a tool for members to post announcements and job opportunities and to access data on other alumni.

Types of networking Web sites available

There are some Web sites that can assist you in accessing information and contacts that can support your networking. `Industryinsite.com` provides a network of professionals from a wide range of industries (accounting to publishing, retail to entertainment) that you can access. It also has helpful business information.

Although nothing can replace face-to-face contact, online networking can help you find people who you want to meet. Sites such as `switchboard.com` and `whitepages.com` can help you locate people you have lost touch with and other people you want to contact.

Using the Internet to Create Community

Humans have a natural need to feel a sense of belonging and to be part of one or several communities. You may have a church community and a neighborhood community. Your family is a community. Your business provides you with a professional community. Any special interests or hobbies that you have also provide you with community.

The Internet allows people to create community as well. No matter what your interests, hobbies, demographics, or career, groups that help you connect with like-minded individuals are available on the Web. By using the Internet, your community extends beyond your physical environment to encompass people around the world. Now you can actually be part of a global community and have a global presence.

Friends of Emily

When my friend Emily became ill with cancer, one of her friends thought of creating an e-group on the Web so that all of us who loved and were concerned about Emily could be in touch and in communication with one another.

We used the e-group to maintain a schedule of friends who offered to take turns providing meals for the family and spending time visiting with Emily. It was a great idea. I could go into the e-group, check the schedule, and sign myself up. It was easy for me to pick a good time to go and easy for Susan (one of Emily's best friends) to know that Emily was taken care of without having to make 40 phone calls, leave messages, and coordinate everyone's schedule.

Occasionally, someone would leave a message about what it was like to be with Emily and give an update on how she was doing. Emily's husband, Scott, began to leave messages about how she was doing and what was needed. When Emily was moved to the hospice, the e-mails picked up in terms of volume and depth.

It became very common for the e-mails to be of the goose-bump variety because there was such a sense of family and community. Even the friends of Emily who had never met each other experienced a sense of knowing one another.

The e-group provided Scott, Emily's husband, with a way to feel connected with family and friends at a time when one can understandably feel very alone, isolated, and disconnected from the rest of the world. Through e-mail, Scott was able to share his experience of being with Emily, touch on the range of emotions that he was dealing with, and also share how much he appreciated the support of everyone.

The Friends of Emily e-group became a community support system, not just for Emily, for all of us as we faced our own grief, gratitude, and appreciation for friends and life. The experience is difficult to put into words. The e-group provided Emily's family and friends with a way to be with her as she completed her life here on earth, and it was a life-changing experience for everyone involved.

Creating community through e-groups

An e-group can be set up on the Internet so that everyone from a designated group has access to member information, meetings, calendars, and so on. An e-group provides each member of the group with the capability to send one message that goes to everyone. It also provides a place where people can review previous messages sent and received by members of the group.

Using the Internet to enhance family community

My family, like most families, is spread out. We range from Texas to North Carolina with cousins and relatives in Tennessee, Ohio, and Missouri. And just like most families, we care about each other and mean to stay in touch and be involved in each other's lives. Unfortunately, just like most families, time can fly by without us seeing or being in contact with one another.

And then came e-mail. I remember when I first approached my Mom about e-mail. She wasn't too sure, but she was willing to give it a try. She had a computer and used it mainly for recipes, finances, and playing computer games (as good a use of computers as anything!). She was willing to set up an e-mail account on a one-month trial basis and I thought that might be as far as it went. However, we began to e-mail each other and I noticed that even though I wouldn't sit down and write out a letter, I would easily sit down and write an e-mail and think of more and more things to say during the writing. Often, we found ourselves sending an e-mail and then calling and pretty much repeating everything we had just sent in the e-mail. To my surprise and pleasure, she was willing to keep the e-mail program after the trial month. That was several years ago. We don't talk any less on the phone than we did before. It's just that e-mail gives us an additional means for being in touch.

Then my brother set up an e-group for our family. We can leave messages for each other and post announcements and photos. We have information (names, addresses, phone numbers, e-mail addresses, birth dates, and so on) on extended family members we would not normally be in touch with (relatives by marriage and their relatives). It's almost like creating an e-group of your family tree and it can be as simple or extensive as you desire.

Again, the family e-group and e-mails will never replace sitting around the table together for a meal or playing games in front of the fireplace. Yet, technology gives you a way to stay in touch with relatives all around the country who you may otherwise lose touch with and keeps you more up to date on what's happening in each other's life.

How professional communities can utilize the Internet

Initiate the development of Web sites or e-groups for the groups and organizations that you belong to so that members and participants can easily disseminate information, stay in touch, and stay abreast of what's happening.

If you don't know how to set up an e-group or develop a Web site, network with some of the people you know to find out who they have used to develop their Web site. You are bound to have some people in your network who have computer knowledge and would be glad to help you out.

The Windsor Club is a professional networking group that I've belonged to for ten years. It meets twice a month on Thursday mornings for breakfast, networking, and programs. Our purpose as a group is to support each other, our businesses, and the community. We have 20-plus members — business owners from all different industries and professions. Don Clerc, owner of Clerc Computer Consulting, took it on himself to get us on the Web. He created a Web site that evolved into an e-group. We can now easily send one message that goes out to all the members as reminders of meetings, social activities, or important news about a member (celebration, tragedy, or request).

Any member can go to the site to check out the schedule of meetings, find out who the speaker is for the next meeting, get a phone number or address of another member, or get the address of last month's speaker in order to send a thank-you. Rather than calling everyone to remind them of meetings or special events, the e-group lists the meeting or event on the calendar and a single e-mail message is sent to the whole group.

The site also includes a directory of information on each member, which helps new members become more familiar with everyone in the club.

Creating a Web site or e-group for your organization provides a way to easily mantain connections and relay information.

I'll Just Send Them an E-Mail . . .

It's quick. It's easy. It's almost like magic. With electronic mail, you instantly send a message and, voilà, it appears in an e-mail box that can be on the other side of the world. In the year 2000, approximately 116 million Americans, or 41.5 percent of U.S. households (according to the U.S. Department of Commerce), had e-mail accounts and e-mail access.

Think about what that makes possible! Information used to take days, weeks, or even months to get to some locations. Now, through the Internet and e-mail, you can access and distribute information within minutes. No sooner is there an event, an idea, a new product release, or a new discovery than e-mails begin to circle the globe with commentaries, photos, surveys, and so on. The Internet is a powerful tool for social interaction, global connection, and marketing promotions.

Networking via e-mail

E-mail can be an efficient way to pass information to the people in your network.

When you discover a Web site that would be of value or interest to someone you know, send him or her an e-mail message passing the information along. Include the address of the site as a hyperlink. Here's an example:

> Larry,
>
> I just came across a Web site that might be of value and interest to you. It tells how . . . If you want to check it out, click on www.xxxxxxx.com.
>
> Donna

You can give referrals and leads via e-mail, such as the following:

> Jim,
>
> I recently met Jake Rogers and wanted to encourage you to contact him about . . . You can reach him at xxx-xxx-xxxx or email@internet.com. Let me know if I can be of any help.
>
> Best wishes,
>
> Jane

You can even make requests via e-mail:

> Jack,
>
> I'm looking for . . . Please let me know of anyone you would suggest that could be of help to me. Any recommendations you can make will be greatly appreciated.
>
> Thanks and let me know how I can be of support to you.
>
> Regards,
>
> Karen

A quick e-mail can keep the communication lines open between you and someone down the street or on the other side of the world. Occasionally, I'll browse through my e-mail address book to notice whom I haven't been in touch with recently and send out a few quick e-mails. Even if I pick just a few people to make contact with every week, I keep my networking up to date.

Pointers for effective e-mail

Subject headings tell the reader the purpose of your message. What you choose for the subject heading can make a big difference in whether the recipient reads your message right away or not at all.

Don't make up a subject head that makes your message sound urgent when it's not. People will not appreciate feeling tricked into opening your message.

If your reply to a message changes the subject of the original message, then change the subject heading accordingly.

Keep your messages succinct and to the point. Be aware that some people will not bother to scroll all the way through a message and may thus miss information towards the end of the message. So be sure to make your point towards the top of the message. Also, if you have more than one topic to address, send two messages — one topic per e-mail — to make it easy for the other person to respond to each subject. This way the recipient can archive or save each message and easily identify messages later by topic according to the subject heading.

When you must send an e-mail to a list of people, make sure that you use the blind carbon copy (bcc) feature so that you are not giving out other people's e-mail addresses and so that the recipients do not have to wade through a long list of e-mail addresses. Do your best to choose e-mail and Web site addresses that are easy for people to remember. When you work for a company you are probably assigned an e-mail address; however, if you have your own business, remember that your Web address and e-mail are part of your marketing materials.

Be professional. Don't use e-mail to gossip or vent. Don't write anything in an e-mail that you wouldn't be able to say in person. Be aware that not every topic is appropriate for an e-mail. If you're upset with someone, pay the person the courtesy of speaking with him or her face-to-face. Doing so also prevents misunderstandings. For more on this subject, see *Communicating Effectively For Dummies* by Marty Brounstein (Hungry Minds, Inc.).

Do not barrage people with lots of jokes and inspirational stories. Once in a while may be okay, but to pass along most of what comes your way can be way too much and a turn off for people. If you send a lot of junk e-mail, people may immediately delete your messages and then you'll have trouble getting their attention when you do have something important to send.

Use both lowercase and uppercase letters, just as you would in a normal letter. The use of all capital letters comes across as shouting and is aggressive and intrusive. The use of all lowercase letters comes across as unprofessional, very informal, and laid back.

Include a signature file with your e-mail so that people have information about how to be in touch with you. A signature file is, in some ways, the Web version of a business card.

Your signature file includes the information that you want the recipient of your e-mail to know about you. Once you set up a signature file, it's automatically included at the end of all the e-mails that you send. (Or your e-mail program may give you the option of attaching the signature.) Information on how to set up a signature file should be available through your e-mail provider, or look for "signature" under the drop-down menus.

Here's an example of what I could include in my signature:

> Donna Fisher, Certified Speaking Professional Author of *People Power, Power Networking, Power NetWeaving, and Professional Networking for Dummies* www.donnafisher.com
>
> *Working with companies who want to bring out the best in their people and people who want to partner and connect powerfully with others.*

E-mail allows you to enhance your relationships. However, it is not meant to be a replacement for face-to-face connections. Electronic connections are great for maintaining contact in the time between face-to-face encounters.

Even with all that technology has to offer, face-to-face networking is a vital part of the networking formula for building powerful relationships. High touch combined with high tech creates unlimited opportunities for accessing information, making connections, and maintaining connections.

Other Internet tips

Make your Web address as available to people as you make your phone number. Include a friendly reminder in your voice mail greeting for people to check out your Web site and give them the Web address. When you leave a voice mail message for someone, consider giving him or her both your phone number and e-mail address, as a way to get back with you.

> Hi, this is Donna. I'm calling you about the article for your December newsletter. Please get back with me to confirm the number of words and date for submission of the article. Call me at xxx-xxx-xxxx or my e-mail address is donna@donnafisher.com. Again xxx-xxx-xxxx or donna@donnafisher.com. Thanks. I look forward to hearing back from you.

Likewise, when asking for someone's phone number, go ahead and ask for an e-mail address as well.

Enhancing Communication through Voice Mail

I hear many complaints about how hard it is to actually reach people because everyone has voice mail. But voice mail was never meant to be a tool for avoiding communication; it was meant to make it easier for people to be in touch with one another. Use voice mail to enhance connections rather than create distance and frustration.

Voice mail is great because it lets you leave your message with exactly the words and tone of voice that you want to communicate to the other person. It gives you an efficient way to let people know that you are attempting to reach them even when they're out of the office or away from home.

Guaranteeing a call back

Leaving effective voice mail messages involves choosing the words and tone of voice that creates the results you want.

If you leave the same generic message all the time: "This is Janet, please call me at xxx-xxx-xxxx," you are less likely to get a call back.

In your message, tell the recipient what you are calling about and give him or her sufficient information to warrant a return call.

> "Hi, this is Mark. I've got an idea for you regarding a contact that may be able to help with your xyz project. Call me at xxx-xxx-xxxx. I'll be in this afternoon 'til 4:00 and tomorrow from about 10 to 2."

> "Hi, this is Susan returning your phone call about the association meeting. I do plan to be there. Please call me back at xxx-xxx-xxxx to verify the time and place."

> "Hi, this is Carl calling to let you know that the meeting time for next Wednesday has been changed from 2 to 2:30. Please leave me a message at xxx-xxx-xxxx to let me know that you got this message."

Notice how the above examples are short and sweet and yet still convey all the important information.

Voice mail tips

Here is a review of tips to keep in mind for both your voice mail greeting and messages that you leave for others. Your words, pace, and tone of voice make a difference in the impression you create and the way people respond to your message.

- Keep your message simple, straightforward, appealing, and professional.

- Choose words that are easy to hear and understand.

- Speak in a tone of voice that is crisp and professional, yet friendly.

- Speak your greeting in such a way that people feel as if they reached you even when they get a voice mail.

- Match your tone of voice with the reason you are calling.

- If you want your message to sound upbeat and inviting, then smile while you speak.

- Always leave a message giving the purpose/reason for the call.

- Leave your phone number (and repeat it twice) even when you know they already have your number. Speak at the same pace that it takes for someone to write the number.

- Don't worry about mistakes. It's okay to be real.

- Change your voice mail greeting on a regular basis to provide callers with a personal touch and current information.

Voice mail greetings

Now, let's talk about the voice mail message that people hear when they call you. Have you called someone who has the same voice mail message every day, day after day, and sometimes year after year? Do you notice how you feel when you get that message?

On the other hand, have you called someone whose voice mail message gives you up-to-date, specific information about where he or she is or when he or she will be available the day that you are calling? Ever notice how you feel when you get that kind of message? You probably feel more connected, informed, and included when someone goes to the effort of leaving a voice mail greeting that is current and keeps you informed.

I travel a lot, and I know that people often get my voice mail when they call. What I want is for them to feel like they reached me, even when they get the voice mail message. Here are some examples of effective voice mail greetings:

"Hi, this is JoAnn. It's Thursday, March 26. I am currently out of the office with a client. I will be back in this afternoon. Please leave a message and I will get back with you."

"Hi, this is Jerry. It's Thursday, April 29th. That you got this message means I'm on the other line. Please leave a message and I will get back with you."

"Hi, this is Dana. Today is Wednesday, February 18th. I'm currently in a meeting; however, I will be back in my office by 3:00 this afternoon. Please leave a message regarding when's the best time to get back with you."

Although this works for the office, be careful about leaving messages on a home voice mail greeting that gives people too much information about you and your whereabouts.

Chapter 16

Networking Etiquette

*E*tiquette is about good manners, common courtesy, and caring behavior. The purpose of networking etiquette is to behave and interact in a way that makes people feel honored and respected.

Although there are rules of etiquette for social, business, and networking functions, networking etiquette is based on guidelines of kindness and respect. If you become so rigid about following the rules that you make people feel uncomfortable, you have missed the purpose of etiquette.

People often say that their networking suffers because they aren't sure what to say, what to do, or what's appropriate. Because of the uncertainty, they don't do anything and choose not to network. The more familiar you are with the etiquette of networking, the more at ease and comfortable you can be when meeting and networking with people.

Making Your Networking Fit the Purpose of the Event

Any event at which people gather has networking potential. In every situation, your networking should support and honor the purpose of the event. Events, whether social or business, typically have a specific purpose or theme. The purpose of the event determines what's appropriate to talk about and do at that event. In this section, you can find information about various social, business, and networking events, their purposes, and the types of conversations that are appropriate at each one.

Social events

Networking can happen anywhere, anytime, with anyone. Even social events, such as weddings, birthdays, and retirement parties, provide an opportunity for networking. The way to network effectively and appropriately is to make your networking style gracious and courteous. Your networking should be expressed as a natural interest in people. The personal characteristics you need to have to network effectively are the same characteristics that make you likeable, trustworthy, and considerate.

When you consider it an honor to meet the other people in attendance and take your attention off of yourself long enough to make others feel like they're important, you're networking. This style of networking is appropriate everywhere; it's a way of relating and connecting. The following list discusses social events to which you may be invited, their purposes, and ways you can support their purposes through your conversations.

Weddings

Purpose: To honor and celebrate the love that two people express by marrying one another. You honor the bride and groom by interacting with grace and respect. Make your conversations reflect and generate love and respect. When meeting people, for example, ask them how they know the couple.

Anniversary parties

Purpose: To honor and celebrate a couple's marriage on the day that commemorates their joining in matrimony. Anniversary parties are an opportunity to honor the couple for their years together and the ongoing love and commitment that the marriage represents. Generate conversations about the couple, your relationship to the couple, and the fun times that you've had with the couple. These parties are times of joy and respect, with light, fun conversation.

Birthday parties

Purpose: To honor and celebrate people's value and life on the date of their birth. Generate conversations about your relationship and your experiences with the birthday person: how you met, how long you've known each other, what you have in common, what you appreciate about your relationship, what the person has done for you or meant to you, and so on.

Going-away parties

Purpose: To express honor and appreciation to people who are making a changes in their lives that involve moving to another city or another company. Honor the purpose of the event with congratulations on the new beginning and fond memories of special times.

Retirement parties

Purpose: To honor people for their years in the workforce and the contribution they have made to a company, city, industry, or community. Generate conversation regarding the difference the person has made in your life, how he or she has been a leader or an inspiration, and how he or she has contributed.

Housewarmings

Purpose: To celebrate a new home. Honor the purpose of the event with a housewarming present and conversations about the decor; elicit people's memories of their first homes or favorite homes.

Holiday parties

Purpose: To celebrate a holiday and what the holiday represents. Each holiday is a celebration of some kind and has its own theme and purpose. Tailor your conversation so that it suits the particular holiday. You can generate conversation by asking people what they plan to do for the holiday.

At most social events, you see people you know and meet new people as well. Networking means being gracious, courteous, and willing to converse. Through your conversations, you can learn more about people you already know and connect with people you just met.

General "best behavior" guidelines for social events

As a guest, help create the kind of environment and conversations that you would want the guests to be having if the event were yours. If it were your wedding, anniversary, or holiday party, for example, what would you want people to be doing? What would you want people to be talking about? What type of feeling would you want people to walk away with?

If you're in a conversation that generates an interest in talking business, remind yourself that you can set up another time to continue the discussion. You may want to discreetly ask for a card so that you can call the person about getting together at another time to talk business. If you decide not to ask for the person's card (or you ask and he doesn't have a card with him), you can always get the person's phone number later from a mutual friend who attended the event.

Remember that at an event, networking is about meeting people and taking the first step toward creating a connection that's of value. You can keep your conversation appropriate to the situation and still network. The basics of etiquette apply in terms of courtesy, respect, and general good manners.

Business events

Business events can be all business or be opportunities to have both business and social conversations. They include company meetings, industry conferences, business open houses, company picnics, business holiday parties, fundraising events, and charity balls, to name a few. Each event has a purpose. Your best guide for appropriate behavior is to have good manners and make sure that your actions and conversations support the purpose of the event. Common courtesy once again is the rule.

Business events are not typically the place for selling, negotiating, or doing deals. Those activities take place during appointments, sales meetings, and contract negotiation meetings. The business events listed in this section are held primarily for the purpose of giving people a chance to meet, establish rapport, get to know each other, discover common interests, and develop relatedness. The events establish a sense of camaraderie and boost morale within the company or organization. The more connected people feel, the more likely they are to work together effectively and enjoy working together.

Business socials

Purpose: To provide people with an opportunity to meet other people, develop contacts, and create visibility for themselves. A business social can be a company picnic, a corporate dinner, or a company outing to a sporting event. These events are opportunities to get away from office conversations and enjoy some informal time with the people you work with. In these events, people can drop their office personae and discover each other as individuals. As a result, the human element becomes more pronounced in the workplace. Conversations at these events are likely to be about everyday topics like the local news, the weather, children, hobbies, and sports.

Charity events

Purpose: To raise money for a charity or community organization. Honor the purpose of the event by generating conversations about the difference that the organization makes in your life or the lives of others, why you support the organization, and what is possible as a result of the organization's work. Be curious about how others got involved with the organization.

Conferences

Purpose: To bring people together who have common interests and to provide educational, motivational, and networking programs. Multitudes of events are likely within the conference setting — receptions, workshops, a banquet, networking time, and so on. The best way to support the overall purpose of the conference is to be an enthusiastic participant. Be friendly. Introduce yourself to people. Be available to people who approach you.

Generate conversations about what people are getting from the conference, and find out where they're from, what they want to accomplish at the conference, and which workshop sessions they recommend.

Corporate meetings

Purpose: To bring people together for a designated purpose that furthers the company and the individuals who are participating. The purpose of a corporate meeting is identified by its agenda. The meeting is a place to network, even if you don't typically think of meetings as networking opportunities. By being a part of the meeting, you enhance your visibility with the other participants. Also, because you're connecting with others at the meeting, you have a chance to gain knowledge by listening and learning. You may also have a chance to network informally before or after the meeting.

Professional associations

Purpose: To bring members together for educational, motivational, and networking opportunities. Professional associations typically have monthly chapter meetings with educational programs and time for mingling. To get value from your membership, you need to show up. Show up physically and then show up by talking to people, meeting new people, and finding out what's new with the people you already know. Generate conversations about people's business and the positive, interesting things that are happening in the industry.

Business open houses

Purpose: To express appreciation to clients, customers, vendors, associates, and so on for the opportunity to work together. Sometimes the purpose of an open house is to announce the opening of a new business or the move of a business to a new location. Often, though, it's just to thank the people associated with the business for their support. Many businesses also have an open house as a holiday party. Many companies have a tradition of holding a certain type of open house that's related to a particular theme, time of year, or holiday.

Develop an invisible networking style that's appropriate everywhere and with everyone. In other words, your networking should be natural and should manifest itself as being gracious toward and interested in other people.

Networking events

Some events are designed to bring people together to meet, mingle, and network. You and all the other people are there to meet and mingle, so jump in and fulfill the purpose of the event. Networking events are a perfect opportunity for practicing your networking skills and developing your networking approach.

Your attitude, your people skills, and your communication skills will greatly influence your experience and success at a networking event. If you go to the event wishing that you were somewhere else, watch out! Your attitude will turn people off.

An attitude is difficult to hide, even if you attempt to cover it up. At some point, it will reveal itself. Because attitude is intangible, we think it's invisible. However, your attitude shows up in your walk, talk, facial expressions, body language, tone of voice, and other mannerisms.

At networking events, people are there to network. That's what is expected of you. If you don't want to network, don't go. If you do go, support the purpose of the event by networking.

Trade shows

Purpose: To provide a showcase of businesses for a particular industry so that the participants can gather information about vendors' products and services. Check the exhibitor directory beforehand to see what companies are represented and to identify those individuals you want to talk to. Make sure that you have plenty of business cards with you because lots of people (including the exhibitors) will ask for your card. Talk with people. Be pleasant and friendly with people. Ask questions so that you know who to call if you plan to follow up with an exhibitor. Get brochures or business cards with the information that you will need to follow through on your networking efforts.

Chamber or association mixers

Purpose: To provide an opportunity for people to meet, learn about each other's businesses, and take the first step toward creating new business opportunities. A mixer is a chance to mingle. Support the event by connecting, conversing, and continuing to move around the room. Generate conversations about the chamber, chamber activities, other people's businesses, and how they are involved in the chamber. Ideally, you want to get other people talking about themselves, and you want to listen. Listen well enough to remember something about each person the next day so that if you wanted to call an individual, you can reference something you talked about.

Seminars/workshops

Purpose: To provide participants with valuable information that can enhance their lives and their successes. Participants can utilize the opportunity to connect with the other participants by generating conversations with people sitting nearby and mingling before and after the sessions and during the breaks. Generate conversations to learn more about other people and their businesses and ask what they're learning from the workshop.

Understanding the Roles of the Host and Guest

What does it take to be a really good host? Number one is the ability to put other people at ease — to make everyone feel included, taken care of, and special. The host's job involves overseeing the event and ensuring that everything runs smoothly. The perfect host is a master at keeping an eye on everything and finding ways to quickly and easily handle any problems that arise so that no one even notices.

The host does the following:

- ✔ Greets people.
- ✔ Introduces people to each other and includes in the introduction some tidbits of information that help people relate to each other.
- ✔ Lets people know where the refreshments are.
- ✔ Mingles and visits with all the guests.
- ✔ Oversees the flow of the event.

The easiest way to put yourself at ease as a guest is to play the role of host. I don't mean taking over the running of the event. I mean taking your attention off of yourself and focusing on taking care of the other people at the event. Even when you aren't the actual host of the event, you can let a sense of service guide your actions. Be there to serve others, and your networking will flourish.

When you arrive at an event, find the host as quickly as possible and say hello. Be sure to find and thank the person who invited you to the event as well if the person who invited you isn't the host.

Stand to greet people unless you're somehow trapped behind a table. Standing brings a sense of honor and importance to the moment. Also, acknowledge the presence of the people around you. Treat all people with equal respect regardless of their perceived position, wealth, and status.

The guest does the following:

- ✔ Seeks out the host upon arrival.
- ✔ If someone is being honored, expresses congratulations.
- ✔ Mingles and circulates.

✔ Is gracious and courteous with everyone.

✔ Goes lightly on the drinks and refreshments.

✔ Does not draw undue attention to himself.

✔ Does not monopolize the attention of any one person or group at the event.

✔ No matter what type of event it is, has her business cards handy and easily reachable (but not visible).

✔ Thanks the hosts.

Your role as a guest is to enjoy the party and help make it a success for the people who are hosting the event or being honored by it.

Practicing Common Courtesies Related to Social Events

All the common courtesies that are appropriate in our society make for gracious networking. Be considerate and gracious with people in all your interactions and you will most likely be adhering to the basics of networking etiquette.

Offering timely responses to RSVPs

The RSVP has always been a request for response, and it still is. An invitation warrants a response, usually by a specific date. When people are planning an event and honor you with an invitation, show them the same respect by responding to their invitation. Let people know that you received their invitation and either accept it or decline it.

Beware of two common RSVP pitfalls:

✔ You receive an invitation and then place it in a stack of "I'll get around to it later" items. "I'll get around to it later" may lead to never rather than later or finding the invitation again after the event has already taken place. The RSVP either gets delayed or ignored.

✔ You put off making plans or wait until the last minute to make plans and do not respond to the invitation in a timely manner.

Making introductions

When it comes to introductions, the main thing is "just do it!" Introduce yourself to people and introduce people to one another. When someone comes over to talk with you and you are talking to someone else, make sure to introduce the new arrival to the person with whom you're conversing.

Train yourself to be professional and at ease when meeting and introducing people to one another. The general rule is to introduce the younger to the elder, the junior to the senior, the nonofficial to the official. Say the name of the person you wish to honor first.

Make sure that both people can hear you when you introduce them to each other. If possible, include something in the introduction that they can relate to and that helps them get to know each other. Here are some examples:

- "Faye, I would like for you to meet Jane. Jane is my publicist, and she's thinking about joining our networking breakfast club."

- "Mark Roberts, this is Glenn Baker. Mark works in the production department. Glenn and I know each other from working together in marketing for six years."

- "You two should know each other. Jack — Harry. You share the same alma mater."

- "I would like for the two of you to meet. Mary, this is John. John, this is Mary. John and I met at the church picnic last week."

- "Professor Smith, I would like to introduce to you my roommate, Steve. Steve and I were discussing my physics project at lunch today. He has some ideas about the material we discussed in your class."

- "Mother, I would like for you to meet my friend Amy. Amy worked with me at the center, and we've stayed in touch as friends ever since."

Introduce yourself to people you don't know. If you see someone alone, go up to say hello. Always acknowledge the presence of the people around you and at least make eye contact and offer a greeting. Even if you don't have a chance to stay around to talk and visit with people, be courteous enough to say hi, shake their hands, and learn their names.

In a networking situation, don't walk by or stand next to people without making some kind of connection. A smile, a nod, a handshake, a greeting, and an introduction are appropriate ways to acknowledge the presence of the people around you.

Writing Thank-You Notes

When someone gives you something tangible or intangible or does something for you, send a note of thanks. This could be a thank you for lunch, a referral, time together, valuable information, business, and so on. Your thank-you note can be anywhere from a few words ("You're the best!") to a few sentences. Keep it simple, and at the same time be sure to express specifically what you appreciate.

If you purchase cards that say "Thanks" or "Thank you" on the front, you're limited to sending them only in certain situations. When you have note cards with your company logo, your monogram, or your emblem or that are blank, you can use those cards for thanks, congratulations, thinking of you, here's a referral, and so on. Consider having cards handy that are professional and multipurpose.

Here are some examples of effective thank-you notes:

✔ "Thank you for referring me to Matthew Wilson. I have contacted him and look forward to learning more about his manufacturing process. You always seem to know exactly whom I need to meet. Thank you for being a valuable resource."

✔ "Thank you for recommending me to Karen Sommers. I appreciate the opportunity to make a proposal to her regarding ABC's upcoming project. With your help, I got in touch with her just in time to take part in the bidding process."

✔ "Thank you for introducing me to Mark Kramer. I have scheduled a meeting with him next week and will let you know how things proceed. Please know that I appreciate your support and will always take good care of the people you send my way."

✔ "Thank you for giving my name to Barbara Maxwell. We talked this morning, and I am sending a packet of information to her this afternoon. Thank you for trusting me with your clients. I assure you that anyone you refer to me will be treated with the utmost care and respect."

Exchanging Business Cards: When, Where, and How

Your business card is the means by which you provide your contact information to others. It represents you when you aren't around and may get passed along to numerous other people.

I recommend that everyone have a calling card of some kind. If you are retired or don't work outside the home, get a personal calling card. If you're in job transition, definitely have a card that has your contact information along with information regarding the job position or industry with which you associate yourself.

Creating a business card

Have a business card that creates the impression you want to make. Your company may have a standard template or style set up for business cards, in which case all you need to do as an employee is fill in the pertinent contact information. The cards are printed and then sent to you. However, if you have the opportunity to create your own business cards, keep the following tips in mind.

- Utilize the services of a good graphic designer to create an image that is visually appealing, impressive, and immediate.

- Make sure that the card contains all the essential information that a person may need to get in touch with you. It should be easy to read, with the most important information (your name and phone number) displayed most prominently.

Being prepared to give your card

Keep your cards handy. You never know when you may meet someone with whom you want to exchange contact information. Can you recall a time when you asked someone for his card and, because he didn't have one, he ended up handing you a scrap of paper on which he wrote his information? Pieces of paper are much more likely to get tossed or lost than business cards. Know where your cards are. Don't wait until someone asks for your card to go searching for it. Preferably, keep your business cards in the same place so that in a split second you can reach for it and hand it to the person. I keep my cards in my right-hand pocket. If I buy a suit that doesn't have pockets, I have a pocket just for business cards sewn onto the inside of the suit. When someone asks for a card, obtaining one is simple and easy.

Keep a backup supply of cards in your briefcase or the glove compartment of your car.

Keeping your cards handy doesn't mean having them in your hand and out in the open. It means that they are reachable. Be able to put your hands on them with little effort, but don't look like you're jumping to pass out cards to everyone as soon as you meet them. Don't mix other people's cards in with your cards, either. You don't want to have to search through a stack of cards to find yours or hand out a card that's dirty, smudged, or has someone else's information written on the back.

Being prepared to receive cards

When someone hands you a card, look at it and read it to yourself. Taking a moment to look at the card conveys the respect that is so important in making a strong impression and a connection. There may be something on the card (a logo, slogan, address, and so on) that would be valuable and interesting for you to comment on or ask about.

Keep a pen handy so that you can make notes on the back of the card that will be helpful with your follow-through. I know that when I'm talking with someone and I offer to send something or call the person about something, I'd better make a note to myself. Even if I think I'll remember later, there's a very good chance that other things will get on my mind and that the follow-through may never happen if I don't have a note.

Have a system for either filing the cards or storing and tracking the data from the cards. A database management system on your computer will provide easy access to information about the people you meet.

Review the cards you gather each day and follow up immediately on any actions you need to take as a result of your conversations.

Asking for a business card

The exchange of business cards ideally happens when some point in the conversation calls for an exchange of information. Ask for a card as a natural part of the conversation. Here are some examples of requests for business cards:

- The other person mentions something that you want to have further conversation about. You ask if you may call her — a perfect opportunity to ask, "Do you have a card handy that I might have?"

- The other person refers to something, and as a result you offer to send her an article or brochure. "I would like to send you that article on home-based business tips. May I have one of your cards?"

> ✔ Based on the conversation, you tell the other person that you would like to know how to get in touch with him. A straightforward "May I have one of your business cards?" is perfectly acceptable.

Offering your business card

Find an opening in the conversation in which offering your card to the other person is natural. Let the person know why you want him to have your card. Give him a reason to want your information.

Here are some examples of gracious ways to offer your card:

> ✔ "I would like to be on your mailing list. Here's my card."

> ✔ "I'd be interested in subscribing to your weekly e-mail tips. Here's my card. Let me know if there's something I need to do to get signed up."

> ✔ "I would like to follow up with you regarding your convention that's coming up. If I might have one of your cards — and here's one of mine — I'd like to get back with you next week."

 Do not walk up to someone and immediately hand her your card. And don't pass a stack of cards around a table (unless someone asks you to do so and a refusal would be rude) so that each person takes a card even if they never have a chance to talk with you.

Business Lunch Etiquette

The value of a business lunch is that the environment is more conducive to relaxed conversation and networking than an office is. Eating together is a common social activity where people feel comfortable getting to know one another.

All sorts of etiquette rules apply to what you should order, who pays, and so on. The main thing to remember is to be thoughtful and polite. If you want all the details, though, check out Sue Fox's *Etiquette For Dummies* (Hungry Minds, Inc.).

Making a good impression

 If you are the guest and you aren't sure how extravagant to get with your order, you may ask the host of the lunch what he recommends. His response will clue you in to his thinking and give you some guidelines.

Cell phones and social situations

Keep your cell phone conversations to yourself. Turn your phone off in meetings — corporate, lunch, dinner, breakfast, conference, church, and any other type of meeting you can think of! When using your cell phone, find a place where your conversation will not interrupt or intrude on others. Speak at a volume that allows the person on the other end of the line to hear you without broadcasting your conversation to everyone around you.

If you need to have the phone on because of an emergency or special situation, make sure that what you're doing works for the people you're with. If you have to leave the phone on, set it to vibrate and then graciously excuse yourself to answer the call somewhere more private.

Start the lunch conversation with general topics and interesting small talk. Take some time for social interaction while ordering and waiting for the meal to be served. After the meal is served, you can find a natural way to segue into business topics.

Knowing who pays for the meal

If you invite someone to lunch and you're using that opportunity to learn from her, gather information from her, or get advice from her, *you* pay for lunch. At a networking or business lunch, who pays is not determined by level of success, influence, wealth, or gender. Typically, whoever initiates the lunch as a means of gaining value is the host for the meeting and thus pays the tab.

When dining with peers, friends, or coworkers, it's common for each person to pay his own way no matter who initiated the meal (unless it's a special occasion, like a birthday or a celebration of a promotion).

When it's your role to pay, be as straightforward and yet discreet as possible. When the bill is brought to the table, place your hand on it immediately and place it next to your plate. Claim it!

Send a note of thanks whether you paid for lunch or were treated to lunch. If you're the one who paid, you still want to thank the other person for his time and the value you received from having a chance to meet with him.

Looking at the Elements of Business Etiquette

Business etiquette and social etiquette are based on the same principles of being considerate, polite, and courteous. The same guidelines of etiquette that work in social settings apply in any business setting — workplace, office, cubicle, or corporate meeting.

Being a time guardian

Respect people's time. Be the timekeeper rather than requiring other people to watch the clock to protect themselves. When you ask for the opportunity to talk with someone, give her a time frame: "Do you have 20 minutes that we could schedule for you to review this report with me?" or "May I come in? I'd like to get your advice on the xyz project if you have about ten minutes."

Here are some other things to say when requesting someone's time while also conveying that you respect and value that time.

- ✔ "Is this a good time, or would you like to schedule a time for me to call you back?"

- ✔ "I have reviewed all the data from last quarter's sales project. It would probably take about 45 minutes for me to give you a recap, answer any questions you have, and outline the next project. When would be the best time for you?"

- ✔ "I know you've got a busy day. How can I best arrange to have about an hour with you?"

When you walk into other people's offices or cubicles, remember that you're entering their space and interrupting whatever they're doing at the moment. Don't just barge in and start talking. Ask for their time and attention and the opportunity to talk with them.

Telephone etiquette and effectiveness

Networking over the phone introduces the challenge of developing a relationship when you have no chance to make eye contact and utilize body language and facial expressions to connect. When you're face to face with people, you can tell by nonverbal cues whether they're having a good day and whether it's a good time to talk with them. When you're on the phone, your words and tone of voice have to carry the whole conversation.

Be friendly and personable and let people know early in the conversation why you're calling. You don't have to say what you're calling about in the first words out of your mouth, but you also don't want to wait 20 minutes to say, "Well, what I really called about is . . . ." You could say, "One of the things I'm calling about is . . . . But first, I'd like to hear a little bit about how things are going." Be friendly, but still clarify the purpose of the call up front.

For much more information on this subject, please see Marty Brounstein's *Communicating Effectively For Dummies* (Hungry Minds, Inc.).

Calling referrals

When calling someone you've been referred to, say who you are, giving your first and last name. Then follow these steps:

1. **Tell this person who referred you to him or her.**

2. **Explain why you were referred to the person and why you are calling.**

3. **Ask if it's a good time to talk. If it isn't, ask when would be a good time for you to call back and, if possible, schedule a call with the person.**

4. **End the call graciously. You might say, "Thank you for the chance to talk with you. I look forward to . . . ."**

Prepare in advance so that you don't have to think about what to say and can give your full attention to the person on the other end of the phone.

What if you don't reach your referral? Is it better to leave a message or to keep calling back? Personally, I prefer to leave a message. I want the person to know that I called. If I don't leave a message, I've wasted my time calling without letting anyone know. Here are some things you may say if you're leaving a message:

✔ "My name is Harry Klein. Mary Jones recommended that I contact you about . . . . I have information about . . . that I would like to present to you. Please call me at xxx-xxx-xxxx. Again, my name is Harry Klein at xxx-xxx-xxxx."

✔ "Hi, my name is Nancy Porter. I got your name and number from Mark Hammond. I understand that you are the person who . . . . I thought you would like to know about . . . . You can reach me at xxx-xxx-xxxx. I look forward to talking with you. Again, Nancy Porter, xxx-xxx-xxxx."

Before you make the call, think of a question to ask to determine whether the person is the best person for you to be talking with: "I understand that you do . . . . Based on that, I have information about how to improve . . . . I thought this information would be of interest and value to you."

Don't ask if the person is interested: "I have xyz to offer. Is that something you would be interested in?" Instead, tell her what you have that would be of interest to her. "I have xyz, which is designed for companies like yours . . . ." Ask questions that help you learn more about her and her needs and interests.

Make sure that you get back with the person who gives you the referral to let him know that you took action based on the recommendation. Let people know the results of their referrals.

Other telephone etiquette tidbits

Don't be so eager to hang up the phone that you leave the person on the other end of the line with a dial tone buzzing in her ear. After you say good-bye, take a second before you disconnect. Some people are so busy smiling and dialing that their fingers are poised to end this call and make the next call, and they hardly get "goodbye" out of their mouths before they hang up.

When you need to put someone on hold, ask "Can you hold for a second?" or "May I put you on hold while I check on that?" Leave people on hold for as short a time as possible. If you're not going to be able to get back to the person until several minutes have elapsed, ask if you can call back. Leave a person on hold only if she asks for it, and even then, check with her frequently in case she changes her mind or needs to get off the phone to take care of something.

Be careful about doing anything that conveys a sense of non-importance to the person you're speaking with. Don't eat or carry on side conversations while you're on the phone. Return phone calls. Obviously, when people call and ask you to call back, the courteous thing is to respond as promptly as possible. If you can't return a call in a timely manner, have a coworker or someone else return the call for you and explain the delay.

Knowing When and How to Say No

You have the right to say no to networking requests that people make. Your decision to say no could be based on the person or what the person is asking. If you're not sure what you're willing to do for someone, say that you need to think about it and arrange to get back to him or have him get back with you.

Here are some factors that may influence your decision to network with people:

- ✔ You have had a negative experience with them.
- ✔ You don't trust them.
- ✔ You don't like the way they do business or interact with people.
- ✔ Your values, styles, and goals are incompatible.
- ✔ You are not familiar enough with them or their business.
- ✔ The time is not right because of previous commitments you've made.

Sometimes, you may say no to what a person is requesting yet offer an alternative. Or you may say no and tell the person why you can't do what she is asking of you. Sometimes you say no because you need more information in order to say yes. Or you may say no and recommend someone else who would be a better source for the person's need. Or you my say no to the person's specific request yet still help him fulfill the request. For example, someone may ask you to help him make contact with someone you know by scheduling a lunch meeting. You may choose not to arrange a lunch meeting, yet you may be fine with giving him the person's phone number.

Here are some tactful and considerate ways to say no:

- ✔ **Saying no to a lunch invitation:** "I would like to be of help, but right now my time is focused on . . . . We could spend ten minutes on the phone if you'd like."

- ✔ **Saying no to getting together until you have more information about the person and what she thinks you can do:** "Let's talk a little bit first about what you think we could do for one another" (or "I could do for you" or "you could do for me," whichever is appropriate to the situation).

- ✔ **Saying no because you had a negative experience with the person:** "I'm not comfortable making that recommendation. What's in the way for me is my experience . . . ." Explain the facts about what happened that didn't work for you. As a result of this type of conversation, you may end up giving the person some valuable information that he wasn't aware of. It's possible that because of the conversation, you may reconsider the request, or the person may ask for another chance.

✔ **Saying no for the time being:** "What I really think is best is if you would send me an e-mail with your information and let me review it. Then call me next week and we'll talk." You're willing to check things out, and at the same time you put the ball back in the requester's court so that he must take the initiative to make something happen. This way, you find out how serious he is and how important getting together is to him.

You might give the person a suggestion and see if he follows through on it. For example, recommend reading a certain book that addresses the issue before getting back with you. In a way, you are playing the role of a mentor, at least momentarily.

Even if you say no to someone's request, wish the person well. Thank the person for thinking of you as someone who could be of value. In saying no, you may still give valuable advice or words of encouragement and end up making a contribution — and that's networking. Networking doesn't always have to look a certain way. Networking is at work whenever information and value are exchanged.

Part V
The Part of Tens

The 5th Wave   By Rich Tennant

SEYMOUR ENCOUNTERS A NETWORKING CHALLENGE

"What do you mean the Poultry Association is tomorrow,
and the Investors Forum is today?"

In this part . . .

This part provides you with information on how to master the art of small talk, develop your memory, become a masterful networker, and avoid common networking turnoffs.

Chapter 17

Ten Ways to Master the Art of Small Talk

In This Chapter

▶ Approaching small talk with the right mentality

▶ Finding ways to click with others

Are you one of those people who say one or more of the following?

- ✔ "I'm not good at initiating conversation with strangers."
- ✔ "I never know what to say."
- ✔ "I don't have anything interesting to say."

I say that's not so. Small talk does not have to be significant. It's designed to give people a chance to connect and to create a bridge to conversations about opportunities. You want to put people at ease, draw them into conversation, and create a comfort zone for a relationship with them to be possible. This chapter gives you ten ways to do so. For more on how to create and engage in small talk, see Chapter 5.

Create a Small-Talk Top Ten List

Identify five things that you enjoy talking about and can talk about easily. List five subjects that you don't know much about but would enjoy learning about from others. You now have a list of ten topics that you can use to generate small talk and create conversations that are fun, interesting, and valuable. Here are a couple of examples:

- ✔ **Jane's top ten list:** Travel, dancing, books, movies, investments, yoga, publishing, e-commerce, recreational vehicles, gardening

- ✔ **Ken's top ten list:** Astronomy, children, venture capital, literacy, soccer, the Internet, jazz, Italian recipes, bicycling, music

If you've ever thought that you don't know what to say or don't have anything interesting to say, look at your top ten list. It will help you see that you have many topics at your disposal that you can use to generate an interesting conversation.

Think of some of the interests that you had growing up that you never got around to pursuing. Think of new opportunities that weren't available in the past that can now add a new dimension to your life (computers, the Internet, travel, and so on). If you pursue any of these topics, you'll have some interesting things to talk about. Even if all you do is ask others about these topics so that you can learn more, you open the door to interesting conversation.

Listen to What People Are Saying and Find Something of Interest to Respond To

Attentive listening is as critical to small talk as it is to, well, talking. Through listening, you know what to say to generate connection and rapport. Let the other person's conversation guide you toward your next comment or question. Here's an example:

> **Mary:** I'm so behind at the office. Taking a two-week vacation is great, but it's difficult to come back from.
>
> **Norm:** A two-week vacation sounds great! Where did you go?

This exchange may lead to more questions:

- What was your favorite port?
- What was the best part of the trip for you?
- Have you been on a cruise before? Would you go again, and where?

Be Curious

Curiosity keeps you attentive. Be curious about who people are both as individuals and as businesspeople. Be curious about what makes them tick, what they dream of, what they can do for you, and what you can do for them.

Don't be curious to the point where you become annoying; be curious enough to explore. Get caught up in your attempt to learn more about people.

If you know someone well enough, ask questions in order to get to know the person even better. Here's a list of possibilities:

- ✔ What do you like most about . . . ?
- ✔ What do you most appreciate about . . . ?
- ✔ What influenced you the most in making that decision?
- ✔ When was the turning point in your business really taking off?
- ✔ Who has been your greatest hero or mentor?

Find out enough about the other person to know what he or she would be interested in talking about, and then direct the conversation toward that topic.

Don't be so focused on other people that you make them uncomfortable. You don't want people to feel like they're being forced to talk or that they're being interrogated, scrutinized, or put on the spot.

Look for Common Interests

If small talk is a game, the object is to find what you have in common with the people you're talking with. Sharing these experiences or interests gives you a bond and fuels your conversation. No matter who the person is, you're bound to have something in common.

You've probably been in a conversation that was going nowhere. However, when you discovered that you followed the same sports team, you attended the same college, or your kids went to the same camp, all of a sudden the conversation took off.

Things you have in common with another person may include

- ✔ Charities you're involved with
- ✔ College you attended
- ✔ Hobbies
- ✔ Professional affiliations
- ✔ Religion

Religion and politics are not normally recommended as small talk topics; however, you may discover during the course of a conversation that you and the other person attend the same church, which can give you lots to talk about in an interesting and friendly manner.

- Schools your children attend
- Sports you follow or participate in
- State where you live (if you're at an out-of-state conference, for example) or were born
- Type of work

Think of three people whom you typically enjoy being and talking with. Write down their names. Next to each name, make a list of all the things you have in common with that person. Include material things (a boat, bicycle, motorcycle, certain kind of car, musical instrument, garden), qualities and characteristics (adventurous, methodical, inquisitive), interests (reading, playing music, home decorating, cooking), and group activities (choir, calligraphy guild, society for the performing arts, sailing group). Notice the common experiences and interests that contribute to your ability to engage in fun and interesting conversations with these people.

Your job is to get to the point where the conversation takes on a life of its own and you can just go with the flow.

Be Interested

Your interest encourages other people to talk openly with you. Whether your interest lies in who they are as people, their business, how they got into business, how they plan to grow their business, or anything else, being interested in other people is often the key that unlocks their personality.

Here's how to show that you're interested:

- Ask other people about themselves and listen when they respond.
- Continue to ask questions to follow up on what they said.
- Say that you're interested!
- Use encouraging body language, such as making good eye contact and nodding your head.

Be interesting as well as interested. If you're constantly learning and growing, engaging in interesting conversation should be easy. Personally and professionally, always strive to expand yourself. You're either growing or stagnating. If you're growing, your networking activities become that much easier.

Remind Yourself that Small Talk Is the Prerequisite to Making a Connection

Small talk lays the groundwork for a connection. Through eye contact, a friendly tone of voice, and topics that are appealing, warmth and energy begin to develop. This energy leads to enthusiasm, more openness, more conversation, and an ever-deepening sense of relatedness and connection.

If you're strictly interested in producing results for your business, you may consider small talk a waste of time. However, small talk leads to trust and rapport, which lead to results and opportunities.

Not all small talk is created equal. Here are some hints on how to engage in small talk that can lead to more important conversations:

- ✔ Be gentle and patient.
- ✔ Be kind and considerate.
- ✔ Give your undivided attention.
- ✔ Stroke the other person with words of encouragement and interest.
- ✔ Discover what the other person likes and talk about that.
- ✔ Allow the small talk to flow and build.

At a business luncheon I attended, several women started talking about golf and their interest in improving their golf games. One person mentioned that she knew the president of a local women's golf association and described some of the activities it sponsored. I was interested in contacting her friend to learn more about the organization and to inquire about opportunities to conduct one of my programs on networking for the members of the association. Because people typically think of golf as a great opportunity to network, I thought it would be a great fit. The conversation at the luncheon then moved on to other topics, and I chose not to pursue the information at the time, but made a mental note to talk to this woman about it later. As we were driving to the location where I was speaking at her company's meeting, I referred to the conversation. After I'd barely finished my sentence and before I could even ask for her help, she offered to contact her friend about me as well as give me her friend's number, and she proceeded to tell me more about what she knew of the organization.

The goal of small talk is friendship and a sense of connection, which can lead to a multitude of possibilities.

Keep Throwing Out Topics until Something Clicks

In Chapter 6, I use a tennis analogy to describe small talk. You may have to "serve" several topics to the other person before she responds. If someone doesn't respond to your conversation right away, don't assume that she's not interested. It may be that you just haven't found a topic that she's able to respond to. Continue to serve until a topic piques her interest and she's able to return your serve. When a topic clicks, it triggers a connection within the other person. It resonates with something she has experienced or thought about and is a topic she can relate to in some way.

There may be times when nothing seems to work and you just don't click with the other person. (Some days, my tennis game just seems to be off.) It may be that it just isn't the right time or place; you may be able to carry on a great conversation with that person another time.

Participate in the Conversation

Have you ever attempted to generate conversation with a person, and all he does is respond with one-word sentences: *yes, no, maybe, sure, kinda*. He refuses to get actively involved, and you become frustrated. Make sure that you don't create that feeling in someone else. When people are attempting to talk with you, respond with more than one or two words.

If you repeatedly receive one-word responses in a conversation, don't interrogate that person or make that person feel like he has to talk. Sometimes, you just have to accept that a conversation isn't going to happen. If the other person is not willing to participate, you can't do much other than find someone else who *is* interested and willing.

There's one technique you can use to spark a conversation that seems lifeless: Prime the pump by talking about something interesting or funny that happened to you recently. Your willingness to talk may help the other person respond in kind.

Ideally, small talk is easy and enjoyable. There's no need to make it serious. Having fun when talking with people helps create the rapport and camaraderie that are important in building relationships that lead to results.

Putting People at Ease

Don't put people on the spot. Your job is to put people at ease, to make them feel comfortable, to allow them to relax and enjoy a casual conversation with you. Don't attempt to teach, preach, or impress. Choose topics that are easy and comfortable for people to respond to. Stay away from jargon, buzzwords, curse words, sexist language, and other inappropriate language.

Religion and politics can be hot topics, meaning that they generate a lot of emotions and opinions. Although you may get an immediate response, the response may create tension and agitation, which could hamper the flow of the conversation. If you happen to find out that you have common beliefs and opinions, however, you may be able to share your interests in a positive way.

Pointed questions or comments may make others feel that they're being put on the spot, while at the same time making you come across as judgmental, unprofessional, or a complainer.

Be with People

Even though I've written a lot about what to say and how to say it, small talk is primarily about being present to people when you're talking with them. You know what it's like to talk with someone who's partially listening while obviously thinking about other things. Instead, be alert to what people are saying.

Networking is more a way of being than it is something you have to do. Small talk happens more naturally when you're being interested and pleasantly curious. You tend to say the right thing when you're interested. When you're willing to be with people, the doing side of small talk falls into place.

Chapter 18

Ten Techniques for Effective Name Recall

*O*ver and over, I hear people say that they're just not good at remembering names. If you and I meet and I can't remember your name later, what good has it done that we met?

I believe that everyone can remember names. Your mind has the capacity to recall billions of pieces of data. It may be that you haven't learned how to fully utilize that capability. It could be a matter of being lazy. For some people, it's a matter of being stuck in thinking that it's not possible. And for many others, developing good memory skills has not been a priority.

Strengthening your "memory muscle," just like any other muscle, takes consistent work. But if you work at it, you will develop your ability to remember names beyond what you ever thought possible.

When you decide to focus on remembering names, one of the side benefits is that you will give people your full attention. By paying attention to people, you increase your chances of making a strong connection. And when you make a strong connection, you not only help yourself remember who they are, but they are more apt to remember who *you* are.

Treat every moment as if you're about to make a connection that will provide you with a once-in-a-lifetime opportunity. If you gave every moment that kind of attention, you would discover more once-in-a-lifetime opportunities!

You can be effective at meeting people and yet still miss out on the value of networking if you haven't developed your ability to remember names, faces, and pertinent information (job, industry, company, and so on).

Make Remembering Names a Priority

Make it a priority to develop your memory skills. Your mind has the ability; it's up to you to develop that ability. It may take a strong commitment on your part and a great deal of practice, but it is doable. If you decide that it's important and you make it a priority, you will do whatever it takes to develop that ability.

Think of someone you know who is good at greeting people by name. Notice how people respond when addressed by their names. What value do you feel this could bring to your networking? How do you think it would enhance your networking results?

Make a list of all the benefits of remembering people's names. What are the immediate benefits? What are the long-term benefits? Identify what would motivate you to improve your ability to remember names.

Start Saying You Can

I hear so many people say, "I'm just not good with names" or "I can never remember people's names." People usually make these comments with great conviction. They have convinced themselves that these statements are not only true, but will be true forever.

Stop saying that you can't remember people's names and consider the possibility that you can. Every time you catch yourself thinking, "I can't remember people's names" or "I'm just not good with names," affirm the following to yourself:

- ✔ I know that I have the ability to remember people's names, and I will work on developing that ability.

- ✔ I can remember people's names when I focus on them and make it a priority to do so.

- ✔ I will at least consider the possibility that I can do a better job of remembering names now and in the future.

- ✔ I know that I can do anything I set my mind to — including being masterful at remembering names.

- ✔ Developing my memory skills is a new priority in my life.

- ✔ Every time I meet someone, I will focus on that person as part of my commitment to remembering names.

> ## Let technology help you remember
>
> Technology provides valuable resources to help you recall and access data. With a computer contact-management system, you can sort and access data by city, state, country, industry, organization, and company. When you're attempting to remember the name of that person you met at the engineering conference in Atlanta back in the spring who works for Harrison Engineering, you can do a search in your contact-management system to find the name by searching for the company name, date, or industry.

It's possible that the only reason you can't do something is that you say you can't. If you continue to reinforce the idea that you can't remember names, you will continue to prove yourself right. *Can't* is a judgment and limitation that you place on yourself. Even if you choose to not develop your memory skills, at least acknowledge that you have a choice.

Focus on Connecting with People

Your ability to focus gives you great power. Distractions are a main reason that you miss out on retaining certain information. When you focus on someone and concentrate on what she's saying, you significantly enhance your ability to remember.

I've noticed that when I lead a corporate training session, there are times when I'm able to call people by name throughout the day, and then there are times when I can't seem to remember anyone's name without prompting. The difference has to do with where I'm focused as I arrive at the corporate site and begin to meet people. If my focus is on gathering my supplies, getting things set up, and thinking about my program, then the chances are very high that I will not be calling people by name by the end of the day. However, if my focus is on meeting and connecting with people and remembering their names, then throughout the day I easily call people by name — which greatly enhances their feeling of being related to and valued. It's all in where I'm coming from and where I place my focus.

Use Your Laser Listening Skills

Listen to what's being said. You can't remember something you never heard. Sometimes you don't remember a name because you never heard it in the first place. Information that goes in one ear and out the other never has a chance to be stored in your memory.

If for some reason you don't hear a person's name when she says it, ask her to repeat it. If the person has an unusual name, you might ask her to repeat it and also to spell it for you. Most people will be flattered that you're showing such an interest in them.

Listening is key to memory because you have to hear the information and register it in your mind in order to recall it later. As you improve your listening skills, you will also — naturally, without working at it — improve your memory skills.

Repeat After Me . . .

Repetition has been and always will be a valuable memorization technique. You may have learned the multiplication tables through pure repetition. In class and at home, you probably practiced over and over 2 times 2 equals 4, 2 times 3 equals 6, 2 times 4 equals 8, and so on. Through repetition, that information became a permanent part of your mental files. Ten, twenty, thirty, and forty years later, you are still able to recite those multiplication tables . . . through the power of repetition.

The power of repetition applies when you're meeting people and attempting to remember names as well. As soon as you meet someone, repetition can begin to work for you. Here's how the process works:

1. You meet someone and he says his name. You hear the name for the first time.

2. You say his name as part of your response to him: "Hi, Dan, nice to meet you."

3. You use his name in a natural way during your conversation with him. "So, Dan, how long have you been a member of the chamber?"

4. If Dan has on a nametag, take a second to glance at the nametag and see his name.

5. When you ask for Dan's business card, take a moment to read the name on the card.

6. Say his name again as you end the conversation: "Dan, nice to visit with you. Good luck with your marketing project."

7. When you get back to your office or house, quickly review the business cards you collected and think about each interaction.

8. Take the business cards and type the information into the database on your computer.

9. Follow through on any action that's appropriate as a result of meeting these people.

This common scenario shows the natural flow of repetition that can happen every time you meet someone. In this scenario, you hear, say, see, read, think, or type the person's name nine times. By incorporating repetition into the process of meeting someone, you store names in your mind for later recall.

However, this repetition makes an impact only if you pay attention. The same scenario can happen, yet if you're thinking about other things, you aren't paying attention when you're handed a business card, or you quickly stuff the business card somewhere and don't find it until months later, you'll still walk away not remembering the person's name. Repetition works when you focus on what's being said. If not, memory doesn't have a chance because the information never even makes it into your mental computer.

The next time you're at a meeting and you want to learn everyone's name, practice the power of repetition by following these steps:

1. **Repeat to yourself (silently) the name of the person directly across the table (or room) from you.**

2. **Repeat to yourself the name of the person next to her.**

3. **Go back to the first person and mentally say her name and then the second person's name.**

4. **Go to the third person and say his name to yourself.**

5. **Go back to the first person and mentally say the names of persons one, two, and three.**

6. **Go to person four and repeat the process.**

   You can continue this process all the way around the room or table.

This exercise incorporates focus, repetition, and concentration in such a way that you can learn and recall the names of everyone at your meeting or lunch table.

Developing your ability to call people by name greatly enhances your ability to develop the trust and rapport that are necessary for masterful networking.

Follow Up Right Away

The power of repetition continues when you get back with people as soon as possible after meeting them. Prompt follow-up makes you think about those people one more time and recall the things you learned about them. Doing so reinforces that information in your mind and at the same time gives you an opportunity to gather new information.

The more quickly you follow up with people after meeting them, the greater the boost you give to placing their names permanently in your memory bank.

Reinforce the Connection with Action

If you take action when you meet someone, you immediately reinforce your connection. Action adds substance. The action can be as simple as asking the person for a business card and then making a note on the card of something you learned about that person.

Being in action — being physically involved in some way — reinforces the information you're receiving. When someone hands you a business card, take a moment to look at it and actually read the information on the card. Notice the company logo, office location, tag line, and Web address and respond by commenting on the card: "I see your office is down the street from me." "Interesting logo. Tell me how you came up with that." "Your card says that you work with people who want to grow their business. How do you do that?"

When you get back to the office, take a few minutes to review the cards you received and think about the interactions. Make note of any follow-through action that you are to take, like sending a newsletter, making a phone call, or passing on a name.

Associate the Person's Name with Something

Association relies on the mind's tendency to remember information that's visual, dramatic, or emotional. You use this technique by forming a mental picture. For example, if you meet Jack and he's an accountant, take a second to picture Jack with a calculator. When you need to recall what Jack does, you can bring up your mental picture. In memory courses, they typically say that the more exaggerated the visual image is, the better your memory of it will be. So picture Jack punching numbers on a gigantic calculator or Jack in an office with piles of calculators all around him.

You can associate people's names with their industries (as in the example of Jack), the events where you meet them, the cities in which they live, the groups they belong to, or the companies they work for. You can also associate names with physical characteristics and words that are already very familiar to you.

Using the technique of association takes focus. Here are some examples of how an association can assist with remembering people's names:

✔ When Robin handed me her card, I noticed the word *musician* under her name. Because I love music and admire people who have musical abilities, I was very interested in hearing about her career. She started telling me about her new CD project, and I got a mental picture of a robin singing, which helped me remember her name and her occupation the next time we met.

✔ When David Kent introduces himself, he says, "Hi, I'm David Kent, Kent like Superman." By giving people an association to relate his name to, he makes it easy for people to remember his name.

✔ When Suzanne was car shopping, one of the salespeople approached her and introduced himself: "Hi, I'm David Kraft, Kraft as in cheese." Suzanne noticed that she had no trouble remembering his name because of the helpful association he used as part of his introduction.

In these examples, names were related to words that were already very familiar. This can make remembering easy.

Use All Your Senses

Using all your senses when taking in information is important: audio (hearing the name and saying the name), visual (seeing the name and reading the name), and kinesthetic (typing the name and writing the name). When you get all your senses involved, you're more likely to embed the information so firmly in your mind that you can easily recall it later. Here are some ways to activate all your senses when you're meeting and talking with people:

✔ Look at people so that you get a strong mental picture of them.

✔ Listen to the sound of people's voices. Notice whether the voice is deep, high, nasal, gravelly, rapid, or slow.

✔ Get in touch with any feelings you have about meeting them or about what they're saying. Notice whether you feel excitement, intrigue, enthusiasm, joy, or frustration.

✔ Make physical contact by shaking hands. As you greet the person and end the conversation with a handshake, you activate the sense of touch.

To make the best impression with your handshake, make it palm to palm. Shake firmly, but don't crunch! You can review handshakes in Chapter 7.

The Sweetest Sound in the World

Someone once said that the sweetest sound in the world is to be called by name. So many things change as we go through life, yet what stay the same for most people are their first names. People respond to the sound of their names. And one of the ways you can honor people is by remembering them and calling them by name. Notice how you feel when someone remembers you and calls you by name. Does it make you feel important, valued, and honored? Does it make you value and appreciate the other person even more?

This week, call everyone you talk to by name. Whether it's a phone conversation or in person, sprinkle the other person's name throughout your conversation. Notice how the other person responds to being called by name. And notice if calling him by name makes a difference in the way you interact, pay attention, and connect.

Being known is important to people. One of the ways you let people know that you know them is to call them by name. Make it your objective that the people in your network feel like you really know them. Give them what's important to them: their names.

Chapter 19

Ten Traits of the Masterful Networker

In This Chapter
▶ Defining the attributes of the most effective networkers
▶ Discovering how to listen and respond to maximize your networking efforts

Masters — of anything — tend to work smart rather than hard. As a result, they go about their business with grace and ease. They look like naturals. People who have developed a supreme level of skill are typically proud of their accomplishments and their level of expertise. Yet that pride is tempered with a humility that keeps them focused on what got them to the pinnacle: practice, dedication, and commitment.

Masterful networkers know that networking is not about time or quantity, but about *quality*. The quality of your conversations, the quality of your relationships, and the quality of your work is what matters. In this chapter, you find tips on how to mimic the best networkers so that you can make your networking efforts as effective as possible.

Masterful Networkers Are Aware

Masterful networkers have a highly developed awareness of what's going on in their world and in the worlds of their friends and associates. They are aware that opportunities are all around, all the time. For them, it's not a matter of whether or not things can happen — can I find this, or can I find someone who can help me with that, or can I get in touch with someone who knows something about what I need to know? Master networkers are confident that things can happen. They know and trust the process of networking. They approach life and other people knowing that anything and everything can happen as long as they're willing to receive and as long as they take the networking action that relates to what they want.

Masterful networkers have an awareness of life's possibilities because they've moved beyond being self-focused. Instead of thinking about their independence, they've adopted the more mature and powerful attitude of interdependence. They think of themselves as being part of a network, part of a community. They have shifted their awareness from *me* to *we*.

That inclusive attitude doesn't mean that they have lost touch with themselves or are unclear about their goals. Actually, it's because master networkers have such clarity and strength in themselves and in their goals and networks that they can expand their focus. They've grown into a place of maturity and strength that allows them to be inclusive. Including others in their thinking has become a habit.

Masterful networkers are interested in success for everyone, not just success for themselves. They realize that accomplishments for themselves don't bring lasting human fulfillment. They derive fulfillment from being connected, valued, and of value to people. They relate to people as human beings rather than as things or as means for getting what they want.

Masterful Networkers Are Responsive

Have you ever offered something to someone and found that she seemed receptive but never really responded to the opportunity? People leave cards on the table. They have offers, support, and opportunities and yet, for whatever reason, they don't pick them up and run with them. Maybe the opportunity is so big that it's too scary for them to pursue. Maybe, at some level, they don't think they deserve the help or support. Maybe their fear of failing is too strong.

Masterful networkers are responsive. They respond to the requests that are made of them, and they respond to the opportunities that are presented to them. Typically, they've trained themselves to respond promptly, and thus they diminish their chances of losing out on the opportunities.

It may seem that masterful networkers get more leads and support than is typical. That may not be true. The real story may be that they follow through and respond to leads and accept support more readily than most people do.

How you respond to a situation makes all the difference in terms of the results that happen around you.

Masterful networkers make it appear that they're at the right place at the right time. But the truth is that the types of networking opportunities that show up around masterful networkers are around *you* all the time.

Put your money where your mouth is

Masterful networkers don't waste time saying things they don't mean. They can be counted on to do what they say. They live their lives as examples of "what you see is what you get." If they say that they're going to call, they do. If they say that they're going to send you certain information, it happens. Their lives are simple because they don't play games. They don't say one thing when they mean another. Being people of their words, their interactions are marked by clarity. Their communications are simple and straightforward.

Masterful networkers do what they say they're going to do, and they do it without a lot of fanfare. To them, it's the only way to be. Their lives look fairly simple and uncluttered. Their results look magical.

Masterful Networkers Make Connections

Masterful networkers have developed their ability to connect with people. They may not meet more people than anyone else; however, their network is much more powerful, productive, and satisfying because they connect with people. Rather than just talking or meeting people, they go a step beyond and connect.

To enhance your ability to connect with people, consider the following questions. Once you have your answers, take action on them.

- ✔ How do you know when you've made the connection?
- ✔ When you don't connect with someone, what typically has gotten in the way?
- ✔ How would you describe what it's like to truly connect with someone?
- ✔ What things can you focus on to be more effective at connecting with people?

Masterful networkers are always building relationships. Rather than waiting for relationships to happen, they develop relatedness with the people around them. They use their conversations to get to know people better and develop greater trust and rapport. They look people in the eye and give them their full attention. They listen for commonalities. They listen for the commitment, passion, and vision of the people they talk with. They create a bond.

Here are some signs that you've made a connection:

✔ You feel a sense of rapport; at some point, you just seem to click.

✔ Your conversation is engaging, easy, meaningful, and fun.

✔ You feel comfortable calling the other person.

✔ When you see the other person later, you remember him or her and want to go over and talk.

✔ You think of the product or service the person offers and recommend the person when you meet a third person who may be able to use that product or service.

Networking is about connecting. If you're creating distance and separation, you are not networking. Judgment creates separation; interest creates connection.

Masterful Networkers Are Laser Listeners

Masterful networkers don't listen just because they think they should. They listen because they're interested. They want to get to know people. They want to do more than just meet people and be able to call them by name; they want to really know them. Masterful networkers listen in a way that creates connections (as I wrote about earlier in this chapter).

One of the greatest gifts you can give someone is your undivided attention. Listening creates powerful trust and rapport. *Laser listening* involves hearing more than just words. When laser listening, you focus on the heart of the matter. You hear through the noise, chatter, and automatic words to get to the person's core. You laser right through the surface conversation to hear the other person's message, the other person's intent.

The following lists show how your attitude affects your listening. The first three items represent the kind of positive attitude that will enhance your listening, and the second list shows three common roadblocks to effective listening.

To laser listen:

✔ Listen from a place of interest and pleasant curiosity.

✔ Listen with suspended judgment and an open mind.

✔ Listen while wanting to empower, serve, and contribute.

Your attempts to laser listen will be ineffective if you

- ✔ Listen while thinking, "This isn't of value."
- ✔ Listen while wanting the conversation to be over quickly.
- ✔ Listen just so that you can impress the other person.

Master networkers uncover opportunities through laser listening. They hear something that piques their attention while in a conversation. Through asking questions and continuing to listen, they uncover more valuable information. Through focused listening, they develop a level of trust with the other person. The other person then opens up even more, which allows the master networker to uncover even more valuable information.

Your laser listening — listening with your full attention and focus in order to get to the heart of the matter and hear the intent of the communication — greatly influences the flow, depth, and value of your conversations.

Masterful Networkers Hone Their Recall Skills

You meet a lot of people in your life. This first step in networking happens no matter what you do. But to capitalize on meeting people, one particular networking skill is crucial: the ability to recall information about other people.

You can train your mind to think in a certain way. And you can train your mind to collect, file, and retrieve information easily. Your mind has tremendous capabilities.

What if every time you saw someone, you were able to recall something about her and her life from your previous conversations? What if, every time you spoke to someone, you remembered to ask about her favorite hobby, her recent trip, her latest promotion, or her child's school project?

On paper, list 20 important people in your life. Next to each name, jot down some of the things you know about them based on conversations you've had with them and activities you've participated in together. This week, every time you talk with these people, reference something that you've talked about with them previously.

Masterful Networkers Are Organized

Masterful networkers never seem to have to search for a business card or wonder what they did with a phone number. They've developed systems that make their lives easier and their networking more effective. When someone asks for their cards, they don't have to search for them because they always keep their cards in a certain place that's easy to access. They don't have to wonder where that phone number is because they have a database, palm device, or daily planner that keeps track of all their information by name, company, industry, or event. And they don't forget to call because they listen, pay attention, and make notes that invariably remind them of what they need to do.

Their networking has become easy because they've organized themselves and efficiently manage their information and activities. Things happen effortlessly and easily for master networkers because they have systems in place.

 If you tend to lose things, decide on a certain place to keep certain things. Keep your business cards in one location. Keep business cards that are handed to you in another place. Keep your palm device in a certain place. When everything has a place, you don't have to think about where something could be or spend time searching for it. You then have more time to be with the people around you, which naturally leads to networking magic.

Masterful Networkers Create Possibilities

Masterful networkers are resourceful. They see and create possibilities when no one else even thinks to. They think that things can be done and that it's just a matter of finding a way or finding the right resource.

They're willing to say, "I'm not sure if this will lead to anything, but I recommend that you give Jerry Smith a call." They're constantly exploring. Rather than deciding that something can or can't be done, they keep their minds open to all possibilities.

Masterful networkers create possibilities by asking questions. Here are some questions that can stimulate a broad range of thinking and open up unexpected possibilities:

- ✔ What if you did . . . ?
- ✔ Have you ever tried . . . ?
- ✔ Have you ever considered . . . ?
- ✔ What do you think would happen if you took the opposite viewpoint?

Journaling your conversations

LaWana Cole has worked in the banking industry for approximately 30 years. During those 30 years, she's worked for four large national banks. Her first seven years were with Ohio National Bank. She had grown so close to the people she worked with there that when she left, she felt as if she were leaving all her closest friends. She was certain that she would stay in touch with her friends from the bank. Yet after she moved on, got involved in a new job, and met new friends, she didn't stay in touch with her old friends like she was so sure she would.

She told herself that she would never let that happen again. So the next time she moved on, she started a journal to help her maintain contact with the people she wanted to continue to be in relationships with.

LaWana says that the journal idea came about partly because she feels like she has "lots of friends and a short memory." She says, "I do it to keep myself honest. I can actually flip back through one of my journals to see whom I talked to three years ago on this day and what the highlight of the conversation was. In fact, oftentimes I will do that and then call that same person and say, 'Hey, Randi, guess what we were doing three years ago on this day? You were picking up your child from the nursery and . . . .'"

People tend to hesitate to call someone because they don't know what to say. LaWana says, "With my journal, I always know what to say, because my journal gives me that information." Every time she calls someone, she makes a short and simple journal entry. She records the date, the name, and the highlight of the conversation. Each entry is brief. There is often only one comment for each conversation. If you were to flip through LaWana's journal, you would see these types of entries:

- 6/12/96 Bar Mitzvah for Leah
- 3/19/98 Lyn, Everett's first 2 teeth
- 9/27/98 Great Aunt Nora, cast for 3 weeks left foot
- 6/22/99 Kris became grandma in April
- 12/10/99 Called Randi, left message thinking about her at Hanukkah
- 2/9/00 Lyn, daughter's pregnancy, 7th month doing well

It's very easy for LaWana to call a friend and say, "Do you know what you were telling me 20 years ago?" Some people know that she keeps her journal, and she says that they seem to enjoy it as much as she does.

LaWana keeps the journal with her in her briefcase. If she happens not to have her journal with her, she makes a note on a stick-on note and then pastes or transfers it into the journal. She makes a note in her journal after phone calls (inbound or outbound), face-to-face meetings with visitors, guests, friends, and so on.

LaWana says one of the benefits of her journal is that staying in touch with people from all walks and paths of her life gives her a rich and diverse network. Her network has truly expanded — and her life has been enriched — because she found a way to maintain old contacts from different phases and cycles of her life while meeting new people.

Masterful networkers have developed a brainstorming mentality, tackling problems by means of a search-and-explore methodology. Their thinking process is along the lines of, "Let's see . . . Who might I know who . . . ? How might I be able to help here?" And they're willing to recommend something or someone without having to know for sure whether the fit is perfect. They don't have to be right all the time, and they aren't networking for glory.

To develop a brainstorming mindset, come up with at least five solutions to every issue, challenge, or problem you deal with. You're brainstorming, so the important thing is to think creatively and spontaneously.

Before giving people advice, ask five questions in order to gather more information, and then offer five options.

Masterful Networkers Know Their Goals

Because masterful networkers have well-defined goals, they're more likely to notice the resources that are all around them that can help them accomplish those goals. Here are some questions that may help you define your goals and, as such, improve your networking abilities:

- ✔ What are your goals as a networker?

- ✔ What vision do you have of how the people in your network would ideally interact with each other?

- ✔ What goals do you have that you believe your network can help you with?

- ✔ What types of goals would you like to help others reach?

After you identify your goals and vision, you're able to turn your focus and attention outside of yourself. You're more likely, then, to inquire about others' goals and visions and discover mutual ways to be of support. Your conversations tend to be more interesting and compelling. People are more likely to gravitate toward you and want to participate in what you're doing. You tend to attract people who are also goal-centered; therefore, you can generate a network of valuable resources who help one another reach their goals and fulfill their visions.

Goals give you direction, focus, and energy. Goals help you identify the actions that help you fulfill what you feel to be your purpose. When you know what you're up to in life and you have clearly defined goals, you have a much better idea of how to produce the results you want.

Masterful Networkers Are Givers and Receivers

Networking involves a flow of giving and receiving. You can initiate the flow of networking by giving to someone or by being receptive and accepting a gift that someone presents to you. Either way, being tuned in to the power of giving and receiving is the core of being a masterful networker.

Some people seem to be natural givers. They like to be of service. They notice what others want and need and respond automatically, without being asked. Even if you're not an automatic giver, you can develop a giving nature. Here are some questions to ask yourself to help you become a better giver:

- ✔ In what relationships do you give freely and without conditions?
- ✔ In what relationships could you be more giving?
- ✔ What resources do you have to give that could be of value to others?
- ✔ What is your current attitude about giving?
- ✔ Are you as available to give as you are to receive?

Networking is about reciprocity, and reciprocity means mutual exchange or influence. Masterful networkers realize that giving, asking, and receiving are all part of the flow that keeps their networks working.

Masterful Networkers Are Consistent

One of the things that you can count on from masterful networkers is that they are consistent with their networking. They truly live networking. It's their lifestyle. They don't use it as a technique to further their careers. They live their lives such that their networking helps not only them, but also everyone around them.

Because networking is an integral part of their lives and their mentality, they don't wait until they have a need to network. They network all the time, so when a need comes along, it's handled almost instantaneously.

LaWana Cole, mentioned earlier in this chapter, has her secretary schedule into her calendar what she calls *touch time*. Touch time can be the time LaWana spends talking with someone from her team, her boss, clients, and friends. All this talking helps her maintain a support team that keeps her motivated and strong. On LaWana's calendar, her secretary actually blocks time slots of 30 minutes at various intervals during the week for touch time.

Chapter 20

Ten Networking Turnoffs and How to Avoid Them

In This Chapter

▶ Sidestepping common networking pitfalls

▶ Remembering what's important and what's not

Networking gets a bad reputation when people "network" in a way that's inconsiderate, inappropriate, or unprofessional. You may not even be aware that what you're doing turns people off and creates a negative impression. Just as little things have a positive impact on your relationships, little things done inappropriately can ruin your chances for developing a strong network. The following behaviors are common networking turnoffs and networking no-nos.

Constant Selling or Overselling

If you're always focused on making a sale, you will turn people off and miss the opportunity to connect. Networking events are not the place to sell. Nurture your contacts, ask for the opportunity to follow up with a phone call, but don't put people on the spot. You must invest the time to get to know people and find out what they need. Networking involves learning about people — their interests, goals, dreams, and hobbies.

You can develop numerous sales opportunities through effective networking. However, knowing and understanding the difference between networking and sales is important. Networking is building relationships, getting to know people, and learning how you can be of service and value to one another. Selling means generating a conversation with someone about purchasing a product or service that you have to offer. Learn the timing of when to network and when to initiate a sales conversation. If people feel used, you've missed the relationship-building process that is essential for effective networking. And you've probably blown the sale.

You can approach people to introduce yourself, your products, and your services without turning them off. The best way to network is to focus on people, listen to them, give to them, and show a natural interest in them. Although networking is not sales, networking does provide an important foundation for generating sales (and results in all areas of life). The truth is that you're always selling something . . . your ideas, your services, or yourself.

You sell yourself by the way you treat people, the way you behave, and the professional manner in which you relate. Through selling *yourself* first and investing in relationships, you open the door to selling your *product* later.

Sales don't come first; people do!

Hogging the Limelight

People who namedrop or feign an interest don't show the authenticity that leads to a quality network. Quality networking requires a willingness to get your attention off of yourself in order to give attention to other people. Have you ever been turned off because someone seemed to give you help just so that he or she could look good or impress you? A masterful networker realizes that networking is not about looking good, but about building a support system for a lifetime. Networking must be sincere and authentic to inspire strong, trusting relationships.

Be aware of the following pitfalls that will make you appear self-absorbed:

- **Namedropping:** Talking about the people you know can turn people off if you do it to impress rather than to be of value. Don't act like you're best friends or buddies with people you barely know. Even if your best friend actually is famous, using that fact to impress others can backfire.

- **Bragging:** Constantly talking about your successes will drive people away. It's great to share your successes with your network; just don't go overboard. Make sure that your conversations include equal time for hearing about, encouraging, and celebrating the successes of others.

- **Exaggerating or embellishing upon your accomplishments.** When you exaggerate or embellish your accomplishments, people begin to take what you have to say with a grain of salt. You create doubt in people's minds regarding how much truth there is to what you say.

✔ **Speaking with an arrogant tone or mannerism.** Expressing arrogance through your tone of voice, words, or mannerisms creates distance rather than connections. Networking requires treating people as valuable equals in terms of possibilities and opportunities.

✔ **Not following through.** When you say that you're going to do something and you don't follow through, you begin to look like you're saying things just to look good rather than because you really want to be of help.

Making Insincere, Shallow Comments

Many people habitually say, "Let's get together" or "Let's do lunch." The comment is made spontaneously, with little if any thought of following through. If you don't intend to follow through, the statement is insincere and ineffective. If you say, "Hey, let's get together sometime," schedule a time and do it. If you say, "Let's do lunch," pull out your calendar and make the lunch appointment right then and there. If you're not willing to take the action, don't say the words.

The following words and phrases represent a commitment to take action. Make sure to follow through on the actions that you say you will take.

✔ "I'll send you . . . ."

✔ "I'll get back with you."

✔ "I'll give you a call."

✔ "I'll check on . . . for you."

✔ "Let's get together."

✔ "Let's do lunch."

✔ "I'll call you with her name and number."

✔ "I'll fax you that information."

✔ "I'll e-mail you with . . . ."

Take yourself seriously when you say that you're going to do something for someone. If that means leaving a phone message for yourself as a reminder, do it. Create a system for keeping track of your promises and being accountable for them.

Whenever you say, "Let's do lunch," include the question, "Are you available on [date]?" Make the most of your interactions by making statements that generate positive actions.

Treating People Like Chopped Liver

Thinking of networking as a business "meat market" is rude, unprofessional, and inappropriate. Yet you've probably been in a situation where someone introduced herself, spent a minute finding out what you do, and then quickly dropped you when she realized that you're not a prospect for her business. And you've probably been in a situation where you were talking with someone and the whole time that person was continuously scanning the room to see who else was there. What a terrible feeling! All the people you meet can be of value, whether they turn out to be business prospects or not. If you decide that *everyone* has value, not just certain people, you'll improve your networking.

Networking events are a place to meet people, make contacts, reconnect with people, and gather information.

You treat people as valued when you give them your attention. Give someone your undivided attention for even one minute, and that person is more likely to connect in a way that could be valuable. Connecting with someone doesn't have to take long, but it will never happen if you're too busy trying to connect with only the "right" people instead of connecting with the person in front of you.

People are much more than potential clients. Someone who doesn't even look like a prospect could turn out to be one of the most valuable friends, advisors, or centers of influence you could have. However, you will miss opportunities if you don't take the time to learn a little bit about the person you just met. Develop that first steppingstone of a relationship and treat the person with common courtesy. It's the right thing to do, *and* it's pragmatic.

Networking is a treasure hunt. Jewels are out there everywhere. And just as many different types of jewels exist (diamonds, rubies, emeralds, sapphires, and so forth), many different types of networking jewels are available to you — customers, vendors, associates, employees, friends, advocates, advisors, mentors, and supportive peers, for instance. Just like you may have to dig for the jewel, you may have to dig to discover enough about people to uncover their value.

Talking Incessantly

Have you ever been cornered by someone who talks so incessantly that you feel hopelessly trapped? Some people have an amazing ability to talk on and on without realizing that they've monopolized the conversation and the other person isn't listening anymore. A conversation is meant to be an interaction between two or more people. Develop dialogues rather than monologues. Make sure your conversations are interesting so that people can easily respond to what you're saying.

You can use gracious and courteous ways to free yourself from a conversation while being respectful to the people you've been talking with. This is true whether you're with someone who goes on and on oblivious to your needs or whether you simply need to move on from the conversation and meet other people.

Here are some ways to give closure to conversations:

- ✔ "I know there's a lot more we could talk about regarding . . . ; however, right now I need to make sure that I say hello to some other people who are here."

- ✔ "This sounds like something we ought to get together to discuss further at another time. How about lunch next Wednesday? (Pull out your date book or Palm Pilot and schedule the time and place for lunch next Wednesday.) I have some other people I need to say hello to. I'll look forward to seeing you next Wednesday."

- ✔ "It's really nice talking with you. I've got to leave shortly and need to handle some other business. Please excuse me. Have a great evening."

- ✔ "I've got to go now; however, it was nice to meet you. Here's my card. If you want to continue this discussion, give me a call at my office."

- ✔ "I need to check on some guests that I invited for this evening. I enjoyed talking with you. Good luck on your project."

The Magically Appearing Business Card

Have you ever found a business card in your hand, and yet you never asked for the card, never met the person, and may not even know for sure how or why the card appeared? The exchange of business cards is best done one-on-one after rapport has been established. Typically, you reach a point in your conversation where it's natural to ask for or offer a card. When you're handed a card, take a moment to look at it. Looking at the card conveys respect and helps you remember the person's name later.

Explaining why you want a card or why you're giving your card to someone is sometimes useful. Here are some things to say when you ask for or offer a business card:

- ✔ "I would like to send you some information about my presentation so that you can consider me for you next conference. Do you have a business card handy?"

- ✔ "I know someone I think would be good for you to call. If you'll give me a card, I'll make a note to call you with his name and number."

- ✔ "I'd be glad to send you an e-mail once I remember the name of that book. May I have one of your cards?"

- ✔ "I would be interested in receiving some information about your services. Here's my card."

- ✔ "Do you have a business card with you?"

- ✔ "Here's my card. Let me know if I can be of support in any way."

- ✔ "I'd be glad to check on that for you. Give me one of your cards and that will be my reminder."

 When at a business luncheon, don't pass a stack of your cards around the table. Instead, find a way to initiate the exchange of business cards while you talk directly with people.

Getting Too Personal Too Quickly

If you are too eager and attempt to get to know people too quickly, your networking approach can turn people off. Asking personal questions about someone's health, relationships, religion, politics, and other private matters may cause people to feel intruded upon and therefore grow cautious. The same holds true for telling people all about your personal opinions and aspects of your life that they may not want to know about. Give people a chance to get to know you, to warm up to you, and to feel comfortable around you. After you have developed a certain level of friendship and trust, discussing more personal matters will be natural and comfortable.

Because networking is about relationship-building, time can be a factor. Yes, there are some people with whom you will just click. But many potentially valuable relationships need time to grow and deepen.

Say you meet a woman who's a buyer for a large business. You've seen her several times at various meetings and events and would like to get to know her better. You sense that you could develop a valuable professional relationship and be of value to each other down the road. The following are some ways in which you could take that relationship to the next level.

- ✔ Offer to be of support to her in some way.

- ✔ Get involved in a common cause.

✔ Participate on a committee with her.

✔ Invite her to an activity — a sporting event, a networking meeting, or any other event that she may enjoy.

✔ Schedule lunch with her.

✔ Introduce her to someone you know who would be a good contact.

Be sure to think carefully about what method will work best for the particular person you're networking with.

Allow your relationships to grow gradually. Although networking can happen easily and quickly with someone you've just met, you will enhance your networking abilities if you focus on building relationships for the long term.

Being Lazy with Relationships

Have you ever been turned off by people who are interested in results but aren't willing to do what it takes to build relationships? Building and maintaining a relationship takes willingness and vulnerability. Some people want results without putting in the effort to get to know people.

The combination of patience and persistence is powerful fuel for successful networking. Be patient so that you don't get frustrated, become overly aggressive, or give up. Know that what you sow, you will have an opportunity to reap. Know that there are many different avenues for generating the results that you want. And be subtly persistent. Continue to prime the pump. Continue to network, give, and ask for results, and you will build relationships with people through your interactions.

When you focus on relationships, results happen naturally and automatically. When you focus on results, your relationships may never develop to the point where they produce ongoing and substantial results.

Here are some ways to create relationships that generate results:

✔ Acknowledge people.

✔ Be encouraging and supportive.

✔ Be a resource — give people helpful information and contacts.

✔ Be willing to spend time with people.

✔ Listen with interest to what people have to say.

✔ Be an advocate for people's success.

Taking It for Granted

Have you ever been around a person who isn't appreciative of the support and networking he receives and seems to take it for granted? Have you networked with someone, given him something of value, and never heard back from him — not only no words of thanks, but no feedback of any type? You're left hanging. You don't really know whether he followed through on your support or utilized it at all. You don't know if your tip led to something great or got dropped along the way.

Always knowing the ripple effect of the networking you initiate is impossible. However, completing the cycles that you start with people is crucial. That includes thanking people for their time, support, ideas, leads, referrals, and so on. It also involves letting people know that their networking with you prompted some action or result.

Even if a lead that someone gives you doesn't generate a new customer, you want to thank the person for the lead. The person did her part simply by giving you the lead. When you thank her, she will be much more likely to continue to give you leads and support. In fact, just the process of thanking her will trigger her mind to begin thinking of other leads or support that she might pass your way.

An attitude of gratitude is the fuel that generates even greater good in your life. What you focus on with appreciation increases and expands.

Being Insincere

Have you ever been turned off by someone whose interest appears to be insincere? Some people seem to go through the motions of networking. They attend networking events with smiles on their faces and plenty of business cards to hand out. However, there may be very little action and follow-through. These people may mean well and just haven't developed their follow-through, memory recall, or organizational skills, so things fall through the cracks. Some people network like it's a technique or a "thing to do." By doing so, they miss out on the opportunity to truly connect with people and generate a fulfilling, lifelong network of support.

You can do all the right things and yet still not have a successful network if your heart and attitude aren't in the right place. You don't have to love everyone, yet treating people with sincere respect and dignity is vital to having healthy relationships, whether they're networking relationships, personal relationships, family relationships, or professional relationships.

Create Your Own Networking Action Plan

· ·

This is the place to write down all the action steps that this book has suggested to you that you plan to implement. Every time that you read something that makes you think of a useful networking behavior, habit, or activity that you'd like to incorporate into your own life, write it down under one of the following sections. You can include dates as timelines for taking certain actions. By the time you finish the book, you will have your own networking action plan.

Implementing your action plan will take your networking to a whole new level of ease and effectiveness. Taking action based on your plan will turn the ideas from this book into realities and create numerous networking success stories in your life.

New habits: (add checks to the boxes as you begin to implement habits you wish to adopt in your daily life)

❑ Sending notes

❑ Using ask-offer-thanks

❑ Speaking up

❑ Reintroducing yourself to people

❑ Calling people by name

❑ Replenishing business card supply

❑ Keeping business cards handy

❑ Inputting contact information in computer

❑ Calling people to stay in touch or reconnect

Here, write some more habits you wish to implement in your daily life.

❑ _____
❑ _____
❑ _____
❑ _____
❑ _____
❑ _____
❑ _____
❑ _____
❑ _____

People to acknowledge:

❑ _____
❑ _____
❑ _____
❑ _____
❑ _____
❑ _____

People to call:

❑ _____
❑ _____
❑ _____
❑ _____
❑ _____
❑ _____
❑ _____
❑ _____

Requests to make:

❑ _____
❑ _____
❑ _____
❑ _____

- ❑ _____
- ❑ _____
- ❑ _____
- ❑ _____
- ❑ _____

Networking events to attend:

- ❑ _____
- ❑ _____
- ❑ _____
- ❑ _____
- ❑ _____
- ❑ _____

Other actions:

- ❑ Order business cards
- ❑ Buy notecards
- ❑ Enter all names and addresses into a computer database
- ❑ Write word-of-mouth marketing plan
- ❑ Write brand identity
- ❑ _____
- ❑ _____
- ❑ _____
- ❑ _____
- ❑ _____
- ❑ _____

Networking success stories (add dates for effectiveness):

_____

_____

_____

_____

_____

_____

Networking success stories, continued

_____

_____

_____

_____

_____

_____

_____

_____

_____

_____

_____

_____

_____

_____

_____

_____

_____

_____

_____

_____

_____

_____

_____

_____

_____

_____

_____

_____

_____

_____

_____

_____

_____

_____

_____

_____

_____

_____

_____

_____

_____

_____

_____

_____

_____

_____

_____

_____

_____

_____

_____

_____

_____

_____

_____

_____

_____

Index

Dummies Books™
Bestsellers on Every Topic!

GENERAL INTEREST TITLES

BUSINESS & PERSONAL FINANCE

Accounting For Dummies®	John A. Tracy, CPA	0-7645-5014-4	$19.99 US/$27.99 CAN
Business Plans For Dummies®	Paul Tiffany, Ph.D. & Steven D. Peterson, Ph.D.	1-56884-868-4	$19.99 US/$27.99 CAN
Business Writing For Dummies®	Sheryl Lindsell-Roberts	0-7645-5134-5	$16.99 US/$27.99 CAN
Consulting For Dummies®	Bob Nelson & Peter Economy	0-7645-5034-9	$19.99 US/$27.99 CAN
Customer Service For Dummies®, 2nd Edition	Karen Leland & Keith Bailey	0-7645-5209-0	$19.99 US/$27.99 CAN
Franchising For Dummies®	Dave Thomas & Michael Seid	0-7645-5160-4	$19.99 US/$27.99 CAN
Getting Results For Dummies®	Mark H. McCormack	0-7645-5205-8	$19.99 US/$27.99 CAN
Home Buying For Dummies®	Eric Tyson, MBA & Ray Brown	1-56884-385-2	$16.99 US/$24.99 CAN
House Selling For Dummies®	Eric Tyson, MBA & Ray Brown	0-7645-5038-1	$16.99 US/$24.99 CAN
Human Resources Kit For Dummies®	Max Messmer	0-7645-5131-0	$19.99 US/$27.99 CAN
Investing For Dummies®, 2nd Edition	Eric Tyson, MBA	0-7645-5162-0	$19.99 US/$27.99 CAN
Law For Dummies®	John Ventura	1-56884-860-9	$19.99 US/$27.99 CAN
Leadership For Dummies®	Marshall Loeb & Steven Kindel	0-7645-5176-0	$19.99 US/$27.99 CAN
Managing For Dummies®	Bob Nelson & Peter Economy	1-56884-858-7	$19.99 US/$27.99 CAN
Marketing For Dummies®	Alexander Hiam	1-56884-699-1	$19.99 US/$27.99 CAN
Mutual Funds For Dummies®, 2nd Edition	Eric Tyson, MBA	0-7645-5112-4	$19.99 US/$27.99 CAN
Negotiating For Dummies®	Michael C. Donaldson & Mimi Donaldson	1-56884-867-6	$19.99 US/$27.99 CAN
Personal Finance For Dummies®, 3rd Edition	Eric Tyson, MBA	0-7645-5231-7	$19.99 US/$27.99 CAN
Personal Finance For Dummies® For Canadians, 2nd Edition	Eric Tyson, MBA & Tony Martin	0-7645-5123-X	$19.99 US/$27.99 CAN
Public Speaking For Dummies®	Malcolm Kushner	0-7645-5159-0	$16.99 US/$24.99 CAN
Sales Closing For Dummies®	Tom Hopkins	0-7645-5063-2	$14.99 US/$21.99 CAN
Sales Prospecting For Dummies®	Tom Hopkins	0-7645-5066-7	$14.99 US/$21.99 CAN
Selling For Dummies®	Tom Hopkins	1-56884-389-5	$16.99 US/$24.99 CAN
Small Business For Dummies®	Eric Tyson, MBA & Jim Schell	0-7645-5094-2	$19.99 US/$27.99 CAN
Small Business Kit For Dummies®	Richard D. Harroch	0-7645-5093-4	$24.99 US/$34.99 CAN
Taxes 2001 For Dummies®	Eric Tyson & David J. Silverman	0-7645-5306-2	$15.99 US/$23.99 CAN
Time Management For Dummies®, 2nd Edition	Jeffrey J. Mayer	0-7645-5145-0	$19.99 US/$27.99 CAN
Writing Business Letters For Dummies®	Sheryl Lindsell-Roberts	0-7645-5207-4	$16.99 US/$24.99 CAN

TECHNOLOGY TITLES

INTERNET/ONLINE

America Online® For Dummies®, 6th Edition	John Kaufeld	0-7645-0670-6	$19.99 US/$27.99 CAN
Banking Online Dummies®	Paul Murphy	0-7645-0458-4	$24.99 US/$34.99 CAN
eBay™ For Dummies®, 2nd Edition	Marcia Collier, Roland Woerner, & Stephanie Becker	0-7645-0761-3	$19.99 US/$27.99 CAN
E-Mail For Dummies®, 2nd Edition	John R. Levine, Carol Baroudi, & Arnold Reinhold	0-7645-0131-3	$24.99 US/$34.99 CAN
Genealogy Online For Dummies®, 2nd Edition	Matthew L. Helm & April Leah Helm	0-7645-0543-2	$24.99 US/$34.99 CAN
Internet Directory For Dummies®, 3rd Edition	Brad Hill	0-7645-0558-2	$24.99 US/$34.99 CAN
Internet Auctions For Dummies®	Greg Holden	0-7645-0578-9	$24.99 US/$34.99 CAN
Internet Explorer 5.5 For Windows® For Dummies®	Doug Lowe	0-7645-0738-9	$19.99 US/$28.99 CAN
Researching Online For Dummies®, 2nd Edition	Mary Ellen Bates & Reva Basch	0-7645-0546-7	$24.99 US/$34.99 CAN
Job Searching Online For Dummies®	Pam Dixon	0-7645-0673-0	$24.99 US/$34.99 CAN
Investing Online For Dummies®, 3rd Edition	Kathleen Sindell, Ph.D.	0-7645-0725-7	$24.99 US/$34.99 CAN
Travel Planning Online For Dummies®, 2nd Edition	Noah Vadnai	0-7645-0438-X	$24.99 US/$34.99 CAN
Internet Searching For Dummies®	Brad Hill	0-7645-0478-9	$24.99 US/$34.99 CAN
Yahoo!® For Dummies®, 2nd Edition	Brad Hill	0-7645-0762-1	$19.99 US/$27.99 CAN
The Internet For Dummies®, 7th Edition	John R. Levine, Carol Baroudi, & Arnold Reinhold	0-7645-0674-9	$19.99 US/$27.99 CAN

OPERATING SYSTEMS

DOS For Dummies®, 3rd Edition	Dan Gookin	0-7645-0361-8	$19.99 US/$27.99 CAN
GNOME For Linux® For Dummies®	David B. Busch	0-7645-0650-1	$24.99 US/$37.99 CAN
LINUX® For Dummies®, 2nd Edition	John Hall, Craig Witherspoon, & Coletta Witherspoon	0-7645-0421-5	$24.99 US/$34.99 CAN
Mac® OS 9 For Dummies®	Bob LeVitus	0-7645-0652-8	$19.99 US/$28.99 CAN
Red Hat® Linux® For Dummies®	Jon "maddog" Hall, Paul Sery	0-7645-0663-3	$24.99 US/$37.99 CAN
Small Business Windows® 98 For Dummies®	Stephen Nelson	0-7645-0425-8	$24.99 US/$34.99 CAN
UNIX® For Dummies®, 4th Edition	John R. Levine & Margaret Levine Young	0-7645-0419-3	$19.99 US/$27.99 CAN
Windows® 95 For Dummies®, 2nd Edition	Andy Rathbone	0-7645-0180-1	$19.99 US/$27.99 CAN
Windows® 98 For Dummies®	Andy Rathbone	0-7645-0261-1	$19.99 US/$27.99 CAN
Windows® 2000 For Dummies®	Andy Rathbone	0-7645-0641-2	$19.99 US/$27.99 CAN
Windows® 2000 Server For Dummies®	Ed Tittel	0-7645-0341-3	$24.99 US/$37.99 CAN
Windows® ME Millennium Edition For Dummies®	Andy Rathbone	0-7645-0735-4	$19.99 US/$27.99 CAN

Dummies Books™
Bestsellers on Every Topic!

 GENERAL INTEREST TITLES

FOOD & BEVERAGE/ENTERTAINING

Title	Author	ISBN	Price
Bartending For Dummies®	Ray Foley	0-7645-5051-9	$14.99 US/$21.99 CAN
Cooking For Dummies®, 2nd Edition	Bryan Miller & Marie Rama	0-7645-5250-3	$19.99 US/$27.99 CAN
Entertaining For Dummies®	Suzanne Williamson with Linda Smith	0-7645-5027-6	$19.99 US/$27.99 CAN
Gourmet Cooking For Dummies®	Charlie Trotter	0-7645-5029-2	$19.99 US/$27.99 CAN
Grilling For Dummies®	Marie Rama & John Mariani	0-7645-5076-4	$19.99 US/$27.99 CAN
Italian Cooking For Dummies®	Cesare Casella & Jack Bishop	0-7645-5098-5	$19.99 US/$27.99 CAN
Mexican Cooking For Dummies®	Mary Sue Miliken & Susan Feniger	0-7645-5169-8	$19.99 US/$27.99 CAN
Quick & Healthy Cooking For Dummies®	Lynn Fischer	0-7645-5214-7	$19.99 US/$27.99 CAN
Wine For Dummies®, 2nd Edition	Ed McCarthy & Mary Ewing-Mulligan	0-7645-5114-0	$19.99 US/$27.99 CAN
Chinese Cooking For Dummies®	Martin Yan	0-7645-5247-3	$19.99 US/$27.99 CAN
Etiquette For Dummies®	Sue Fox	0-7645-5170-1	$19.99 US/$27.99 CAN

SPORTS

Baseball For Dummies®, 2nd Edition	Joe Morgan with Richard Lally	0-7645-5234-1	$19.99 US/$27.99 CAN
Golf For Dummies®, 2nd Edition	Gary McCord	0-7645-5146-9	$19.99 US/$27.99 CAN
Fly Fishing For Dummies®	Peter Kaminsky	0-7645-5073-X	$19.99 US/$27.99 CAN
Football For Dummies®	Howie Long with John Czarnecki	0-7645-5054-3	$19.99 US/$27.99 CAN
Hockey For Dummies®	John Davidson with John Steinbreder	0-7645-5045-4	$19.99 US/$27.99 CAN
NASCAR For Dummies®	Mark Martin	0-7645-5219-8	$19.99 US/$27.99 CAN
Tennis For Dummies®	Patrick McEnroe with Peter Bodo	0-7645-5087-X	$19.99 US/$27.99 CAN
Soccer For Dummies®	U.S. Soccer Federation & Michael Lewiss	0-7645-5229-5	$19.99 US/$27.99 CAN

HOME & GARDEN

Annuals For Dummies®	Bill Marken & NGA	0-7645-5056-X	$16.99 US/$24.99 CAN
Container Gardening For Dummies®	Bill Marken & NGA	0-7645-5057-8	$16.99 US/$24.99 CAN
Decks & Patios For Dummies®	Robert J. Beckstrom & NGA	0-7645-5075-6	$16.99 US/$24.99 CAN
Flowering Bulbs For Dummies®	Judy Glattstein & NGA	0-7645-5103-5	$16.99 US/$24.99 CAN
Gardening For Dummies®, 2nd Edition	Michael MacCaskey & NGA	0-7645-5130-2	$16.99 US/$24.99 CAN
Herb Gardening For Dummies®	NGA	0-7645-5200-7	$16.99 US/$24.99 CAN
Home Improvement For Dummies®	Gene & Katie Hamilton & the Editors of HouseNet, Inc.	0-7645-5005-5	$19.99 US/$26.99 CAN
Houseplants For Dummies®	Larry Hodgson & NGA	0-7645-5102-7	$16.99 US/$24.99 CAN
Painting and Wallpapering For Dummies®	Gene Hamilton	0-7645-5150-7	$16.99 US/$24.99 CAN
Perennials For Dummies®	Marcia Tatroe & NGA	0-7645-5030-6	$16.99 US/$24.99 CAN
Roses For Dummies®, 2nd Edition	Lance Walheim	0-7645-5202-3	$16.99 US/$24.99 CAN
Trees and Shrubs For Dummies®	Ann Whitman & NGA	0-7645-5203-1	$16.99 US/$24.99 CAN
Vegetable Gardening For Dummies®	Charlie Nardozzi & NGA	0-7645-5129-9	$16.99 US/$24.99 CAN
Home Cooking For Dummies®	Patricia Hart McMillan & Katharine Kaye McMillan	0-7645-5107-8	$19.99 US/$27.99 CAN

TECHNOLOGY TITLES

WEB DESIGN & PUBLISHING

Active Server Pages For Dummies®, 2nd Edition	Bill Hatfield	0-7645-0603-X	$24.99 US/$37.99 CAN
Cold Fusion 4 For Dummies®	Alexis Gutzman	0-7645-0604-8	$24.99 US/$37.99 CAN
Creating Web Pages For Dummies®, 5th Edition	Bud Smith & Arthur Bebak	0-7645-0733-8	$24.99 US/$34.99 CAN
Dreamweaver™ 3 For Dummies®	Janine Warner & Paul Vachier	0-7645-0669-2	$24.99 US/$34.99 CAN
FrontPage® 2000 For Dummies®	Asha Dornfest	0-7645-0423-1	$24.99 US/$34.99 CAN
HTML 4 For Dummies®, 3rd Edition	Ed Tittel & Natanya Dits	0-7645-0572-6	$24.99 US/$34.99 CAN
Java™ For Dummies®, 3rd Edition	Aaron E. Walsh	0-7645-0417-7	$24.99 US/$34.99 CAN
PageMill™ 2 For Dummies®	Deke McClelland & John San Filippo	0-7645-0028-7	$24.99 US/$34.99 CAN
XML™ For Dummies®	Ed Tittel	0-7645-0692-7	$24.99 US/$37.99 CAN
Javascript For Dummies®, 3rd Edition	Emily Vander Veer	0-7645-0633-1	$24.99 US/$37.99 CAN

DESKTOP PUBLISHING GRAPHICS/MULTIMEDIA

Adobe® In Design™ For Dummies®	Deke McClelland	0-7645-0599-8	$19.99 US/$27.99 CAN
CorelDRAW™ 9 For Dummies®	Deke McClelland	0-7645-0523-8	$19.99 US/$27.99 CAN
Desktop Publishing and Design For Dummies®	Roger C. Parker	1-56884-234-1	$19.99 US/$27.99 CAN
Digital Photography For Dummies®, 3rd Edition	Julie Adair King	0-7645-0646-3	$24.99 US/$37.99 CAN
Microsoft® Publisher 98 For Dummies®	Jim McCarter	0-7645-0395-2	$19.99 US/$27.99 CAN
Visio 2000 For Dummies®	Debbie Walkowski	0-7645-0635-8	$19.99 US/$27.99 CAN
Microsoft® Publisher 2000 For Dummies®	Jim McCarter	0-7645-0525-4	$19.99 US/$27.99 CAN
Windows® Movie Maker For Dummies®	Keith Underdahl	0-7645-0749-1	$19.99 US/$27.99 CAN

Dummies Books™
Bestsellers on Every Topic!

GENERAL INTEREST TITLES

EDUCATION & TEST PREPARATION

Title	Author	ISBN	Price
The ACT For Dummies®	Suzee Vlk	1-56884-387-9	$14.99 US/$21.99 CAN
College Financial Aid For Dummies®	Dr. Herm Davis & Joyce Lain Kennedy	0-7645-5049-7	$19.99 US/$27.99 CAN
College Planning For Dummies®, 2nd Edition	Pat Ordovensky	0-7645-5048-9	$19.99 US/$27.99 CAN
Everyday Math For Dummies®	Charles Seiter, Ph.D.	1-56884-248-1	$14.99 US/$21.99 CAN
The GMAT® For Dummies®, 3rd Edition	Suzee Vlk	0-7645-5082-9	$16.99 US/$24.99 CAN
The GRE® For Dummies®, 3rd Edition	Suzee Vlk	0-7645-5083-7	$16.99 US/$24.99 CAN
Politics For Dummies®	Ann DeLaney	1-56884-381-X	$19.99 US/$27.99 CAN
The SAT I For Dummies®, 3rd Edition	Suzee Vlk	0-7645-5044-6	$14.99 US/$21.99 CAN

AUTOMOTIVE

Title	Author	ISBN	Price
Auto Repair For Dummies®	Deanna Sclar	0-7645-5089-6	$19.99 US/$27.99 CAN
Buying A Car For Dummies®	Deanna Sclar	0-7645-5091-8	$16.99 US/$24.99 CAN

LIFESTYLE/SELF-HELP

Title	Author	ISBN	Price
Dating For Dummies®	Dr. Joy Browne	0-7645-5072-1	$19.99 US/$27.99 CAN
Making Marriage Work For Dummies®	Steven Simring, M.D. & Sue Klavans Simring, D.S.W	0-7645-5173-6	$19.99 US/$27.99 CAN
Parenting For Dummies®	Sandra H. Gookin	1-56884-383-6	$16.99 US/$24.99 CAN
Success For Dummies®	Zig Ziglar	0-7645-5061-6	$19.99 US/$27.99 CAN
Weddings For Dummies®	Marcy Blum & Laura Fisher Kaiser	0-7645-5055-1	$19.99 US/$27.99 CAN

TECHNOLOGY TITLES

SUITES

Title	Author	ISBN	Price
Microsoft® Office 2000 For Windows® For Dummies®	Wallace Wang & Roger C. Parker	0-7645-0452-5	$19.99 US/$27.99 CAN
Microsoft® Office 2000 For Windows® For Dummies® Quick Reference	Doug Lowe & Bjoern Hartsfvang	0-7645-0453-3	$12.99 US/$17.99 CAN
Microsoft® Office 97 For Windows® For Dummies®	Wallace Wang & Roger C. Parker	0-7645-0050-3	$19.99 US/$27.99 CAN
Microsoft® Office 97 For Windows® For Dummies® Quick Reference	Doug Lowe	0-7645-0062-7	$12.99 US/$17.99 CAN
Microsoft® Office 98 For Macs® For Dummies®	Tom Negrino	0-7645-0229-8	$19.99 US/$27.99 CAN
Microsoft® Office X For Macs For Dummies®	Tom Negrino	0-7645-0702-8	$19.95 US/$27.99 CAN

WORD PROCESSING

Title	Author	ISBN	Price
Word 2000 For Windows® For Dummies® Quick Reference	Peter Weverka	0-7645-0449-5	$12.99 US/$19.99 CAN
Corel® WordPerfect® 8 For Windows® For Dummies®	Margaret Levine Young, David Kay & Jordan Young	0-7645-0186-0	$19.99 US/$27.99 CAN
Word 2000 For Windows® For Dummies®	Dan Gookin	0-7645-0448-7	$19.99 US/$27.99 CAN
Word For Windows® 95 For Dummies®	Dan Gookin	1-56884-932-X	$19.99 US/$27.99 CAN
Word 97 For Windows® For Dummies®	Dan Gookin	0-7645-0052-X	$19.99 US/$27.99 CAN
WordPerfect® 9 For Windows® For Dummies®	Margaret Levine Young	0-7645-0427-4	$19.99 US/$27.99 CAN
WordPerfect® 7 For Windows® 95 For Dummies®	Margaret Levine Young & David Kay	1-56884-949-4	$19.99 US/$27.99 CAN

SPREADSHEET/FINANCE/PROJECT MANAGEMENT

Title	Author	ISBN	Price
Excel For Windows® 95 For Dummies®	Greg Harvey	1-56884-930-3	$19.99 US/$27.99 CAN
Excel 2000 For Windows® For Dummies®	Greg Harvey	0-7645-0446-0	$19.99 US/$27.99 CAN
Excel 2000 For Windows® For Dummies® Quick Reference	John Walkenbach	0-7645-0447-9	$12.99 US/$17.99 CAN
Microsoft® Money 99 For Dummies®	Peter Weverka	0-7645-0433-9	$19.99 US/$27.99 CAN
Microsoft® Project 98 For Dummies®	Martin Doucette	0-7645-0321-9	$24.99 US/$34.99 CAN
Microsoft® Project 2000 For Dummies®	Martin Doucette	0-7645-0517-3	$24.99 US/$37.99 CAN
Microsoft® Money 2000 For Dummies®	Peter Weverka	0-7645-0579-3	$19.99 US/$27.99 CAN
MORE Excel 97 For Windows® For Dummies®	Greg Harvey	0-7645-0138-0	$22.99 US/$32.99 CAN
Quicken® 2000 For Dummies®	Stephen L. Nelson	0-7645-0607-2	$19.99 US/$27.99 CAN
Quicken® 2001 For Dummies®	Stephen L. Nelson	0-7645-0759-1	$19.99 US/$27.99 CAN
Quickbooks® 2000 For Dummies®	Stephen L. Nelson	0-7645-0665-x	$19.99 US/$27.99 CAN

Dummies Books™
Bestsellers on Every Topic!

GENERAL INTEREST TITLES

CAREERS

Cover Letters For Dummies®, 2nd Edition	Joyce Lain Kennedy	0-7645-5224-4	$12.99 US/$17.99 CAN
Cool Careers For Dummies®	Marty Nemko, Paul Edwards, & Sarah Edwards	0-7645-5095-0	$16.99 US/$24.99 CAN
Job Hunting For Dummies®, 2nd Edition	Max Messmer	0-7645-5163-9	$19.99 US/$26.99 CAN
Job Interviews For Dummies®, 2nd Edition	Joyce Lain Kennedy	0-7645-5225-2	$12.99 US/$17.99 CAN
Resumes For Dummies®, 2nd Edition	Joyce Lain Kennedy	0-7645-5113-2	$12.99 US/$17.99 CAN

FITNESS

Fitness Walking For Dummies®	Liz Neporent	0-7645-5192-2	$19.99 US/$27.99 CAN
Fitness For Dummies®, 2nd Edition	Suzanne Schlosberg & Liz Neporent	0-7645-5167-1	$19.99 US/$27.99 CAN
Nutrition For Dummies®, 2nd Edition	Carol Ann Rinzler	0-7645-5180-9	$19.99 US/$27.99 CAN
Running For Dummies®	Florence "Flo-Jo" Griffith Joyner & John Hanc	0-7645-5096-9	$19.99 US/$27.99 CAN

FOREIGN LANGUAGE

Spanish For Dummies®	Susana Wald	0-7645-5194-9	$24.99 US/$34.99 CAN
French For Dummies®	Dodi-Kartrin Schmidt & Michelle W. Willams	0-7645-5193-0	$24.99 US/$34.99 CAN

TECHNOLOGY TITLES

DATABASE

Access 2000 For Windows® For Dummies®	John Kaufeld	0-7645-0444-4	$19.99 US/$27.99 CAN
Access 97 For Windows® For Dummies®	John Kaufeld	0-7645-0048-1	$19.99 US/$27.99 CAN
Access 2000 For Windows For Dummies® Quick Reference	Alison Barrons	0-7645-0445-2	$12.99 US/$17.99 CAN
Approach® 97 For Windows® For Dummies®	Deborah S. Ray & Eric J. Ray	0-7645-0001-5	$19.99 US/$27.99 CAN
Crystal Reports 8 For Dummies®	Douglas J. Wolf	0-7645-0642-0	$24.99 US/$34.99 CAN
Data Warehousing For Dummies®	Alan R. Simon	0-7645-0170-4	$24.99 US/$34.99 CAN
FileMaker® Pro 4 For Dummies®	Tom Maremaa	0-7645-0210-7	$19.99 US/$27.99 CAN

NETWORKING/GROUPWARE

ATM For Dummies®	Cathy Gadecki & Christine Heckart	0-7645-0065-1	$24.99 US/$34.99 CAN
Client/Server Computing For Dummies®, 3rd Edition	Doug Lowe	0-7645-0476-2	$24.99 US/$34.99 CAN
DSL For Dummies®, 2nd Edition	David Angell	0-7645-0715-X	$24.99 US/$35.99 CAN
Lotus Notes® Release 4 For Dummies®	Stephen Londergan & Pat Freeland	1-56884-934-6	$19.99 US/$27.99 CAN
Microsoft® Outlook® 98 For Windows® For Dummies®	Bill Dyszel	0-7645-0393-6	$19.99 US/$28.99 CAN
Microsoft® Outlook® 2000 For Windows® For Dummies®	Bill Dyszel	0-7645-0471-1	$19.99 US/$27.99 CAN
Migrating to Windows® 2000 For Dummies®	Leonard Sterns	0-7645-0459-2	$24.99 US/$37.99 CAN
Networking For Dummies®, 4th Edition	Doug Lowe	0-7645-0498-3	$19.99 US/$27.99 CAN
Networking Home PCs For Dummies®	Kathy Ivens	0-7645-0491-6	$24.99 US/$35.99 CAN
Upgrading & Fixing Networks For Dummies®, 2nd Edition	Bill Camarda	0-7645-0542-4	$29.99 US/$42.99 CAN
TCP/IP For Dummies®, 4th Edition	Candace Leiden & Marshall Wilensky	0-7645-0726-5	$24.99 US/$35.99 CAN
Windows NT® Networking For Dummies®	Ed Tittel, Mary Madden, & Earl Follis	0-7645-0015-5	$24.99 US/$34.99 CAN

PROGRAMMING

Active Server Pages For Dummies®, 2nd Edition	Bill Hatfield	0-7645-0065-1	$24.99 US/$34.99 CAN
Beginning Programming For Dummies®	Wally Wang	0-7645-0596-0	$19.99 US/$29.99 CAN
C++ For Dummies® Quick Reference, 2nd Edition	Namir Shammas	0-7645-0390-1	$14.99 US/$21.99 CAN
Java™ Programming For Dummies®, 3rd Edition	David & Donald Koosis	0-7645-0388-X	$29.99 US/$42.99 CAN
JBuilder™ For Dummies®	Barry A. Burd	0-7645-0567-X	$24.99 US/$34.99 CAN
VBA For Dummies®, 2nd Edition	Steve Cummings	0-7645-0078-3	$24.99 US/$34.99 CAN
Windows® 2000 Programming For Dummies®	Richard Simon	0-7645-0469-X	$24.99 US/$37.99 CAN
XML For Dummies®, 2nd Edition	Ed Tittel	0-7645-0692-7	$24.99 US/$37.99 CAN

Dummies Books™
Bestsellers on Every Topic!

GENERAL INTEREST TITLES

THE ARTS

Art For Dummies®	Thomas Hoving	0-7645-5104-3	$24.99 US/$34.99 CAN
Blues For Dummies®	Lonnie Brooks, Cub Koda, & Wayne Baker Brooks	0-7645-5080-2	$24.99 US/$34.99 CAN
Classical Music For Dummies®	David Pogue & Scott Speck	0-7645-5009-8	$24.99 US/$34.99 CAN
Guitar For Dummies®	Mark Phillips & Jon Chappell of Cherry Lane Music	0-7645-5106-X	$24.99 US/$34.99 CAN
Jazz For Dummies®	Dirk Sutro	0-7645-5081-0	$24.99 US/$34.99 CAN
Opera For Dummies®	David Pogue & Scott Speck	0-7645-5010-1	$24.99 US/$34.99 CAN
Piano For Dummies®	Blake Neely of Cherry Lane Music	0-7645-5105-1	$24.99 US/$34.99 CAN
Shakespeare For Dummies®	John Doyle & Ray Lischner	0-7645-5135-3	$19.99 US/$27.99 CAN

HEALTH

Allergies and Asthma For Dummies®	William Berger, M.D.	0-7645-5218-X	$19.99 US/$27.99 CAN
Alternative Medicine For Dummies®	James Dillard, M.D., D.C., C.A.C., & Terra Ziporyn, Ph.D.	0-7645-5109-4	$19.99 US/$27.99 CAN
Beauty Secrets For Dummies®	Stephanie Seymour	0-7645-5078-0	$19.99 US/$27.99 CAN
Diabetes For Dummies®	Alan L. Rubin, M.D.	0-7645-5154-X	$19.99 US/$27.99 CAN
Dieting For Dummies®	The American Dietetic Society with Jane Kirby, R.D.	0-7645-5126-4	$19.99 US/$27.99 CAN
Family Health For Dummies®	Charles Inlander & Karla Morales	0-7645-5121-3	$19.99 US/$27.99 CAN
First Aid For Dummies®	Charles B. Inlander & The People's Medical Society	0-7645-5213-9	$19.99 US/$27.99 CAN
Fitness For Dummies®, 2nd Edition	Suzanne Schlosberg & Liz Neporent, M.A.	0-7645-5167-1	$19.99 US/$27.99 CAN
Healing Foods For Dummies®	Molly Siple, M.S. R.D.	0-7645-5198-1	$19.99 US/$27.99 CAN
Healthy Aging For Dummies®	Walter Bortz, M.D.	0-7645-5233-3	$19.99 US/$27.99 CAN
Men's Health For Dummies®	Charles Inlander	0-7645-5120-5	$19.99 US/$27.99 CAN
Nutrition For Dummies®, 2nd Edition	Carol Ann Rinzler	0-7645-5180-9	$19.99 US/$27.99 CAN
Pregnancy For Dummies®	Joanne Stone, M.D., Keith Eddleman, M.D., & Mary Murray	0-7645-5074-8	$19.99 US/$27.99 CAN
Sex For Dummies®	Dr. Ruth K. Westheimer	1-56884-384-4	$16.99 US/$24.99 CAN
Stress Management For Dummies®	Allen Elkin, Ph.D.	0-7645-5144-2	$19.99 US/$27.99 CAN
The Healthy Heart For Dummies®	James M. Ripple, M.D.	0-7645-5166-3	$19.99 US/$27.99 CAN
Weight Training For Dummies®	Liz Neporent, M.A. & Suzanne Schlosberg	0-7645-5036-5	$19.99 US/$27.99 CAN
Women's Health For Dummies®	Pamela Maraldo, Ph.D., R.N., & The People's Medical Society	0-7645-5119-1	$19.99 US/$27.99 CAN

TECHNOLOGY TITLES

MACINTOSH

Macs® For Dummies®, 7th Edition	David Pogue	0-7645-0703-6	$19.99 US/$27.99 CAN
The iBook™ For Dummies®	David Pogue	0-7645-0647-1	$19.99 US/$27.99 CAN
The iMac For Dummies®, 2nd Edition	David Pogue	0-7645-0648-X	$19.99 US/$27.99 CAN
The iMac For Dummies® Quick Reference	Jenifer Watson	0-7645-0648-X	$12.99 US/$19.99 CAN

PC/GENERAL COMPUTING

Building A PC For Dummies®, 2nd Edition	Mark Chambers	0-7645-0571-8	$24.99 US/$34.99 CAN
Buying a Computer For Dummies®	Dan Gookin	0-7645-0632-3	$19.99 US/$27.99 CAN
Illustrated Computer Dictionary For Dummies®, 4th Edition	Dan Gookin & Sandra Hardin Gookin	0-7645-0732-X	$19.99 US/$27.99 CAN
Palm Computing® For Dummies®	Bill Dyszel	0-7645-0581-5	$24.99 US/$34.99 CAN
PCs For Dummies®, 7th Edition	Dan Gookin	0-7645-0594-7	$19.99 US/$27.99 CAN
Small Business Computing For Dummies®	Brian Underdahl	0-7645-0287-5	$24.99 US/$34.99 CAN
Smart Homes For Dummies®	Danny Briere	0-7645-0527-0	$19.99 US/$27.99 CAN
Upgrading & Fixing PCs For Dummies®, 5th Edition	Andy Rathbone	0-7645-0719-2	$19.99 US/$27.99 CAN
Handspring Visor For Dummies®	Joe Hubko	0-7645-0724-9	$19.99 US/$27.99 CAN

FOR DUMMIES
BOOK REGISTRATION

Register This Book and Win!

We want to hear from you!

Visit **dummies.com** to register this book and tell us how you liked it!

✔ Get entered in our monthly prize giveaway.

✔ Give us feedback about this book — tell us what you like best, what you like least, or maybe what you'd like to ask the author and us to change!

✔ Let us know any other *For Dummies* topics that interest you.

Your feedback helps us determine what books to publish, tells us what coverage to add as we revise our books, and lets us know whether we're meeting your needs as a *For Dummies* reader. You're our most valuable resource, and what you have to say is important to us!

Not on the Web yet? It's easy to get started with *Dummies 101: The Internet For Windows 98* or *The Internet For Dummies* at local retailers everywhere.

Or let us know what you think by sending us a letter at the following address:

For Dummies Book Registration
Dummies Press
10475 Crosspoint Blvd.
Indianapolis, IN 46256

...FOR DUMMIES™

BESTSELLING BOOK SERIES